Greed

Greed

Gut Feelings, Growth, and History

A.F. Robertson

Polity

First published in 2001 by Polity Press in association with Blackwell Publishers Ltd

Editorial office:
Polity Press
65 Bridge Street
Cambridge CB2 1UR, UK

Marketing and production:
Blackwell Publishers Ltd
108 Cowley Road
Oxford OX4 1JF, UK

Published in the USA by
Blackwell Publishers Inc.
350 Main Street
Malden, MA 02148, USA

ISBN 0-7456-2605-X

A catalogue record for this book is available from the British Library and has been applied for from the Library of Congress.

Typeset in 10½ on 12 pt Sabon
by Best-set Typesetter Ltd., Hong Kong
Printed in Great Britain by TJ International, Padstow, Cornwall

This book is printed on acid-free paper.

Contents

List of Illustrations

Plates

Figures

Acknowledgments

I offer my sincere thanks to the many people who have advised, assisted, and encouraged me during the lengthy process of producing this book: Viviane Alleton, Apostolos Athanassakis, Ryan Balot, Barbara Bray, David Brokensha, Leonard Broom, Donald Brown, Michael Carrithers, David Crawford, Dano, Roger Friedland, Juan Gamella, Ramon Guardans, Ed Hagen, Keith Hart, Tim Ingold, Gustav Jahoda, Lucy MacKay, Fiona Magowan, Mat Mines, Harvey Molotch, Stephen Murray, Tetsuro Nakaoka, Robert Patterson, Sikopasi Poggo, Bernard Riley, Anthony Robertson, Elizabeth Stanger, Don Symons, John Tooby, Phil Walker, and Dick Whittaker. My debts range from help with monitoring the media to very detailed criticism of successive drafts. My biggest debt by far is to my wife Francesca Bray, who has walked every inch of the way. Although the compliment seems entirely backhanded, I dedicate these thoughts on greed to her.

The author and publishers would like to thank the following for permission to reproduce copyright material:

Artephot / A. Allemand (plate 2: detail of Romanesque tympanum from Sainte Foi, Conques);
the Bayerische Staatsgemäldesammlungen, Alte Pinakothek, Munich (plate 4: detail from Pieter Brueghel the Elder's *The land of Cockaygne*);

the Galleria Doria Pamphilj, Rome; *www.doriapamphilj.it* (plate 5: detail from Quinten Massys' *Caricature of four usurers*, all rights reserved);

the *New Yorker* Collection (plate 6: cartoon by Robert Weber 1998, all rights reserved);

the Universal Press Syndicate (plate 7: Garfield cartoon by Jim Davis, © PAWS, Inc 1996, all rights reserved);

W. W. Norton & Company Inc (quotation on p. 18 from William Langland's *Piers Plowman: An alliterative verse translation*, transl. E. Talbot Donaldson, © W. W. Norton & Company Inc 1990).

Plate 1 Puss in Boots meets the ogre, by Gustave Doré (1833–83); illustration to Charles Perrault's tale "Puss in Boots" in *Contes du temps passé*, first published in 1697

Synopsis
Miller dies: eldest son gets mill, middle son gets ass, youngest son just gets cat. But cat is smart. Cat traps rabbits and pheasants, sends them to king as gifts from young master, whom he dubs the "Marquis of Carabas." Sundry tricks, boosting identity of "Marquis of Carabas" to king. Cat visits famous ogre, ogre shows cat how he can turn into lion. Cat impressed, challenges ogre to turn into mouse. Ogre obliges, cat eats mouse. Cat claims ogre's palace for his master. King impressed, gives hand of daughter to "Marquis of Carabas." Cat becomes "great lord." Happy ever after.

Interpretation
MILLER'S YOUNGEST SON: No patrimony, can't grow. Fate resolved by wily beast. Acquires new name, major property, patronage, princess, opportunity for *legal* supergrowth.

OGRE: Product of unnatural and illegal supergrowth. Outrageous overconsumption (eats babies). Entitlement rests on bestial force – but is outwitted by beast (cat).

CAT: The magic link: trans-species agent (language, boots, and hat), licensed trickster, outwits and *eats* ogre.

KING: political authority, sanctions transfer of ogre's corrupt acquisitions to youth, *and* gives him princess to marry, go forth and multiply, prosper.

1

Introduction

My brain's convinced that greed has made America better.
But my stomach still tells me something else.
Greed – with John Stossel, a one-hour ABC-TV program
aired Tuesday February 3, 1998

"*Greed*" is an insult which strikes right to the gut. The overstuffed
child or the overcompensated executive may beg for kinder words,
but there it is in the parental scorn or the banner headlines. *Greedy!*
The word doesn't fuss around the head or the heart, it jabs just below
the navel. It sounds angry, taunting, emetic. It cuts back at the fancy
talk of the self-fixated, the rich and powerful. It is a nice little weapon
of the weak.

Greed is a tell-tale, pointing to the presence of our bodies and our
guts in contexts where we would prefer to ignore them or deny their
relevance. For centuries, we have been trying to find nicer ways of
talking about greed, but our best efforts ("self-interest", "egoism")
look puny and apologetic. Western scholars have gone to great
lengths to refine our minds and take them out of our bodies, and as
a result our accounts of "Economy," or "History," or "Culture" have
become lifeless and apathetic. Worse, we have created the lethal illusion that modern institutions like banks, businesses, or governments
have transcended human passions, and can thus absolve us from
blame.

This book takes popular understandings of greed as a guide for putting feeling back into our scholarly explanations. Greed monitors the relationship between desires and growth, measuring our expansive urges against our living bodies. Ordinary people know that greed is as much a gut feeling as an idea, but can we, as scholars, learn anything from this common-sense perception?

Greed looms large in modern life. The word pops up in all forms of communication – novels, movies, cartoons, graffiti, political and religious rhetoric, and casual conversation. Greed is a favorite topic of satirists and cartoonists. It has inspired a surprising amount of poetry, and quite a few popular songs.[1] We see evidence of greed everywhere in our consumer societies: in lottery frenzy, day-trading, and Pokémon fever, in the hedonistic advertising which envelops our daily lives, in kickbacks to public officials, in excessive damage claims in the lawcourts, and in exorbitant fees collected by the lawyers. The word appears frequently both in religious tracts and in criticism of television evangelists. The idea that more is better is not simply futile because it keeps satisfaction out of reach, it is disgusting and it is unfair. The so-called "wealth effect" rebukes the new super-rich at the turn of the millennium: excess breeds excess; the more you get, the more you want. The urge to accumulate and consume is at best a guilty pleasure, and today the anxiety it generates is painfully evident in the fences, locks, guards, and alarms which draw the lines between the extravagance of the wealthy and the relentlessly expanding misery of the poor.

Are we greedy because we are modern, or are we modern because we are greedy? The notion that it is something new in human history at least offers us some hope of redemption. Perhaps we imagine that if we could revert to our older, simpler selves, the future of our children and our planet would be more secure. But do we really have a sweeter, more generous nature to which we can return? The alternative proposition, that we are modern because we are greedy, may seem less naive but it is certainly more disheartening. There is now so much more of everything for greed to get its beastly teeth into, and so much less in the way of moral restraint. But if we are all greedy at heart, how can we save ourselves?

"Greed, gluttony and over-indulgence" purrs an advertisement for diet crackers. "Like Ryvita, they're totally natural."[2] A sampling of the 63,000 Web pages on "greed" selected by the search engine Alta Vista in March 2000 indicates that it is generally regarded as a force deeply rooted in our constitution as human animals. Its effect is to make people "want more than they need." If greediness is built into every body everywhere, the moral issue is whether and how we can contain these urges. This is the age-old war between the beastly passions of the individual and the moral constraints of society. As an urge to take for oneself rather than to give or to share, greed is contrasted with generosity. Abstention or self-denial are ways of recognizing its boundaries. Yet there is ambivalence: although greed may eventually destroy us all, without it we would probably not have progressed beyond pond scum. "We need greed," says Tony Hendra. "Greed makes the world go round. Greed drives history. The greedy fish wriggled up onto shore, looking for more, and its greedy spawn grew feet and arms and waddled about looking greedily for food, becoming in the fullness of time Rush Limbaugh . . ."[3]

Greed is never an absolute judgment (a third spoonful of sugar, three million dollars). It is an assessment of changing circumstances, hence the equivocations about needs and wants. We may find it respectable to be greedy for our family, or on behalf of other real and imagined communities from the bowling club to the nation. A good citizen has the right to be a bit greedy: "You have a certain amount of money," says a Bank of America advertisement coyly. "You would like more. This is the American way."[4] Public indignation about greed waxes and wanes according to shifts in the economic barometer. The 1980s were often described as "the greedy decade" – "Greed is the Juice That Gets Things Going in U.S." reads a typical headline.[5] One of the most quoted apologists of the period is Gordon Gekko, anti-hero of the movie *Wall Street* (1987):

> Greed – for lack of a better word – is good. Greed is right. Greed works. Greed clarifies, cuts through, it captures the essence of the evolutionary spirit. Greed in all of its forms: Greed for life, for money, for love, knowledge, has marked the upward surge of mankind, and greed – you mark my words – will not only save Teldar Paper, but that other malfunctioning corporation called the USA. (*Applause*)[6]

In 1996 a Harris poll found that 61 percent of Americans believed Wall Street is "dominated by greed and selfishness," and yet 70 percent of them also agreed that "Wall Street benefits America."[7] Recession in the 1990s brought some contrition, but with the technology boom at the end of the millennium the word returned with youthful swagger and a lot of irony. Greed Engine is one of the more successful bands touting the vice. In 1998 the Planet nightclub in

Adelaide made a big hit with *Greed*, "the first '80s retro show in Australia." *In Pursuit of Greed* is "a kickin' new multi-player 3-D game from Softdisk." The web publicity urges: "There are two types of people in this world; Haves and HaveNots. Be a Have. Purchase your copy of GREED!"[8] A curious byproduct are the numerous web pages explaining how to cheat at this and similar games. The web is salted with ironic spoofs: *Greed* is "The magazine for those who want more than their fair share." The editor, "Randall Hogmore II," promises no political correctness, no trickle-down public benefits, just "sure-fire ways of boosting your personal wealth by ripping customers off, exploiting your employees, scamming the tax office, rolling your shareholders, fooling lenders and basically lying and cheating to get what you want."[9] Disgraced several decades ago, big-money TV shows have returned in the US with a vengeance. In 1999, in response to the ABC network's grossly successful *Who Wants to be a Millionaire?*, Fox-TV launched *Greed: The Multi-Million Dollar Challenge*. Contestants – frequently praised for their courage – are urged to "Climb that Tower of Greed," which stacks the prize money up to two and a quarter million dollars. At critical steps, they are asked, amid pulsating music, "Do you want to keep the cash or do you *feel the need for greed*?"

As the stock market flickers with anxiety about the value of new technology enterprises, the question is often asked: should these tycoons be getting so much *so young*? This perturbation in the normal pattern of age-entitlement is the theme of the movie *Boiler Room*, which measures the college drop-out who has been drawn into the get-rich-quick frenzy of a shady stock trading firm against his father, the hard-working, sober judge. The vacuity of the easy-come lifestyle is signalled by one of the juvenile brokers entertaining his cronies in his empty mansion. Devoid of family, furniture, and inhibitions, they sit on the floor, eat pizza, drink beer, and chant-along to a video of *Wall Street*, much as an earlier generation chanted-along to *The Rocky Horror Picture Show*.

The meaning of greed is locked into moral judgments about real, bodily growth. Greed is not concerned with what you want or what you think you deserve. It reckons what you need, and if you want to argue that you need more, your best justification is that you are growing. You may not grudge the adolescent his third helping of dinner, but you know that adding half a dozen chocolates to your middle-age spread is *greedy*. And if you want to plead that it is your bank account, or your business, or your prestige which must grow, beware that greed will see through your ruse: it won't accept growth in this metaphoric sense (corporate development, blooming portfolios) as an alibi. Glance at any piece of corporate or national publicity and you will see images of "growth" being squeezed to bloodless metaphoric pulp.[10] You may argue about whether Michael Eisner was entitled to the $565 million in stock options he raked in one day in December 1997, but if you accuse him of *greed* you are talking about his body, not his contract. You are expressing your feelings, you are not, as Mr Eisner might wish, making a rational economic judgment. Markets, he might say, don't have feelings, which is why they will eventually allow the benefits of economic growth to trickle down to everybody (more cars, better food). It may also be why markets, in bearish times, can strike fear into the heart of the toughest trader.

An early invitation to consider greed more closely came from my philosophical barber in California, who was going broke giving people like me long, thoughtful haircuts. Aware of his scepticism about academics, I asked him what he thought social scientists like me ought, for the good of society, to be studying. He is a Vietnam veteran with New Age, maybe-back-to-school intellectuality. After a bit of rumination he fixed on this topic – greed. Its bearing on the American Dream bugged him. The question, as it emerged in conversation, turned on whether greed was a positive, expansive force which had made us what we are, or a congenital defect of humanity, a spreading cancer which would soon engulf us all. He was dismayed by my admission that this was one of the oldest and most chronically unresolved questions at the heart of social philosophy. Jabbing his scissors at my reflection in the mirror, he urged me to get off my butt and find an answer.

Why should it be so difficult for modern, paid-up, professional intellectuals to come to terms with "greed"? Keyword searches in library catalogues have proved, in a negative way, revealing. Greed appears frequently in the vocabulary of journalism and rarely in scholarly analysis (although academics in journalistic mode use the word freely enough). Between 1988 and 1998 the word occurred 236 times in *Los Angeles Times* headlines, dealing with topics as diverse as electoral behavior and serial murder, everywhere from Albania to Zaire. Objects of criticism run from drug barons to basketball players, from paparazzi to royalty, from the "Deep Blue" chess computer to the whole human race. "Greed" pervades Letters to the Editor, bristling with particular intensity around the behavior of local officials, businessmen, and professionals. The most conspicuous target is "executive overcompensation." Understandably, the word appears least frequently in the business sections of newspapers, but when it does it is used with special vitriol.

A large proportion of library holdings with "greed" in the title or catalogue key are novels. The nineteenth-century classics (Trollope, Dickens, Balzac, Zola, Jarry) deal extensively and graphically with greed, and writers like Tom Wolfe (*Bonfire of the Vanities*), Norman Mailer (*The American Dream*), A. S. Byatt (*Possession*), and Michael Lewis (*Liar's Poker*) have continued the theme into the twentieth century. Erich von Stroheim's monstrous movie epic *Greed*, the original version of which was nine hours long, has a bibliography of its own, regular marathon screenings for cinema buffs, and at least one remake.[11] Most of the "serious" books are critical commentaries on politics, economics, and current affairs: the word recurs in titles dealing with Margaret Thatcher and Ronald Reagan, Teamsters, city affairs in Chicago and San Francisco, the biographies of oil and grocery barons, scandals on Wall Street, and the private lives of the super-rich. The 1980s, with executive payoffs, banking scandals, and ecological disasters, produced a rich crop of titles. In almost every case, "greed" is there on the front page as a hook for the reader, its absence from the index an indication that it has no part to play in scholarly analysis.

This gap between public and scholarly interest in greed tells me that there is something wrong with how professional intellectuals have come to explain the world. Until a few hundred years ago, greed was a central issue in social theorizing, a deeply problematic aspect of our relationship with God, nature, and our fellow men. It was a passion built into our living, interacting, reproducing, eating, thinking, breathing, dying *bodies*. Greed was a moral concept which drew together the vices of gluttony, envy, lust, and anger, and was explained as an interaction of the humors (melancholy, choler, phlegm) which linked body, society, and cosmos. Feeling was an inextricable part of the meaning of greed, but over the last thousand years or so we have quite literally explained that meaning away. How and why did this happen?

The people who were most troubled by this beastly, undignified, and irrational passion were the merchants, who made and remade our modern world. They were the experts in wanting and getting more, and it was they who were driven to put a nicer face on greed. The merchant class produced and funded the scholars who translated greed into more acceptable terms like "self-interest," and developed the logics that made it OK with nature, God, and our immortal souls. But despite these painstaking cosmetic efforts, ordinary people have always known greed when they saw it, and preferred the sound of that old, visceral, in-your-face monosyllable.

If you isolate feeling from meaning, greed (along with many other interesting things) simply loses its significance. This was the effect of separating "mind" and "body," the most radical shift in scholarly thinking about people and the world around them. We have broken up our intellectual world into mental topics (broadly, the "humanities") on the one hand, and material and bodily topics (the "sciences") on the other. The ramifications of this division determine how we organize academic institutions – colleges and courses, books and libraries, disciplines and the careers of professors. There have been great gains in understanding: driving a wedge between what we think *with* (mind) and what we think *about* (matter) has helped us figure out how to navigate in space, cure diseases, produce astonishing substances and machines, and explain the workings of ancient trade or modern poetry. But many things which matter to us have got lost in the great divide: an understanding of pain, violence, madness, shame, love, greed. The separations which drive mind and body apart continue to ramify. A symptom of this is that "the body" has come to mean very different things to physiologists or biologists on the one hand, and historians or sociologists on the other. And arguments about "mind" have driven philosophers from one extreme (it's a physical property of the brain) to the other (it has no physical properties at all).

The persistence of powerful notions like greed indicates that "Ordinary People" (the phrase already sounds patronizing) do not separate mind and body in the same ways or to the same extent as well-disciplined intellectuals. Meaning and feeling flow into one another: we know things not just because we think them, but because they are sensations (smells, warmth, a prickle on the skin, a knot in the stomach). The most important reason for this fusion of feeling and meaning is that bodies and minds do not develop separately, they *grow together*. Making meaning is a lifetime's work for each of us, and a big responsibility for the communities and societies in which our brief lives are led. And because communities and societies consist of growing people, their histories and cultures are also laden with feelingful meanings and meaningful feelings. "Home" or "school" or "mother" have a small amount of general, standard meaning which can be captured in a dictionary, and a very large amount of fluid, living meaning which depends on who you are, how old you are, and how you have lived.

Moral notions like greed develop within us and, because human development is necessarily social, within the communities in which we live. Greed is doubly interesting because it is both an aspect of our own growth (I can feel greedy) and one of the ways we come to terms with growth socially – measuring, criticizing, commenting on one another. In chapter 2 I shall explain how this flexible and useful moral device is rooted in gut feelings, most basically hunger and disgust. And later, in chapter 6, I shall make the connection between meaning and growth, explaining how the moral metric of greed is kept alive within our growing bodies, evoked in such images as the infant glutton, the lusting adolescent, and the aging miser. These are the living definitions of greed we refer to in sizing-up ourselves and other people in daily life, and which are passed on from one generation to the next through the knowledge systems we call "culture."

When I ask people to define greed they always begin by talking about persons, not institutions. Even when we accuse banks or governments of greed, the word never loses its grip on our guts. What greed does is remind us that bad behavior is always about real, eating, shitting, mortals. Greed flushes the guilty out of the crowds in which they hide and exposes them in all their individual human frailty. Greed reaches into the family, the business corporation, government, and holds the guilty overstuffed body up for inspection. "*Greed!*" The word brushes all fancy talk of "rational choice" or "corporate welfare" aside. It is a graphic exposure of the behavior of people in public places who might like us to believe that their bodies are none of our business. Greed is no washed-out metaphor, a merely playful allusion to fatness and prosperity. It insists that all human behavior is reducible to bodily proportions, and that wickedness cannot be justified by declaring that we are bigger and better than the sum of our individual parts. It resists the tide of official and scholarly blather because it cuts the privileged and the pretentious down to size with a crisp and satisfying monosyllable. It is "self-interest" which is the enfeebled metaphor, not greed.

Instead of applying modern theory to reveal the ambiguities of greed I want to attempt the opposite: to keep greed intact, regard it as a coherent analytical device, and use it to draw attention to some of the ambiguities and inconsistencies in scholarly explanation. In the long history of scholarly separations and specializations, growth has come to mean very different things to a biologist and an economist, a psychologist and a historian. Because it does not operate with such a fragmented understanding of growth, greed presents a view of human behavior which modern philosophy has generally rejected: growing bodies are not simply the raw material of society or passive objects which are "constructed" by historical forces, they are profoundly implicated in the making of history and impose upon it moral as well as physical conditions.

To explain how feeling gets into meaning, and thus how bodies are implicated in culture and history, I shall re-examine the long and continuous trans-generational process of human growth. For human beings, growing is not a private affair, because we grow and make meaning simultaneously through the interlocking of our lives with other people's. From this perspective many of the distinctions between "feeling" and "meaning" start to dissolve. As we progress from egg to adult to dust, we do not cross any boundary between biology and culture, or between the somatic and the semantic. These are just ways professional academics have carved up aspects of a single, seamless process for their own analytical convenience.

Why academics think this way (and why most ordinary people don't) is a piece of history which has to be told. Since greed is such a vivid example of a "feelingful meaning" I want to use it to show what has got lost in modern scholarly theorizing. The question is: would philosophers who have worked so hard down the years at inventing and defending terms like "egoism" or "self-interest" be willing to reconsider a "primitive" notion like greed as a source of revitalizing ideas? The twist here is that "greed" is not an exotic object from another culture or from our own primitive past, but a bit of our everyday vocabulary which scholars, when they are behaving like ordinary citizens, are as likely to use as anybody else. What is at issue, therefore, is the specialist language of scholarship itself. Scholarly progress will always depend on coining new words and changing the meanings of old ones, but it also depends on explaining and justifying precisely why these are to be preferred to commonplace terms.

Translating "greed" into more forgiving notions of "self-interest" or "rational choice" is not just a technicality, it's a moral deed. None of us in the ivory tower would like to think we are propagating selfish, repressive, partisan, useless, or untruthful knowledge. But outsiders have increasingly mixed views of our self-detachment. At worst, academics are conceited, narrow-minded, patronizing, over-privileged, and downright non-commonsensical. It is sobering that in common parlance the word "academic" has come to mean "irrelevant" ("it's all academic now," we say, when one football team is being thrashed incontrovertibly by another). Meanwhile, academics are queasy about the ways in which science captures the popular imagination, and gets turned to passions for things alien and mysterious – visitors from space, crop circles, etc. The message is that we have to be *studiously* suspicious and dispassionate in dealing with what ordinary people think or do. In their quest for objective truth, neither physicists nor philologists are supposed to take their own bodies or their own feelings into account (there is even something scandalous about the biochemists of an earlier generation who experimented on themselves). It is interesting that when it comes to "great discoveries" (gravity, relativity, the double helix) we take biographical detail very seriously, and yet we take such little interest in the life processes within which *every* scientist makes meaning: the recurrent, massive, cumulative creation of knowledge in its grandest historical forms.

And so to the embarrassing question: Are scholars greedy? Tony Hendra shows us no mercy:

> On greed feed parasites such as think tanks, coalitions, citizen action groups, Centers for the This and That; greed pumps good dollars after bad into querulous quarterlies and meretricious monthlies. Greed hosts weekend retreats, conferences in Aspen, Institutes for Heavy Thinking, Club Meds for the head. Greed provides the panelling, the snow-white linen, the heavy silver, the obsequious illegal aliens that make it possible for neo-Augustans to sit around deep into the night waffling about Virtue.[12]

Are we all complicit in the very vice we seem so studiously to ignore? We are, after all, embedded in the professional class whose asset-stripping roles have been the topic of so much complaint – sometimes, uneasily, by ourselves. Is it just old-fashioned envy that fills my scholarly gut with indignation when I hear about Bill Gates's billions, or Michael Eisner's share-option bonanza? Is that why I reach with grim pleasure for that old, visceral epithet *"greed"*? Or is it because my own privileges and security have been dwindling during the twentieth century as my value to society, and the usefulness of my academic ideas, have been called to question?

I shall pursue this venality as honestly as I can in the last part of the book. I shall explore the accusations of greed which have revolved around our ancestors the childish peasants, our elders the pensioners, and ourselves, the mature, adult professionals. The purpose of these three bio-historical sketches is to show how confused we have become about the meanings of growth, creating false and morally hazardous distinctions between biology on the one hand and history on the other. We have been duped into into imagining, on the one hand, that corporations are real bodies and persons rather than just devices for doing business, and on the other, that corporate expansion measured in stock values, sales, and towering office blocks is actually "growth" in any vital and durable sense. So impressed are we by the expansion of modern social institutions that we have come to think that they make us, rather than we them. This is dispiriting, and it is also untrue. Social institutions are made in the long, slow, trans-generational rhythm of human growth, not just in the heat of the historical moment. The metaphoric shift from the human body to the body politic confuses us: it asserts the connection between physical growth and society, but removes the traces of flesh and blood from our understanding of social institutions. The metaphor is a freakish distortion of human life processes, encouraging us to imagine growth unconstrained by mortality. The marvel of *greed* is its capacity to cut through these delusions, to point to our frail bodies and remind us of feelingful meanings which we – the intellectuals – have worked so hard to disinvent.

How to get feeling back into scholarly meanings is an urgent philosophical and moral question. But is a scholarly explanation of greed possible? Have our disembodied thoughts weakened our moral judgments? Is modern thinking really as dispassionate as we would like to believe? Is it the business of scholars to put commonplace theories like greed out of business, or to find ways of learning from them? Can the human body can be reinstated as the living instrument, rather than just the passive object, of history?

Let me begin by considering what I, and perhaps you too, seem to understand by "greed."

2

What do We Mean by Greed?

Greed: to the modern educated mind it seems brutishly simple, a crude epithet, a sour comment on the human condition. Anything academically interesting about it has been translated into other more palatable terms (self-interest, preferences, emotion, instinct). And yet these refinements have not dislodged the word from everyday use, nor diminished its powers of criticism.

What is there about "greed" upon which we can all agree? Probably that it is an unpleasant, dangerous, but inevitable thing; that it is a passionate, excessive desire; that it is to the detriment of other people and thus potentially damaging to the self; and that it therefore requires personal and collective restraint. Ambivalence is central to the fascination of greed: it is a gratifying but potentially lethal passion at the core of our being; it is poised exquisitely between our natural and our social selves.

Greed is also a strategic device in our power-plays with one another; it emerges as accusation rather than fact. I shall argue that for all its monosyllabic bluntness "greed" analyses, compares, and judges as well as – if not better than – many fancy modern social theories. But it does so largely in a dimension which the scholarly mind resists – *feeling*. This puts me in a quandary: trying to put greed into scholarly words leaches out those sensational meanings that I want to capture. Rather than proceeding from a definition, I shall feel my way towards one. But I must begin with the word.

Semantics

Greed is a very old word, with roots deep in the English language (*graed, groedig, graedig*) and with cognates in a wide range of northern European languages. All of them bear the same visceral stigma. Greediness, in the *Oxford English dictionary*, is an "Excessive longing for food or drink, or avidity in the consumption of it; gluttony, voracity, ravenousness." Greed lurks menacingly at the threshold between man and beast. The beastliness comes through most clearly in words like the German *Fressgier, fressen* referring to the feeding of animals rather than humans (*essen*).

The classic modern dictionaries build up the history of the word as a series of strata. On top of gluttony comes a second, closely related set of sexual meanings: lust, rapacity, cupidity. At this level the meaning converges with words in the Romance languages such as the Spanish *voraz* and *codicia*. These are evidently extensions of the notion of consumption, the "gobbling-up" of sexual gratification (*Fresslust* in German).[1] As in English, the etymological development is from gluttony to lust, rather than in the opposite direction. If you want to be graphic you might lust after a chocolate éclair or ravage a gateau, but you are more likely to gorge yourself on sexual pleasures.[2]

The older meanings of greed cluster around consumption, the more recent around material accumulation. The classic modern dictionaries portray an extension from thoughtless, primitive beastliness, towards greed as a more self-conscious material vice: "Excessive eagerness or longing for wealth or gain . . . avaricious or covetous desire" (*Oxford English dictionary*). Again, there are parallels for this expansion of meaning in many other languages.[3] The *Readers' Digest dictionary* illustrates this modern overlay:

GREED *n* Selfish and grasping desire for possession, especially of wealth; avarice; covetousness.

GREEDY *adj* (1) Excessively eager for acquisition or gain; covetous; grasping. (2) Having an excessive appetite for food and drink; voracious; gluttonous [OE graedig].[4]

This additional newer layer of meaning coincides with the growth of mercantile and industrial societies of Europe. Nevertheless, the most recent dictionaries still acknowledge that the old gut feelings are not merely semantic traces from the distant past, they are the indispensable, living, sensual roots of the contemporary meaning of greed. Greed has not lost its center of gravity in our bellies ("greedy-guts"). Although today we may be more likely to say someone is greedy for money than food, the meaning is conveyed from gluttony to avarice rather than in the other direction. It is as if the definition of the word has expanded from the inner to the outer man, from the belly to social reputation.[5] When we accuse the bribed politician of "greed" (rather than "avarice" or "self-indulgence") we are still making an allusion to his guts rather than to his purse or his wardrobe or his dwelling.

The dictionaries note two further essential qualities of greed: *vice* and *excess*. You can be greedy about almost anything; what matters is how much you want it, and how much of it you want. This is what gives greed its moral color and distinguishes it from more moderate desires. Food, sex, or money are not inherently bad, but wanting too much of any of them assuredly is. This fundamental relativity in the meanings of greed – its "more-ishness" – adds to the complexities of definition.[6] The notion of excess is not a simple question of quantity – the third helping, the eighth concubine – it is above all a relative judgment about people, who they are and how they relate to one another.

Gut feelings

Modernity has added to the connotations of greed, and it has modified the way we explain it, but the basic meanings remain very much alive. The visceral power of greed is ultimately beyond words, which makes it an interesting lexicographical challenge. In everyday usage, greed is not just a selfish preference or an irrational urge, it is *disgusting*. It remains what it has been for centuries: a gut feeling, stirring up other sensations like anger, envy, or shame – *passions*, as they were once called. Loaded with these sensations, it refuses to be squeezed out of our modern vocabulary.

Greed is rooted in feelings, two in particular: hunger and disgust. They are visceral in that we associate them with input to and output from the belly, with gorging at one extreme and vomiting or excretion at the other. The most direct physical signal of greed is the nausea of overconsumption, the remedy being a violent disgorging. On the twelfth-century tympanum of the Last Judgment, over the front door of the abbey at Conques in France, the glutton is up-ended and being forced to spew by three devils. From the vomitoria which are the historic emblem of Roman excesses to the closing sequences of the Monty Python movie *The Meaning of Life*, the theme is evidently timeless. But it would be hard to match the stylish gut response of King Mithridates of Pontus who, in 88 BC, rewarded the imperial greed of the Roman general Manius Aquillius by pouring molten gold down his throat.[7]

In human experience, hunger has surely been a more frequent and more life-threatening experience than glut, and we have been more generally preoccupied with getting food into our stomachs than keeping it there. (For present purposes I take hunger to include thirst, although there are some slight distinctions in relation to greed.) But we need to strike a comfortable balance, to satisfy the vital urge to feed while avoiding doing so to the point of nausea and regurgitation. The ambivalence in our ideas of greed reaches back to this inner reckoning with the pleasure–pain threshold, first of starvation, and then of satiation and the discomfort of retention. Although for purposes of communication I have to use the labels "hunger" and "disgust," we do not need words to be aware of and to distinguish between these two feelings. Infants discover the pleasures and miseries of gorging and vomiting without instruction, and learn from their experience. What they do not yet know is any of the permutations of meaning which people around them attach to these feelings, such as the notion of "greed." This does not imply that hunger or disgust are "meaningless," only that the meaning of these two terms includes bodily sensations.

What makes greed so interesting is the moral complications which accumulate around those basic feelings. There is a perplexing chicken-and-egg relationship between greed as we experience it and as we observe it. On the face of it, we are more likely to perceive greed as a vice in others than in ourselves. Nevertheless, we are perfectly capable of "feeling greedy" and thus in varying degrees unhappy. Indeed, it is this distress which gives the word so much of its semantic power. A common but unconvincing apology for greed is that if it does not harm anyone else, it is all right. But somehow this never expiates the feelings of guilt which prompt this excuse in the first place: we may not be hurting anyone else, but we are probably hurting *ourselves*.[8] Greed, as several people have told me, is a

Plate 2   The fate of the glutton; detail from the Romanesque tympanum of the abbey-church of Sainte Foi, Conques, France (photo Artephot/ A. Allemand)

Get stuffed

The Big Texan Steak Ranch in Amarillo, Texas, has become a magnet for heroic gluttons. Patrons get their $50 deposit refunded if they can eat a 72-ounce (2,041 grams) steak with a baked potato, shrimp cocktail, salad, and roll, all within an hour. Since 1959, there have been about 27,000 contenders, 4,600 of whom have succeeded, including an 11-year-old boy and a 63-year-old grandmother. Professional wrestler Klondike Bill ate two dinners within the hour, and Frank Pastore, a pitcher for the Cincinnati Reds, cleared his plate in 9½ minutes. No one has died, but quite a few have thrown up, right there, on the table.

Los Angeles Times, September 27, 1997.

self-critical notion, a complaint about other people which is intensified by our awareness of the vice in ourselves. In its chronic form greed is "never being satisfied with what you've got," a perpetual discontent which one informant calls "moral damage." We are all susceptible, he says, to "the easy lie" of assuming that esteem can be accumulated in the form of material goods, or romantic happiness in the form of sexual gratification. The result can only be a deepening spiral of self-loathing.

When the critical notion of greed is aroused, it quickly implicates a range of other sensations. In the medieval imagination, greed had the capacity to recruit all or any of the deadly sins beyond gluttony and lust: envy, anger, and pride, and even sloth. These implicated different body parts, from the envious eye and spleen to the arrogant and wrathful heart. Mercantile guilt seems to have intensified the feelings of invasion. The fusion of gluttony, a vice rooted in consumption, and avarice, a vice rooted in retention (saving) extended the meaning of greed to the full length of the alimentary tract. Eating and shitting are "uncomfortable manifestations of our animality," a subjection to nature which Renaissance man was very anxious to escape.[9] A motif dating back to the Middle Ages is of apes (or men watched by apes) shitting coins into a golden bowl.

Piers Plowman

On his way to Church to confess, GLUTTON is intercepted by Betty the brewer. A mob of tavern regulars treat him to snacks and "drinks of good ale." Amid much swearing and gambling they inveigle Glutton to swig "a gallon and a gill":

> His guts began to grumble like two greedy sows;
> He pissed four pints in a Paternoster's length,
> And on the bugle of his backside he blew a fanfare
> So that all that heard that horn held their noses after
> And wished it had been waxed up with a wisp of gorse.
> He had no strength to stand before he had his staff in hand,
> And then he made off moving like a minstrel's bitch
> Some times sideways and some times backwards,
> Like some one laying lines to lime birds with.
> But as he started to step to the door his sight grew dim;
> He fumbled for the threshold and fell on the ground.
> Clement the cobbler caught him by the waist
> To lift him aloft and laid him on his knees.
> But Glutton was a large lout and a load to lift,
> And he coughed up a custard in Clement's lap.
> There's no hound so hungry in Hertfordshire
> That would dare lap up that leaving, so unlovely the taste.

His wife and maid lug him home to bed, where in a "fit of sloth" he sleeps over the weekend. Waking, he asks brightly for his bowl, and his wife sends him straight to the church to repent. He confesses that he has often

> ". . . over-stuffed myself at supper and sometimes at midday,
> So that I, Glutton, got rid of it before I'd gone a mile,
> And spoiled what might have been saved and dispensed to
>   the hungry."

William Langland, *Piers Plowman*, passus V lines 340–56, 371–3. From *Piers Plowman: An alliterative verse translation* by William Langland, translated by E. Talbot Donaldson. Copyright © by W. W. Norton & Company, Inc. Used by permission of W. W. Norton & Company, Inc.

The idea that greed is *uncivilized* persists: in the Dark Ages we were obliged to live like animals in an "oscillation between extremes of gluttonous gorging and enforced fasting," because food supply and the conditions of life itself were so insecure.[10] From the medieval period onward fatness was no longer an acceptable sign of prosperity. The merchant elite, seeking relief from the dictates of the body, replaced quantity with quality, the belly with the palate, glut with gastronomy, satiation with good taste, brutish hunger with a more discerning *appetite*. Puritan anxieties about self-control as expressed in piety, righteousness, self-discipline, self-purification, self-deprivation – healthy leanness, not bloat – only seem to have intensified the visceral link from gluttony to avarice. Bourgeois guilt was now hemmed in between two rival caricatures, one fat and the other skinny, the raunchy consumer capitalist and the sour, abstemious ascetic, John Bull and Scrooge.

Greed: the word itself may be nasty, brutish, and short, but its moral complexities are dense. Its meaning does not have to be created from scratch for each manifestation (your confrontation now with a third slice of cake). We have experienced it and talked about it, and can evoke it rapidly in our assessment of passing events. Conspicuous consumption of cake may be explicitly labelled "bad manners," a judgment we can pluck at a moment's notice off the moral shelf. But "knowing" greed still depends on feeling greedy, whether that sensation is immediately gastric, or a visceral memory.

Moral mechanisms

Although we tend to think of it as the epitome of selfishness or introversion or egotism, greed is meaningless without reference to others, without some sort of social framework. Some speculation about how the meaning of greed "works" or "develops" in the transactions within and between ourselves may help us to figure out how a notion which is so fundamentally about the body (gorging, lusting, retaining) can be extended to criticism of political and economic excesses.

We know what we mean when we accuse other people of greed because it is backed up by sensations in our *own* guts. It is powerful because it is also inescapably a *self*-critical notion. Observing a piece of gluttonous or avaricious behavior arouses sensations of disgust or anger which, when referred back to judgments about our own actions, engender further sensations of anxiety, shame, or guilt. These sensations are in turn projected onto observed behavior: "this is how that greedy person feels, or ought to feel." We can conjure up bug-eyed, open-mouthed, wet-lipped, chubby-cheeked caricatures of gluttony, or slit-eyed, dour, retentive-lipped visages of avarice. A new layer of fear, indignation, or anger may then be added to the complex. It may include invidiousness, feelings of self-reproach that someone else's acquisitive behavior has aroused my envy. Greed gets really nasty, says Berke, when it joins forces with envy, "a state of exquisite tension, torment, and ill will provoked by an overwhelming sense of inferiority, impotence, and worthlessness." The new compound, which he calls "Grenvy," is aggressive and consciously malicious: it "devours and defiles."[11] It sounds like hard work, which may be why self-improvement courses for businesspersons stress boldness and even ruthlessness. Suze Orman's bestselling book and revivalist TV series *The Courage to be Rich* urges that you must rid yourself of "thoughts of poverty," and cultivate the *feeling* that it is good to be rich.

Greed shows little respect for the boundaries we like to draw between body, mind, and society. Just as it projects feelings out into society, so it draws social experience back into bodily sensations. Pondering how this happens, Bernard Williams reckons that feelings of shame and guilt, both of which seem to play a part in the meaning of greed, are mediated by "internalized figures," simplified moral characters drawn into our selves from our social experience. In the case of shame, the figure is "a watcher or witness," whose special talent is to make us feel powerless in the face of its critical gaze. If this is indeed the way we think about how greed works within us, it may help explain the discomfort aroused by guzzling, in private, six chocolates when three would have been quite enough.[12] Somebody, something, is watching. Furtive gluttony can still make you feel ashamed. For guilt, the internalized figure is "a *victim* or an *enforcer*," who summons up the "primitive materials of anger and fear." The dreadful face of the predator (feeding, lusting) is very much present in the semantics of greed ("Of spoil, prey: greedily pursued" (*Oxford English dictionary*)). Vigilant, compassionate, or scolding, these characters, or caricatures, help us draw our feelings out to explicit, communicable levels incorporating "reactions that are progressively more structured by social, ethical, or moral notions." We can talk about the things that make us feel nasty, but the polysyllables in which we clothe our feelings of weakness, pity, or rage do not dispel the primal feelings on which these "internalized figures" play.[13]

Experiencing greed may, in Williams's imagery, be like entertaining a little crowd of dissenting personae, all pointing in various ethical directions. We may even feel "ourselves" getting defensively detached from the fray, the "others" lumping into a single body-within-our-body, like the ravenous "Inner Man" who is often blamed for greed.[14] The meaning of greed is drawn in large measure from a process of denial: we do not like to be regarded as greedy. If all meaning is in some sense derived by contrast (we know things largely because we can distinguish them from other things), then the opposites of greed (generosity, altruism, abstemiousness, asceticism, etc.) provide the positive ground against which we can perceive more starkly the vicious figure. We play tricks with this, using the negative to accentuate the positive: people can profess to be "greedy" for something virtuous (love, justice, fame). "I'm greedy for the poor," says Nancie Mintie, a Los Angeles populist lawyer.[15] "Greed," says the sardonic Tony Hendra, "founds religious orders, greed speeds missionaries to martyrdom, greed caters charity lunches, greed creates the homeless and the kitchens for their soup." Even Mother Teresa, as she ministers to the starving leper, "is doing all this only because it makes her in some profound way feel good. If she didn't do it she wouldn't feel good. She's looking out for Number One."[16] Shakespeare's Henry V makes much the same point:

> By Jove! I am not covetous of gold,
> Nor care I who doth feed upon my cost;
> It yearns me not if men my garments wear;
> Such outward things dwell not in my desires:
> But if it be a sin to covet honour,
> I am the most offending soul alive.[17]

Consider the popular modern pastime, *collecting*. What may start as an innocent, trivial pursuit can easily become a greedy obsession. Collectors rationalize their urges in many ways: it's an investment, a clever way of conveying value to virtually anything that would otherwise be "junk" – used stamps, old furniture, bottletops, gum wrappers, paintings. Less materialistic excuses emphasize conviviality and difference: philatelists are a nicer class of people. Art collecting, according to the Oxford don Angelica Goodden, is "The greed that can be glorious." "The 'real' collector, as is well known, has an obsessive desire to possess that may be simply a different version of an earlier, less reputable, lust for accumulation." But the guilt of wealth can be expiated in "the enduring art of acquisition." According to Goodden, "luckily, the odium attached to wealth lessens when the cash is channelled into art, since art confers a kind of spiritual respectability."[18] It does so, of course, because so many rich and powerful people have, for so many centuries, made charity one of their defining habits: the collection is morally justified when it is finally dumped in a public gallery.

If the meaning of greed allows such scope for play, the lesson must be that before we jump to conclusions we have to know something about who is being greedy about what, when, and in relation to whom. This works both ways: other people can convey to me the true nastiness of my personal greed, but if we all want the same thing in equal measure, greediness is unlikely to be an issue. This raises the question of boundaries: the "self" in selfishness can be plural, a group or category of persons whose actions are judged together. Viewed from within, struggling to get more food for your family, or more wealth for your nation, is an honorable ambition. Your children or your subjects will admire you, and greediness will be essentially in the eyes of other families or other nations who feel relatively deprived. The question, to which I shall return often, is what "greed" at this collective, political-economic level has to do with the visceral feelings which drive the meaning of the word.

Finding words: needs, wants, and deserts

There is a school in the hills north of Santa Barbara whose fundamental pedagogical creed is to teach its pupils to distinguish their wants from their needs. Emphasizing spartan simplicity in the US frontier tradition, it encourages students to form personal judgments about what they really need and what they merely desire. While it is recognized that there can be no absolute rules for the need : want calculus, many of the desirable things of Southern California are placed outside the students' reach, to help them narrow their perception of need. The only "luxury" they are allowed to bring with them is a horse. Opinions among the students vary as to whether this relative deprivation stimulates or suppresses desires, and their acceptance of the school's philosophy seems to depend mainly on the extent to which they sympathize with their parents' wish to isolate them from urban depravity. A specific assumption of this experiment to allay greed is that wants are ideas about ourselves we pick up from the contexts in which we live – Los Angeles, Hicksville, wherever. Needs, our internal moral yardstick, cannot be taught, they must be *learned* by personal experience in an environment stripped down as close to nature as possible.

The trouble we have in defining greed is that the visceral feelings tend to get lost when we try to put them into words. The explanation which people most usually offer, *"wanting more than you need,"* seems on the face of it clear and succinct. However, this apparently simple opposition is a product of deeply ingrained modern intellectual habits which separate mind and body, and thus split the "feelingful meaning" of greed. This does not help us understand greed better. It reduces it to ambiguity, and lays it open to moral evasion and deceit.

Let us explore some of the logic of talking about greed in terms of "wants and needs." The basic idea is that wants do not themselves explain why we want *more*. Only needs can do that. Greed is not the only way of distinguishing among wants: buying an expensive rather than a cheap car may evoke all manner of moral judgments (pride, extravagance, prudence). It is when the criterion of need is evoked that greediness becomes an issue. If we are consciously moralizing about greed, we are more likely to be thinking reductively about wants (how "needful" they are) than expansively about needs (how "wantful" they are). A corollary of this seems to be that we attach more moral weight to the feelings associated with need and distrust those associated with wants. The most ascetic conviction would be when we *feel* that we have stripped away our wants right down to the core of absolute needs. This seems to be what the Santa Barbara school is aiming for.

In this reckoning, greed measures wants against needs, it is not concerned to discriminate one *need* from another. It is not "greedier" to need carbohydrates rather than proteins, or even sex rather than food. If eating meat is judged greedy (rather than just cruel to animals) it is because this urge is construed as a *want* which, compared with eating vegetables or simply consuming less, is considered a morally inferior way of fulfilling our needs. When moralists down the ages have urged that greed can and must be controlled by acts of will, they have had in mind the regulation of wants, not needs.

An implication of this line of argument is that wants imply some degree of choice, and that greed is the stigma of making the wrong decision. A need, however, is compulsive, implying no option: I must have this, and nothing else will do. According to Plato, needs *(creia)* are conditions of the body *(sôma)*. Their fulfillment, and the prevention of unhealthy excess, depends on the "cooperative inter-dependence" of society – the *polis*.[19] Wants are aspects of the ma-terial and social environment in which we live. In this reasoning, if a want turns into a need it does so by being understood as essential to the body. An example is drug use, which is usually thought of as beginning as a desire and a choice ("just say no," Nancy Reagan advised) but upon which the body comes acutely to depend. Actor Robert Downey, sentenced to six months jail in 1997 for violating probation, apologized for his drug relapse thus: "I really need to do this, even if I don't want to, I need to."[20] A drug user whose chronic "habit" is legalized in the context of treatment is unlikely to be described as "greedy," although the epithet is widely applied to those who "push" drugs. Bringing hunger and disgust into agonizing con-junction, bulimia and obesity have acquired symbolic potency in our societies, with lingering public uncertainty about whether they are diseases of biological need or of social desire. Similar considerations are raised by kleptomania.

Needs are more limited but more compelling than wants. If we do not attend to them we suffer physically. Wants, which are not defined by physical necessity, are boundless and therefore, as philosophers down the centuries have pointed out, are never satisfied. At the extremity of need, any desire may be indistinguishable from dire necessity, which is doubtless why in a particular archaic usage *"want"*

Kleptomania

Andrew Rickards' lawyer says that his client is "neither needy nor greedy. He is an old-fashioned kleptomaniac". On 26 August 1997, the 40-year-old factory worker arrived for his hearing "on a red bicycle which he carefully chained to the front railings of Gloucester police station". The "neatly itemised" hoard in his "neat, well-organised house in Say Little Mews" included 194 cans of fish and dozens of tubes of toothpaste. Rickards admitted more than 2,300 offences – probably a record. A sticker on his front door said "Burglars Beware – Our Property is Postcoded".

The Times [London], August 27, 1997.

Preneed Greed

Need and *death* are closely linked in Indo-European etymology, for example the Anglo-Saxon *nyd*, and the Germanic *nau*. The connection lingers in euphemism. Mortuaries in the US still talk of "the time of need" rather than "death" in their sales pitches. The California Casket Company offers savings "preneed or at the time of loss" on coffins. With prior purchase, Direct Casket of California stores your coffin free of charge "until the time of need" (*Los Angeles Times*, November 9, 1996). "The Neptune Pre-Need Cremation Plan — The Sensible Solution," from the Neptune Society, "Eliminates confusion at time of death" (undated advertising flier, California 1996). The Funeral Consumers' Alliance in the US ("dedicated to a consumer's right to choose a meaningful, dignified, affordable funeral") has mounted an assault on *"Preneed Greed"*, quoting the industry's Sales Counselor Reference Guide (10 July 1997). For example: "The family service counselor must maintain a significant preneed sales volume by pursuing leads obtained as a result of at-need arrangements . . . A structured program should be employed for at-need lead follow-up."

www.vcul.or/famsa/sciprene.html

Ojibwa trials

Native Americans like the Ojibwa have obliged their youths to fast ritually at puberty, not, as often supposed, to give them fancy ideas, but to help them put their lives into perspective. While the adolescent is encouraged to discover the boundaries of need in the proximity of death, overdoing it (fasting unto death) is regarded as simply stupid. Hallowell tells the cautionary tale of an Ojibwa boy who, in his puberty fast, declared he wanted to dream omnisciently of " 'all the leaves on all the trees' ". The fast was supposed to instil a "sense of proportion" (Hallowell 1955: 395, n. 82) not megalomania. The implication of this story is that at the ritual moment when the boy's near-mortal reckoning with need was supposed to have helped him put his normal entitlements into perspective, he expressed an extravagant desire for "more power". Outraged, the *pawaganak* spirits snuffed him out: "He did not live to enjoy the blessings he had been given".

Hallowell 1955: 110.

connotes dearth and poverty. Death marks the extremity of need. A painfully effective way of bringing desires into perspective is to force the body close to this mortal baseline by disciplines of abstention and self-denial. The Santa Barbara school was inspired by native American initiation customs in which a combination of fasting and isolation was supposed to bring physical, mental, and moral growth into closer conjunction. Good judgment in these matters is a metabolic as well as a social imperative: to outgrow your needs (get fat) is ultimately as morbid as starvation; and in Platonic terms, a population which does not balance "healthy needs" and the unhealthy, "insatiable appetite" of superfluous desires falls victim to moral "inflammation."[21]

As Christopher Berry remarks in his book on *Luxury*, "While it makes little sense to say that individuals can want something without knowing they are so wanting, it is sensible to say that individuals can have needs of which they are unaware."[22] Needs are all the more powerful because they can be known and communicated wordlessly, but the fact that they are not acts of will poses a fundamental difficulty in concocting a *rational* explanation of their function in greed. Trying to draw up a list of needs inevitably takes us away from the central references of bodily feeling into particular languages, histories, and geographical settings. Even the classic list of food, clothes, and shelter seems suspect: clothes presumably matter more in northern Europe, where the list originated, than in southern Sudan. If the list is in order of priority it suggests once again an outward progression from the body, to which we could add almost indefinitely. Starting from scratch, Braybrooke abstracts our most basic needs thus: "to have life-supporting relation to the environment," food and water, to excrete, to exercise, to rest and sleep, and whatever else "is indispensable to preserving the body intact in important respects." But he feels obliged to add to this list things which are necessary for *social* rather than just *physical* functioning: companionship, education, "acceptance and recognition," "sexual activity," freedom from harassment and fear, and fun – "recreation."[23] But how are we to draw the line between needful and needless fun? Presumably by weighing up what people say they *want* rather than searching either their bodies or their social environment for clues.

The needs–wants calculus lends itself to word play. If you want something very badly you can talk it down to the level of life-sustaining needs. Thus the business executive may justify his impressive car with the leather upholstery on the grounds that this is what he needs to "make a living." This is the stuff of advertising. In these hedonistic times I can urge you to "pamper" yourself, or treat yourself to the luxury car you "deserve," but if I can convince you that owning a Volvo is a bodily, life-and-death issue for you and your children, how can you resist? If I am sufficiently glib, I can make anything from ketchup to mobile phones sound vital. But evoking needs too freely in the classification of wants soon devalues the currency of necessity. Ironically, one of the perils of putting needs into words, rather than leaving them as simply felt, is to make them harder to distinguish from wants. "Wanting too much" is how civilized people talk about the beastliness of greed. But as soon as any of us opens our mouths to explain what we *need*, we expose ourselves to critical attention. Do we really need what we say?

An implication of this logic is that while animals have many *needs* which they share with humans, only humans have wants, because only humans have the reflexive self-awareness and the meaning systems (languages, cultures) to articulate them. Until children can say what they want, perceiving their needs is a parental challenge. Thereafter, learning to *distinguish* wants from needs is one of the moral hazards of growing up. Moral codes help us sort out which desires or actions are good or bad, tolerable or unpardonable, greedy or generous. We might say that they implant those "internalized figures" which stir up the sensations of guilt, shame, or anger which are symptomatic of greed. But one thing is certain: moral codes are seldom even-handed in their judgments about what people need, want, and deserve.

One of the best ways of justifying luxuries is to declare that they are needs. Obviously, this works best in proportion to the power you wield in your society. Saying who deserves what has been one of the prime functions of political ideology down the ages. To the extent that you are entitled to put yourself first, you will be more generous in your assessment of your needs than mine – unless you are being pointedly humble. What you have the power to claim and the right to get obviously affects what you are allowed to hope for in the first place. A corollary is that if your wants, however modest, exceed your entitlements (perhaps because you are an immigrant, or a girl) you are a political threat. But to be accused of *greed* in these circumstances is political trickery: *your* (inferior) body is being evoked to justify *my* (superior) entitlements. Such imputations of bodily inferiority are, of course, at the heart of categories of both race and gender.[24]

In translating needs into ideas, moral codes leach out the physical parts of meaning. In this maneuver *hunger* ("a body drive which recurs in all human beings in a reasonably regular cycle") becomes the selective, menu-driven phenomenon of *appetite* ("basically a state of mind").[25] We do not need a concept of hunger in order to experience it or to justify the urge to eat, but to say we want chapatis or crêpes we have to know something about Indian or French cuisine. On the other hand it makes little sense to say that it is "greedier" to want chapatis than crêpes: it not the cuisine which is at issue, it is our bodies. However much we persist in this dualistic way of thinking, wants alone will tell us nothing about greed, because wants are ideas, not feelings. Ideas (or cultures, or morals, or cuisines) do not feel – bodies do that. Herein lies the power of a feelingful meaning like greed. Because it is rooted in the gut rather than in ethical codes it carries extra critical leverage, challenging and subverting those very codes that try to put it in its place.

The political coding of *deserts* carries with it the assertion that one person's body is fundamentally different from another's.[26] If we believe this, we can carry greed as an accusation and an excuse to any level. On the outer reaches of the political community, the meaning of greed dissolves into amorality: beyond the line which distinguishes "us" from "them," where people become animals, any kind of gluttonous self-indulgence – plunder, rape, murder – becomes morally possible. Only through some sharply focused image of the victim (the Kosovar child, the stack of Holocaust corpses) will the universal, visceral shock of greed return. The political chicanery to which this dialectic of wants and needs can be turned is boundless, but the vital element of feeling serves as a moral brake. As Rousseau put it: "Greed considers some things wrong which are not wrong in the eyes of reason."[27] Entitlement prevaricates about needs but when greed is evoked in political contexts it has the levelling effect of reducing comparison to the human body. Asking whether the queen deserves the pomp of a state banquet and asking whether she needs to eat all that fancy food are two different questions, but only because we have learned to keep the queen and her body in two different conceptual compartments. "Kleptocrats" around the world, like Emperor Bokassa or President Marcos, have profited hugely from this deception, scaling-up their needs to fit their own estimation of their political status.[28]

Turning wants into entitlements can be hard political and ideological work, and changing the configuration of deserts can involve revolutionary upheaval. Ideologies pull themselves up by their own bootstraps: they work because they are self-validating, constructing a monopoly on truth about the order of things. Their last resort is that they are statements of physical or natural necessity. But this is where words confront the final test of gut feeling. Woe betide the monarchy when the public no longer respects this strategic distinction between what one class of body and another deserves.

These equivocations about needs and wants put us in an intellectual quandary. Do we have any reliable, scholarly means of distinguishing fraudulent needs from real ones? Simply wanting something badly enough does not give it the moral force of a need.[29] Have we any criteria for insisting that needs as asserted by one individual or group or society are more valid than another's? If needs are to be a reliable yardstick for wants, they have to be truly distinct from, and more universal than, "mere ideas." This is the sort of difficulty confronting international experts in their efforts to identify "Basic Needs" for aid or development purposes.[30] The quest is further confused by the innumerable ways in which basic needs may be satisfied. Although for the provision of food we no longer "need" the digging sticks our distant ancestors used, for modern farming we certainly need tractors. The problem is that, as soon as we feel we have fixed on something which looks like a basic need we are foxed by doubts that it is "merely" a want.

A result of splitting feeling from meaning is that virtually no intellectual discipline today – least of all in the humanities – has anything definitive to say about human needs, and thus how they might be prescribed, satisfied, or controlled. No amount of information about calories and vitamins can in itself define greed and thus relieve us of the moral anxiety. We get a lot of relativistic advice about food groups, norms for "average" bodies, and the rather lame insistence that "variety" and "balance" are what matter most.[31] All science can do is ratchet up our anxiety, adding powerful new words like cholesterol to our moral vocabulary. A recent advertisement for a sugar-substitute tries to reassure us: "No calories. No guilt. *EQUAL*."[32] On the other hand, many disciplines have a great deal to say about wants, for which we have an inexhaustible vocabulary, but which do not in themselves offer any moral guidance. Neoclassical economics, for example, makes a science of wants or desires in its utilitarian models of preference, but has no theory of need. It is a thoroughly modern political-economic principle (sorely tested in the selling of tobacco and alcohol) that whatever it is that people say they want is what they need.

The other side of this treacherous needs–wants coin is that, however much biologists may be interested in specifying needs (calorie intake, ambient temperature) for medical or humanitarian purposes, they will make no progress in defining greed unless they can discriminate among wants (glutinous rice cake, fast cars). More fundamentally, their quest will be frustrated because there is one vital aspect of the need threshold with which they cannot, under present scholarly conditions, come to terms: *how it feels*. But to suggest that our bodies can tell us what to think goes deeply against the modern philosophical grain. The problem is that if we insist that "the body" is an *idea* just like any other, its function in the needs–wants calculus falls apart. If needs are merely ideas, varying from one social context to another, what authority can they have over our desires?

Measuring greed

If we *feel* needs to be such an effective moral index for wants, it is because needs are so evidently somatic: they are aroused, sensed, and alleviated through the physical processes of the human body. Our basic understanding of how needs vary comes from experiencing changes in our own bodies through time. Inevitably, our most immediate encounters with greed are in the context of the circadian rhythms which structure our appetite and our need for warmth and secure shelter. Accordingly, our most vivid images of greed may be the extra helping of dessert or a bigger share of the blanket. We reckon needs reflexively by comparing two bodily conditions of our own, in the short term (before and after dinner), but also in the longer term (in sickness and health, in youth and age). These more protracted experiences of need are the most difficult to put into words – and to theorize.

Greed puts these feelings to work in the critical assessment of other people. We do so mainly by comparing intuitively the condition of one *body* with another (the needs of a baby and an adult, or a starving and a well-fed man, are plainly different). We also perceive that needs diverge according to the sexual dimorphism which transects all social systems: women and men need different things at different times. Sporadic acts of greed may be forgivable, but make a habit of it and you will establish your reputation as a greedy person. As William Godwin put it two centuries ago: "Our virtues and vices may be traced to the incidents which make the history of our lives."[33] In the longer term in which personalities are formed and judged, we will not simply compare you with other people, we will compare you with your former self: do you deserve more now than you did a few months or a few years ago? Your best justification will be that you have *grown*, or are growing. While the imagery of greed reduces these larger life processes to the immediacies of eating and copulating, the judgment centers on an implicit awareness of the body-in-time.

Bodies grow, and in so doing they continually disturb every moral calculus. Growth affects all of us, in any population, at any time, and in fundamentally the same ways. How we describe the progression from infancy through adulthood to senescence may differ from one social context to another, but the variance itself is beyond doubt. It obliges us to recalibrate our judgments about each person's behavior. The vital index of capacity, in its most basic form a recognition of divergences in body weight, muscular strength, and available energy, is an important component of our assessment of what people deserve. Nowadays we tend to think that judgments of greed are driven by the multiplication of new objects of desire (digital video, time-shares in Florida). But the older and more systematic provocation of such judgments is the somatic change in needs – the escalating appetites of puberty, the demands of parenthood, physical decline with approaching death.

The historical implications of this bodily dynamism and the demands it places on social systems are enormous, but largely concealed. The meanings of greed (and virtually everything else) change along the axis of growth, making its significance much richer than any static, dictionary-style definition will allow. Growth is the best apology for greed. Greed does not merely assess what I want for lunch, it is a commentary on the expansive urges in my whole life. Young people need to grow, but not indefinitely. Aging brings with it the obligation to devolve, divest, and finally to vanish – or face charges of greed.

As an alibi for greed, growth becomes weaker the further it is removed from its feelingful, bodily frame of reference. Business corporations, we are often told, "need" to grow, but just how far should a "young" business expand before its corpulence becomes disgusting? Greed is not duped by the metaphoric shift. What it does, in these circumstances, is to pursue its quarry into the corporate shell, plucking out the mortals who take refuge there and holding them physically accountable. It brings capitalist voracity down with a jolt to the personal level where a multi-million dollar share option is physically repulsive. An interesting variant of this logic emerges in public attitudes to sports stars and others in the entertainment industry whose admirable bodies are their best alibi against accusations of greed. For the stars, aging is not an asset, and it is widely recognized that they have to get as much wealth as they can while they are physically able. Typically, media criticism of "greedy" stars focuses on their managers and agents – as though sports personalities themselves were all innocent airheads.

The subtlety of greed as a moral tool turns on the fact that it measures our desires against something so intrinsic, dynamic, and protracted as bodily growth. Growth makes an endless moral crisis of our lives, and challenges any notion we may have of the timeless, homogeneous nature of moral systems. It is the dynamism of human growth, fixed in our understandings through bodily experience but obscured in our modern explanations of wants and needs, that makes greed such a potent and versatile epithet. It is a persistent, visceral reminder of the inconstancy of morality, and a moral reminder of the inconstancy of the body. The anxiety which greed generates makes it a sharp instrument in our ethical confrontations with modernity.

Denials and Apologies

3

Beastly Passions and Legitimate Desires

Accusations of greed have been a persistent thorn in the flesh of the merchants, industrial barons, and software tycoons who have flourished during the expansive periods of human history. In the interests of progress, greed has to be talked down, denied, excused. This has been one of the main jobs of the scholarly profession, and their most useful device has been the separation of our noble and creative minds from our beastly and corruptible bodies. The privileged mind has been freed to conjure up new desires, but separating thinking from feeling has not been enough to dispel the guilt of greed – which is why ordinary people continue to use it as a moral tool.

Until very recently physical hardship, disease, and the brevity of life made the unity of our psychic and physical selves painfully evident. Thought, motive, personality, even the immortal soul itself were reckoned to have substance, which mingled with the fluids, organs, structures, and physical processes of the body.[1] While modern Westerners seem to think of thoughts as electrical activity concentrated somewhere behind the eyes but capable of flitting about between people, other people at other times have reckoned that they occur in the heart, the belly, the blood, or in the tissues of the whole body. As recently as the nineteenth century in Europe, expert medical opinion regarded temperament as organically secreted liquids: bad humor was an excess of bile, a deficiency of phlegm, or an overactive spleen. This was no metaphor – anger *was* bile: it emerged from the liver, seat of the "deeper" emotions, and could heat up and invade the heart and the lungs with crippling effects.[2] In the Hippocratic Corpus and its Galenic refinement, healthy *growth* depended on fine-tuning the humors on a daily, seasonal, and lifetime basis. This was vital to the integration of people into the cosmos, whose basic constituents of water, fire, earth, and air paralleled the bodily humors.[3]

Such theories are far from extinct. They persist in the vast popular counter-science which links bodily structure, tissue, and fluids to "well-being" in "holistic" therapies and medications, resisting the assertion that our bodies and our thoughts are two completely different sorts of thing. Sensitive ethnographic interpretation suggests that feeling and meaning are not (as we may thoughtlessly have supposed) separated in other peoples' idea systems, just as they are in ours. A recurrent example is the location of particular sorts of thought in particular parts of the body (liver, heart, stomach, bowels) and the direct association of moral qualities or aspects of personality with these organs and the sensations associated with them ("have a heart," "plenty of guts").

The humors

Humor	Blood	Yellow Bile	Black Bile	Phlegm
Organ	heart	liver or gall	spleen	head
Temperature	hot	hot	cold	cold
Humidity	moist	dry	dry	moist
Season	spring	summer	autumn	winter
Growth stage	childhood, development	youth, maturity	adulthood, decline	old age, decrepitude
Temperament	*sanguine* optimistic, rash	*choleric* angry, jealous, presumptuous	*splenetic* melancholy, spiteful	*phlegmatic* calm, resigned

See Nutton 1993. Note that there were many theoretical variations on this basic scheme.

Dignifying the mind

The patron saint of intellectual splitters must be Plato. He rejected the lumping ("monism") of Epicurus and the mainstream philosophy of his time, and revived some obscure Orphic doctrines about the distinctness of the soul, which is trapped in the body, gives life to it, and is delivered from it to eternity at death.[4] This notion of the detachable, immortal soul resonates with Christian doctrines and has made Plato a pillar of European philosophy for fifteen centuries. From its earliest chapters, the Bible provides an excellent charter for splitters. The story of Adam and Eve lays out a pattern of separations: needs and desires, body and soul, nature and society, good and evil, innocence and shame, power and freedom, rules and choice, growth and history. In the paradise garden the Maker met all man's needs including, as an afterthought, Eve, "a help meet for him" to save him from his loneliness. And "in the midst of the garden" God the inscrutable trickster planted man's downfall, "a tree to be desired to make one wise." A slithery fragment of nature got to work on man's weaker side, illegal fruit was consumed, sex, shame, and guilt were discovered, and desires were unleashed. Doomed by their first act of will, man and woman were cast from the mindless certainties of Eden out into the doubts and anxieties, the sweat and the rot, of the real world. Body and soul were separated, and human reproduction with all its physical and social repercussions began in earnest.[5]

Genesis is a story about the moral agony of physical growth and material progress, and the costs of claiming the right to know what we want and to manage our own affairs. This is the bind in which the merchant classes, more than any other segment of society, have always been enmeshed. They have given us our most elaborate apologies for greed, because it is they who have had the anxiety of getting and keeping wealth, the leisure to fret about it, and the literacy to record their anguish. Aristotle's word for mercantile greed was *pleonexia*, a corrupting, enslaving, demoralizing, and socially disruptive desire for more and more things. Much the same beastly passion lingered in the breasts of the merchant classes that emerged from the Dark Ages in Europe, and like their ancient predecessors they wished devoutly to banish it outside the city gates. In this struggle the Church was not a reliable ally. Not only did it hold the merchants' immortal souls hostage, with its monasteries and vast ecclesiastical estates the Church was their main rival in the accumulation of wealth. However, it was the merchants who bred the clerics, not the other way around, and it was to their surplus sons that the bourgeois families gave the scholarly task of making the pursuit of wealth respectable.

An early inspiration was Augustine (354–430), a magistrate's son from Tagaste in what is now Algeria. An intellectually voracious student, well versed in classical scholarship, he settled in Milan as a teacher of rhetoric. There he was baptized at the late age of 33, and made it his mission to develop a new rationale for Christianity from the wreckage of the Roman Church. His detailed knowledge of Plato convinced Augustine that our best prospects for saving our immortal souls was to exercise the God-given capacity to reason for ourselves. This insertion of the *mind* as a mediator between body and soul became the essential tool in sorting out the accumulation of wealth on the one hand, and spiritual salvation on the other.

The next major agent in God's reconciliation with material prosperity was Thomas, son of the Count of Aquino. In a series of debates *On evil*, Thomas defended the proposition that reason must be the best judge of greed. He also offered the comforting assurance that since it is unreasonable to suppose that you would *literally* worship your belly, gluttony was a venial rather than a mortal sin.[6] His daring views, inspired mainly by Aristotle, on the divine right of man to think for himself, were hotly contested by other clerics who insisted that will was not free, and that only God knows what we need. In the arguments which raged at the universities (which were funded by the merchant guilds) in Oxford, Paris, and Cologne, the "Thomists" soon held sway. Saint Thomas, as he duly became a mere fifty years after his death in 1274, was lionized by the emerging bourgeoisie for his gratifyingly down-to-earth concerns, and Toulouse won a vigorous international competition for the civic honor of possessing his remains.

The debate about free will reopened another split which the classical philosophers had already explored: the relationship between God (the invisible power) on the one hand, and nature (our palpable source of sustenance) on the other. The argument about who controlled what resolved itself into a discussion of three sorts of *rules*: God's, nature's, and ours. The Thomists reckoned that because God's law was supreme it was also very much his business, not ours. The best we could do was seek clues in the scriptures about what he wanted. God delegates to *nature* other laws which are implanted in our bodies and – although we may not always be aware of them –

in our minds. We have to use our minds to regulate our own lives, and so long as we do not directly contradict the laws of God or nature, this third level of mundane, "positive" rules is our own business.[7]

However, this new trinity of laws raised more questions than it could answer. It did not, for example, resolve the age-old ambiguity about man being simultaneously a part of nature and apart from it. Puzzling about this produced divergent images of human history which are still with us: one as rational progress, the other as natural evolution. Plato built up his picture of the ideal cooperative republic as an exercise in logic. The smart way of satisfying our many needs is to specialize, and in the proto-community it would soon make good sense to have a full-time shoemaker. This logic appealed to the merchant class, heavily committed to the task of dividing economic and political labor. They were less comfortable with the alternative, darker view which put nature before reason. In this mode, the Jesuit Juan de Mariana and the sixteenth-century humanist George Buchanan both imagined our earlier lives in nature as solitary wanderers, struggling to stay alive and rear children. The predations of animals and other humans forced us to cooperate. These two images of human history, of the convergence of rational minds, or of a struggle for bodily survival, remain the bases of the humanist's and the natural scientist's understandings of society today.

The ambiguity of "human nature" raised other questions: if it is natural to be reasonable, is it not also natural to be greedy, selfish, or murderous? Thomas Hobbes reckoned that if we were so impertinent as to believe that God no longer had a direct hand in political affairs, we could naturally expect to be governed by perfectly reasonable tyrants. It was certainly not reasonable to assume that ordinary people would naturally rise up and beat a tyrant to death. From what Hobbes knew of human nature the prospects of being ruled by a beastly prince were, on balance, just a little better than being ruled by a mass of beastly peasants.

A response to Hobbes's cynicism emerged in a fourth sort of rule which emanated from the daily lives of the merchants: the studiously rational law of *numbers*. This helped to shift the moral liability for greed from individual conscience to bookkeeping. The calculation of probability, so important in helping the trader reckon with the caprices of nature and his customers, was set to work in the organization of *civil* law, the governing of city and state. The most important product was liberal democracy, the ideal world of the merchant, which makes it a matter of faith that a majority vote will add up to good government. This "utilitarian" creed brings individual decisions and public welfare together: the greatest good flows not *from* God or nature but *to* the greatest number. Closely similar statistical principles were applied by the scholars to the emerging ideology of science: truth was to be found in quantities.

It is not difficult to imagine the mercantile mind which these theories were striving to set at rest. In the inherently hazardous world of trade, the ancient conflict between free will and the need for collective restraint has the character of a neurosis. Business communities are both fascinated by the pragmatics of individual behavior, and indignant about its excesses. They ask for government which is strong and steady enough to protect private property and wealth, but not so strong that it stifles personal advantage. They want laws to boost the mutual trust which sustains complicated long-term transactions, but not regulations which cut into profits. Trade is built on the expansion of personal desires – stimulating wants, not just satisfying needs – and collective restraint should never jeopardize the individual's freedom to make money.

While liberating the mind made it much easier to get on with the business of laying the foundations of the modern state as "an omnipotent yet impersonal power," God and the soul were not to be dispelled so easily.[8] The diehard critics of reason drew the guilty figure of *conscience* into the moral arena. The invidiousness of trade, the envy and extravagance on which it thrives, had to be balanced by public postures of generosity and compassion. One way of resolving these conflicts was by drawing lines of space and time between them: you go to church to take care of the soul, you look after your body at home, and you reserve the library, office, or laboratory for your mind. But in the context of any community, especially the trading elite of a small town or city, these facets of yourself will always be reassembled as your *personality*, a composite of spiritual, moral, intellectual, and other characteristics firmly attached to your body, which you yourself have a practical interest in cultivating. Thomas Aquinas inveighed against this: if you took a pride in your well-rounded personality you should be warned that it is your immortal *soul*, pure and simple, stripped of all personal adornments, which God repossesses in the fullness of time.[9]

Prised away from the soul, the mind now seemed very ephemeral, morally exposed, and lethally bound to the body. "I say again that the body makes the mind," declared John Donne in one of his audacious Paradoxes, composed around the end of the sixteenth century. "Not that it created it a mind, but forms it a good or bad mind. And this mind may be confounded with soul, without any violence or injustice to reason or philosophy. Then our soul (me seems) is enabled by our body, not this by that." And so, he concludes, giving the screw another sardonic turn, if nice bodies make good souls, and riches make nice bodies, do riches not make good souls?[10]

What was needed was a magician to get the rational, constructive mind out of this agonizing tangle. Such a philosopher appeared in timely fashion in the seventeenth century, in the person of René Descartes. Born to the French landed gentry, he had plenty of money to publicize his ideas and to travel around the intellectual capitals of Europe. His role was to separate mind and body once and for all, and to put mind in the driving seat. There was little use appealing to the classical philosophers, because for them mental detachment was not a problem. From Homer to Aristotle, they reckoned that reality was "out there" waiting for our bodily senses to perceive it and our smart minds to explain it. "*Idein*" meant to see, and Plato used it to explain the forms and types we attribute to things as they appear to us. It was not until the seventeenth century, abetted by Descartes, that "*idea*" became a thought or concept distinct from reality. "The mind–body problem" is produced by trying to change direction and figure out *from* the mind how sensations are conveyed *to* the mind. This creates a loop in which it is easy to lose track of cause and effect. To deal with this Descartes felt obliged to go back to square one, to the principle of the ancient Greek sceptics that everything should be doubted, especially the "evidence" of the senses. The career of every serious philosopher, says the pioneer phenomenologist Edmund Husserl admiringly, should proceed "in absolute poverty, with an absolute lack of knowledge" from this point of "transcendental subjectivity."[11]

If philosophy were not such an adult business, we might call this a retreat to intellectual infancy. For all the influence it has had, Descartes's reason for giving the mind its separate and privileged status looks astonishingly flimsy. The only thing about which he could be certain was that he was thinking; and the only reason he could be certain he was thinking was because there he was, entertaining *doubts* that he was actually thinking. Descartes reckoned he could pretend he had no body, but to pretend he had no mind was an impossibility, for there it was, busily imagining that it might not really be there.

> I thereby concluded that I was a substance, of which the whole essence
> or nature consists in thinking, and which, in order to exist, needs no
> place and depends on no material thing; so that this "I," that is to say,
> the mind, by which I am what I am, is entirely distinct from the body,
> and even that it is easier to know than the body, and moreover, that
> even if the body were not, it would not cease to be all that it is.[12]

Descartes's ideas about mind and body were hardly new and his
explanations were much disputed during and after his lifetime. His
determination to think primitively produced a thought of the sort
which occurs to many children: the shocking discovery that "I'm Me"
(rather than, for example, somebody else).[13] Descartes, a shy and
sickly bachelor, had his shock rather later than usual at the age of
23, and in the more drastic, solipsistic form that everything, including his own body, might be a figment of his own mind.[14] Turning the
mind–body coin, we might say that in looking for meaning at its most
primitive levels, Descartes had stumbled on what having thoughts
feels like. These feelings of alienation and isolation were at least as
important as the doubt-ridden thoughts themselves in convincing him
that his mind was something distinct.

Descartes's fame rests on his memoirs of this process of self-
exploration, published in twin volumes of *Methods* and mature *Meditations* twenty years after the original flash of inspiration. "Socrates
used to meditate all day in the snow, but Descartes's mind only
worked when he was warm" – either in bed or, in the case of the
famous *cogito ergo sum*, snug in his "*poêle*," his warm-room.[15]
Descartes recounts the physical and emotional details of his discovery of this marvellous new out-of-body method for science. He
went to bed in great excitement, dreaming fitfully of his career in
philosophy.

The agony of his convictions about doubt permeate Descartes's
Meditations. The trouble with philosophizing is that tends to take us,
willy-nilly, out of our bodies. But the splitting doesn't stop after we
have detached our minds. Thinking about thinking makes a new division, and wondering about our selves adds another. Before long, a
clutch of psychic entities – mind, soul, consciousness, personality –
are jostling for our attention.[16] Pretty soon we lose track of the one
thing that holds them all together: the living body. Modern Cartesians who take the mind–body split for granted seem to forget that
Descartes's goal was a better understanding of physical reality, and
that the ultimate philosophical question was not *whether* but *how*

mind and body are linked. Sometimes he sounds like a lumper: "Nature teaches me by these feelings of pain, hunger, thirst, etc. that I am not only lodged in my body, like a pilot in his ship, but, besides, that I am joined to it very closely indeed, so compounded and inter-mingled with my body, that I form, as it were, a single whole with it." The trouble is that nature, through the senses, passes unreliable information about proportions, textures, etc. to the mind. With "all the errors to which my nature is subject" I must be grateful for the superior judgment of my mind – "being able to make use of my memory to link and join present knowledge to past, and of my under-standing which has already discovered all the causes of my errors."[17] Since the evidence of the senses is unreliable, rational thought (fun-damentally, for Descartes, geometrical measurements of "extension") is the key to knowing the external, material world. One must reach out from the abstraction of the idea to the thing, not (like the more empirically-minded Aristotle) from things to specific mental abstractions.

The trouble with doubt as a method, says Bertrand Russell, is that it can only work if scepticism stops somewhere.[18] But where do we break the loop from mind back to mind? The great unresolved ques-tion of Cartesian thought is what sort of relationship the mind ulti-mately has with the body, and thus with other matter in the "real world." Lumpers would simply solve the equation with an equals sign: "mind = body."[19] While Cartesians have piled more and more oppositions on top of the mind–body split (thinking/feeling, ideal/material, etc.), most are vague about how and why things "pair off" in this way.[20] If we split mind–body, why not also make a fetish of shape–body, or motion–body, or behavior–animal, or prop-erty–thing?[21] The best theoretical sense that can be made of the mind–body separation is that they work "in parallel," that there are "thoughts that depend for their existence on the existence of suitable referents for their subjects": to say "that bird is a chaffinch" depends on there being a bird *out there*, not just flitting around in my mind.[22] Huge amounts of ink have been spilled on how and why this "iden-tification" of an idea and an object does, or does not, happen.[23]

Descartes himself was greatly exercised by this problem of how something with no substance connects with the material world. The link, he deduced, must be within our bodies, must be physical, and must involve "motion" (a topic of consuming interest to mathemati-cians and philosophers of his time). It consisted, he thought, of tiny particles (*"les esprits animaux"* – the animal spirits) produced by and racing around in the bloodstream between all parts of the body including the brain. Those dealing with routine body functions and attending to its needs were different (more "*animaux*" than "*esprits?*") from those produced in the brain by the process of thinking. The tricky question, for a devout Catholic like Descartes, was how these more "subtle" *esprits* connected with that troublesome third entity, the soul. Treading the fine line of religious heresy, Descartes thought this was handled by a special "little gland in the brain," probably the pineal.[24] There the soul exerted its influence over thought, and thereby over the *passions* (which were not to be confused with other sorts of thought) presented to it by the messenger *esprits*. The God-given, moral task of the soul was to provoke the mind into rational corrective responses: "there is no soul so feeble that it cannot, being well led [*étant bien conduite*], acquire absolute control over the passions."[25] *Our* task as thinkers in all this hectic activity was to keep a tight grip on our ideas, exercising "premeditation" in "correcting natural faults by striving to separate within oneself the movement of the blood and the *esprits* from the thoughts to which they are customarily connected."[26] Learning to run the body-machine this way would keep beastly vices like greed at bay.

The trouble with explanations like the "*esprits animaux*" is that they take the mind–body ambiguity down to a microscopic level without in any way resolving or explaining the split. Faced with the implausibility of all this, it is little wonder that Descartes resorted to the lame and oft-repeated assurance that it is simply in the body's *nature* to be connected with mind. When the sharp-witted Princess Elizabeth of Bohemia pestered him about this, he told her just to relax and *feel* the union of body and soul.[27]

In the centuries since Descartes's death, the difficulties of explaining the split have been vastly outweighed by the usefulness of separating mind from matter. From the independent control center of the mind, the material world can be authoritatively observed, known, and manipulated. The rational mind can now explore reality without the encumbrance of bodily feelings. This "ingenious removal of the Archimedean point into man himself" has been both the revolutionary premise of modern science and the biggest obstacle to its quest for objective truth.[28] Science has Descartes to thank for its central neurosis: a working principle of doubt masked by a demeanor of certainty. From this ambivalence has emerged the schizophrenic hierarchy of "pure" versus "applied" science, the cogitators and the doers.

Putting science and philosophy into a respectable partnership has guaranteed Descartes his celebrity. The separation and dignification of the mind was also important in the building of the professions, asserting a discreet distance between the thoughts and hands of the doctor, the strategizing and killing of the soldier, the computations of the accountant and the greed of his clients. The mind was freed to think creatively about the differences between metal and wood, or why objects fall down rather than up. But if there is a positive science of physics, why should there not also – as Descartes himself urged – be a positive science of mind? Alas, placed at the center of human existence the privileged mind has been robbed of the capacity to make objective sense of *itself*. Disciplines like psychology and moral philosophy have labored mightily against this disadvantage. If there can be no reliable way of thinking about thoughts, the explanation of ideas is left to gyrate around the periphery of respectable science.[29] Matter cannot argue, that is what minds do. This poses special problems for thinking about someone *else's* mind – one dubious entity confronting another. Descartes was too wrapped up in his own mind to have many thoughts about its relations with others, which is partly why Cartesian logic has been such a fragile basis for modern *social* science. Disembodied science can still tell us little about what thought is, and absolutely nothing about what we *should* think. Little wonder that the liberal defense of science, that it makes a virtue of doubt, should have met with so much skepticism.

Ironically, even those modern "materialists," who reject the notion that ideas come first, are still destined to argue from within the premises of the mind–matter split. In Cartesian logic, this is arguing from incoherence: Descartes insisted that the mind is 'entirely indivisible,' whereas matter is dispersed, fragmented, and awaiting the attentions of the organizing genius of mind.[30] But this notion of mental "integrity" – so full of wholesome moral resonances – is a sham. It takes its cue from the immortal unity of the soul, that divine ally of the mind which "helped to get the religious authorities off scientists' backs."[31] Mental unity assumes that we are all perfect logicians, that our thoughts all connect meaningfully and consistently with one another. This is surely denied by our daily experience ("I'm in two minds," "I can't make up my mind"), in which unaccountable feelings and unthinking routines play such an important part.

Most scientists are too busy to fret about philosophy, even when scientific discoveries shed doubt on the Cartesian premises of science

Guttals and inklings

In taped testimony made public on October 2, 1998, Clinton's personal secretary Betty Currie insisted that although she was aware of the impropriety of telephone calls between Clinton and Lewinsky, "I didn't want to know anything or be able to say I knew anything." Pressed hard by Independent Counsel Kenneth Starr to explain in what sense she knew about the affair, Mrs Currie declared "It was guttal . . . I had a feeling, but I had nothing to base it on, other than a gut."

Not even packages passed from Lewinski to the President, or the fact that they were often alone together, or the fact that she addressed him as "Handsome"?
Mrs Currie insisted "I had nothing to base it on except a guttal."
Counsel persisted:

> Q: Well, Mrs Currie, you've testified now several times that you had inklings, suspicions; you wanted to avoid the appearance of impropriety with respect to their relationship. You had inklings that, in fact, they had a sexual relationship, isn't that true?
> A: No, I did not have inklings.
> Q: So when you testified before that you had inklings, what did you have inklings about?
> A: There was a crush of some sort. I didn't have any inklings of sex.

> *Los Angeles Times*, October 3, 1998.

Much philosophical energy has been devoted to what may and may not be admitted as "thoughts," and the extent to which they depend on "consciousness." Crane's illustration that you and I "think" that President Clinton wears socks, even though that thought may not have crossed my mind, seems spurious to me. Crane argues that this thought was *latent* in my mind. I think it was put there by Crane – I didn't think it, he did, and when he mentions it, it is the counterfactual suggestion that Clinton might *not* wear socks that surprises me. I am "conscious" that I believe his sock hypothesis is correct, but hitherto I had not so much as an inkling* – nor even a guttal – about Clinton's socks. The closest I could get was the knowledge that he had a cat of that name.

Crane 1995: 27–8.

> *Inkling*: a hint or whisper, intimation, "a dim notion or suspicion"
> – Middle English *inclen* to hint at (*Chambers dictionary*).

itself. An interesting example is Descartes's insistence that the mind exists in time but not in space. This possibility is disproved by Einsteinian relativity: if the mind has a "when" (remembering, connecting one idea to the next, adjusting inconsistencies) it must also have a "where" – some coordinates in physical space (perhaps the brain?). The "motion" of a one-dimensional mind, how it actually works, has sorely taxed the ingenuity of Cartesian philosophers. If one disembodied idea simply clings to the coat-tails of another in a string of "serial co-consciousness," the fabric of mental integrity seems very flimsy.[32] But the conception of mind as a mesh of logical strands (algorithms) lingers on in computer images of the mind as "software", and of the brain as a self-contained machine, operating and readjusting itself.[33]

These puzzles about dimensions make it difficult to imagine mind as both a structure and a process – a set of parts changing through time. We usually end up talking about "mental states," without having a clear idea how or why one "state" leads to another. Removing the mind from the body makes it truly lifeless, but it also deprives us of the one good reason we have for regarding it as a separate entity in the first place (which was, of course, how Descartes identified his own individual mind: *I* think, therefore *I* am). Moreover, disembodying the mind makes it much harder to contemplate *other* minds: whether yours might in any sense be "the same" as mine, what distinguishes them and how they interconnect, and how minds come and go – how they *grow*, and how they shape each other in a wider community of minds. Aristotle would not have approved of this disembodied mind. For him mind/soul was consonant with life – *anima* – and thus with the vitality of the body. But through *growth* it transcended individual bodies, first in the reproductive nucleus of the family and then in the political association of the community. By contrast, political growth in the Platonic and Cartesian mode is a convergence of rational minds, something studiously remote from the indecencies of birth, copulation, and death.

We have paid a heavy price for abstracting the mind and putting it in charge of a separate material world. Since Descartes, the mind has gathered a retinue of positive psychic associations (thought, meaning, stability, integrity, character), leaving other attributes (passion, change, decay) with the body. The danger of proceeding in this Manichean mode is that moral qualities soon get drawn into the dyadic scheme, producing infinite regressions of polar opposites: mind/body, good/bad, right/left, white/black, male/female . . . These contrasts belie the fleeting shades of grey which are the real measure of our daily lives.

The greatest damage has come from the wider uses to which this notion of a detached, superior, self-generating, self-regulating, systematically integrated, feelingless mind has been put. I am most concerned by the unthinking transfer of this concept from the tight little mental box in which Descartes imagined it, out to the synthetic supermentalities of "*a* culture," "*a* nation," "*a* society." Composed not of human bodies, but of some narrow and dubious ideas about the integrity of "us" and our separation from "them," these ideas have encouraged sectarian violence on an increasingly large scale. At best, this expansion of the Cartesian mind is a misplaced metaphor. By comparison, "greed" has a penetrating directness which refuses to let your fancy ideas fly free of your old-fashioned, mortal body.

Obliterating feelings

We should remind ourselves that this painstaking abstraction of meaning from feeling was basically about the right to make money with a clear conscience. The next step in this historic project of making up our modern minds was the translation of the mercenary passions like greed into morally acceptable terms like *self-interest* and *preference*. Descartes had laid down some basic principles for arguing that these were *reasonable*, the motives and choices of free minds. John Locke made his reputation as the founder of modern liberalism by insisting that money-making, the expansion of trade, and the necessity of the state emerged *naturally* and benignly from cooperative relations in the bosom of the family. These efforts to put a positive spin on the expansion of wealth and trade met with a good deal of cynicism. The satirist Bernard Mandeville was repelled by the bourgeois social moralizing of the Enlightenment, and argued that whatever progress we had made owed more to the social effects of our natural vices than our intellect. In his famous allegory, when the bees try to live by principles of virtue alone, the hive falls apart.[34]

It is ironic that in arguing that primeval greed is the driving force of modern society, Thomas Hobbes, a near-contemporary of Locke's, provided one of the strongest positive rationales for *self-interest*. According to Hobbes, we have both the self-preserving need and the egalitarian right to go for as much as we can get: "Every man by nature hath right to all things, that is to say, to do whatsoever he listeth to whom he listeth, to possess, use, and enjoy all things he will and can." The catch, of course, is that everyone else can do likewise: "that right of all men to all things, is in effect no better than if no man had right to any thing. For there is little use and benefit of the right man hath, when another as strong, or stronger than himself, hath right to the same." Since "men by natural passion are divers ways offensive to one another," "Reason therefore dictateth to every man for his own good to seek after peace."[35] The choice is between cooperation or mutual destruction. Although Hobbes is best known for his grim characterization of man's life *in* nature,[36] it is the need to associate meaningfully with others, the passionate mind at work in society, which is the essence of *human* nature. Thus, it is in our nature both to be greedy and to have to moderate greed: co-operation is "natural" in the dual sense that we need it because of our animal weaknesses, and can do it because of our human mental advantages.

There has been much discussion of what Hobbes actually meant by "nature": evidently not one but many things, ranging from physical and mechanical processes, to life in primitive communities, and to the structure of logic.[37] Hobbes's natural science of man reaches down to the physics which underlie psychological mechanisms on the one hand, and up to the legal mechanisms of the state on the other. Accordingly, *body* is a triple-entendre in Hobbes's work. It is an elementary physical notion, roughly equivalent with "matter" or "mass," and contrasted with *motion*, in the manner of a structure/process distinction. It is also the assemblage of organs, limbs, needs, and capacities which we think of familiarly as "the human body." In this framework, sensations are "motions" detected by touch, sight, etc. and conveyed (as "*endeavour*") by nerves to the brain. From there they proceed to the heart where they cause pleasure or pain, and are thus attractive or repulsive, depending on whether or not they assist vital motions. The third sort of "body" is the political corporation, the main object of all this conjecture. Hobbes is vague about the "motions" which connect one human body to others in the body politic, but the process apparently begins when we make our own minds up about the morality of a selfish impulse. This involves some compounding of different sorts of passion. Love, for example, combines sexual lust and the pleasure of gratifying another: it "consisteth of two appetites together, to please and to be pleased."[38] We then legislate against greed by entering into contracts with others in the context of civil society. While Hobbes regarded moralizing at the individual level as entirely natural, he was less sure about civil laws (the critical test was whether they were "reasonable"). He did not doubt, however, that the *need* for regulation was "natural."[39]

In his quest for a down-to-earth explanation of human nature, Hobbes reveals the dilemma of the urges to lump and to split. Part of his confusion about "nature," and thus its moral influences, arises from his obligation, as a philosopher of his time, to factor in God. Thus, "body" in its most abstract senses (mathematics and supreme power) gets equated with the deity. Nevertheless, to the extent that he sought to argue relationships between what we sense and how we sense it, and how that determines how both our minds and our societies are made up, Hobbes brought us as close as we may ever have come to an integrated scholarly theory of greed. Given the massive compass of his endeavor, he may be forgiven for mechanical failures in the way he traces the connections, and for thinking of sociality as immediate, self-interested deals rather than a moral process extending through lifetimes and through history.

Although in several respects David Hume brought us even closer to a scholarly understanding of greed, he ultimately left us much further away. Like Hobbes he has been criticized for fuzziness in his ideas of nature, but he too insisted that knowledge of man in the political mass must derive from an understanding of basic physical feelings. Hume was convinced that you cannot figure out human morality by focusing, like Descartes a century earlier, on "pure reason" – natural, God-given, or whatever. Determined to dissolve the "combat" in moral philosophy between reasonable virtues and natural vices, Hume proposed that we are moral beings because of, rather than in spite of, our basic passionate nature. But morality could not, he insisted, be deduced *directly* from the social mechanics of Hobbes's primeval "self-love."

Developing a psychological explanation of how this happens, Hume embarked on a series of analytical separations, beginning with feeling and meaning. "Human nature" is "composed of two principal parts, which are requisite in all its actions, the affections and understanding."[40] The former are "impressions" deriving from physical sensations ("necessities"), most basically pain and pleasure. Since they depend on "natural and physical causes," they are the proper business of "the sciences of anatomy and natural philosophy."[41] Although they are logically prior, these "original" affections are "reflected" into "secondary" impressions through our ideas or "understandings." Hume pursues a "vulgar and specious division" of these secondary impressions into the "calm" (beauty, composition) and the "violent" (a motley collection of passions ranging from joy and love to fear and hatred). He distinguishes some of these further as "indirect," to the extent that they are blends of other more "direct" violent passions which are the components of our "natural temper." Thus, he classifies desire, fear, and joy as violent passions of the *direct* sort; and love, hate, pride, and humility as *indirect*.[42]

The main object of this elaborate breakdown is to show how a moral idea as complicated as "justice," which other Enlightenment philosophers would regard as a strictly rational construct, can be traced to basic physical sensations. However, when they are elevated to the level of ideas like justice, passions are reduced to "faint images," which Hume was concerned should not be mistaken for the beastly motives on which Hobbes's "selfish system of morals" was based.[43] The effect of this analysis is to disconnect the passions from the body, and to turn them into something very insubstantial – tenuous mental "reflections." Hume directs anyone who wants to know more about "real" bodies, in all their animality and indecency, to the anatomist's table, where no amount of picking and probing will tell you the meaning of "justice." Meanwhile, liberated from flesh and bones, the passions can be thought of as independent psychic agents *working on each other*, producing new and useful compounds such as "sympathy" and "trust."

In the crucible of the rational mind, even unpleasant passions can combine into positive moral outcomes. Pushing this Enlightenment rationale a step further, Hume declared that a passion might actually work *to restrain itself*, somehow bringing its own contrary forces into equilibrium. Selfishness was the prime example of a passion which could *only* be controlled by itself. In the following paragraph Hume is trying to sort out the justice of holding private property:

> It is certain, that no affection of the human mind has both a sufficient force, and a proper direction to counterbalance the love of gain, and render men fit members of society, by making them abstain from the possessions of others. Benevolence to strangers is too weak for this purpose; and as to the other passions, they rather inflame this avidity, when we observe, that the larger our possessions are, the more ability we have of gratifying all our appetites. There is no passion, therefore, capable of controlling the interested affection, but the very affection

itself, by an alteration of its direction. Now this alteration must necessarily take place upon the least reflection; since it is evident, that the passion is much better satisfied by its restraint, than by its liberty, and that in preserving society, we make much greater advances in the acquiring of possessions, than in the solitary and forlorn condition, which must follow upon violence and an universal licence. The question, therefore, concerning the wickedness or goodness of human nature, enters not in the least into that other question concerning the origin of society; nor is there anything to be considered but the degrees of men's sagacity or folly. For whether the passion of self-interest be esteemed vicious or virtuous, it is all a case; since itself alone restrains it; so that if it be virtuous, men become social by their virtue; if vicious, their vice has the same effect.[44]

In this paragraph, the self-regulating integrity of Descartes's mentality meets, and prevails over, the nastiness of Hobbes's physicality. Greed is sanitized, first as the "love of gain," then as an "affection of the mind," and finally as "the interested affection." Thus reconfigured, greed controls itself, by logical necessity and "upon the least reflection" by ourselves. Whichever way it works on itself, the effect is the same: reducing an unruly passion to a calmer and more genteel interest, befitting the self-disciplined demeanor of a good citizen. If the action of the passions was hectic and unpredictable, Humean *interests* joined together in a stabilizing web. Thus, says Hirschman in his account of this transformation, "the term 'interests' actually carried – and therefore bestowed on money-making – a *positive* and *curative* connotation."[45]

Recasting greed as a disembodied, self-modulating, beneficial interest helped clear the way for the most materially expansive episode in human history, industrial capitalism. In Hume's account, the reconstruction of greed acquires the force of objective, scientific fact.[46] In times of rapidly expanding political-economic scale, it was important to assert the universality of these material interests – again by allusion to their "natural" origins and society-making logic.[47] Detached from the passions, the interest in accumulation became objectivized as a relentless, self-generating force. The purpose of wealth was not to serve human needs, but to beget more wealth.

Inventing rational self-interest

Adam Smith provided the most influential justification for "the emancipation of economics from morality."[48] In his earlier speculations on moral sentiments (1759), Smith made much of the essential and redeeming, but rather feeble human passion of *sympathy:* "the great precept of nature to love ourselves only as we love our neighbour, or what comes to the same thing, as our neighbour is capable of loving us." A key function of "sympathy" was to hold feelings in check: the expression of passions arising from the body is "indecent," because "the company, not being of the same disposition, cannot be expected to sympathize with them." Thus "to eat voraciously is universally regarded as a piece of ill manners."[49] In *The wealth of nations* (1776) this idea of sympathy as social logic has hardened into a theory of self-interest: "It is not from the benevolence of the butcher, the brewer, or the baker, that we expect our dinner, but from their regard to their own interest. We address ourselves not to their humanity but their self love and never talk to them of our own necessities but of their advantages."[50] The ideological force of Smith's account turns on the cumulative social benefits he thought would derive from the unfettered operation of this motive. Nature disposes us to take pleasure in "wealth and greatness," and these "insatiable desires" are the prime vector in history. They stimulated agrarian civilization with its landlords and peasants, and were at work in the making of industrial society. But, in an unexpected appeal to the belly as the ultimate leveller, Smith declares that there are limits to what the rich man can *consume:* "The capacity of the stomach bears no proportion to the immensity of his desires, and will receive no more than that of the meanest peasant." True, "The rich only select from the heap that which is most precious and agreeable," but they are still compelled to

> divide with the poor the produce of all their improvements. They are led by an invisible hand to make nearly the same distribution of the necessities of life, which would have been made, had the earth been divided into equal portions among its inhabitants, and thus without intending it, without knowing it, advance the interest of all society, and afford means to the multiplication of the species. When Providence divided the earth among a few lordly masters, it neither forgot nor abandoned those who seemed to be left out in the partition.[51]

Hirschman comments that "There seems to be no place here for the richer concept of human nature in which men are driven by, and often torn between, diverse passions of which 'avarice' was only one." The monolithic construction of self-interest – "simplification on a grand scale" – had stripped people, with all their complex visceral motives, locked in time through bodily growth into specific social networks, down to uniform economic agents.[52] This is a great analytical convenience, but the cost in understanding has been immense.

The Smithian model of self-interest is at the heart of Western ideologies of liberal democracy, in which efficient and morally neutral markets (and by analogy ballot boxes) link the abstract, rational individual to the benign state. The unleashing of desire, the growth of markets, and the freedom to choose all go hand in hand, and are enshrined in ideas of "good government" – that is, government which guarantees individual freedom and the uninhibited expansion of wealth. In this ideal world, institutions (firms, lawcourts, fiscal systems) are elaborate "contracts" which result from everyone trying to strike the best possible deals for themselves. The liberal leap of faith is that rational self-interest, efficiently mediated, produces the best, not the worst, of all possible worlds. If things turn out badly, it is because competition was "imperfect." This is not an inherent fault of self-interestedness nor of markets, but the result of external interference, usually human tinkering (unfair tariffs, nepotism, socialist policies). But by insisting that self-interest must be taken on face value and its freedom of expression guaranteed as a political right, neither liberal economists nor "efficient" markets can discriminate which sorts of self-interest are more disruptive than others. The best that can be done is to blame "irrational" motives (greed) which are not the business of economics.

Despite decades of criticism from within liberal ranks of the dangers of reducing virtually any aspect of behavior to analogues of trading, this logic is tenacious and contagious. Increasingly elaborate models of "rational choice" bear diminishing resemblance to how ordinary people seem to think, behave, and *feel*. Criticizing the economist's understanding of rationality in terms of "the acceptability of the assumption of the invariable pursuit of self-interest in each act," Sen has remarked that "the *purely* economic man is indeed close to being a social moron."[53] Lacking any theory of what people need, the liberal analyst can only take at face value what individuals say they want. However, ordinary people cannot define their wants with the sort of precision an economist requires, far less rank them on a single, analyzable scale of negotiable *preferences*. Advertisers are frustrated to discover that modern consumers buy impulsively, on what Midgley calls "direct desire," although we have all learned to accept spurious economic rationales for these gut feelings ('I am 30 percent less likely to want carrots than potatoes').[54]

The irony is that for all its analytical complexity, modern economics can only accommodate the simplest images of human motivation. By now, there is far too much at stake institutionally for economists to dismantle the analytical framework of the market. The best that can be done is to press the existing explanatory apparatus to its limits.[55] Struggling with the paradox that "in many situations the conscious pursuit of self-interest is incompatible with its attainment" (it doesn't make economic sense), Robert Frank has invoked the passions, but always with the intention of readmitting them to the conventional economic mill. What interests him is how emotional or moral behavior, although apparently irrational, can be turned to strategic advantage.[56] This simply continues the Enlightenment quest to reduce the passions to positive, rational logics.

When Adam Smith was barely 10 years old, Alexander Pope, rhymer to the English bourgeoisie, had already put a cheerful holistic spin on the new sanitized version of greed:

> Thus God and Nature link'd the gen'ral frame
> And base Self-love and Social be the same.[57]

A more down-to-earth commentator in the nineteenth century might say that God had been sidelined, nature was being raped, and self was fast becoming alienated from the emerging industrial society. Smith's simplified view of economic agents grappled with a new and morally stark split between microcosm and macrocosm: the disembodied, undifferentiated but rational *individual* on one side, and the overwhelming and mystifying mass of modernizing *society* on the other. The emerging social science of the nineteenth century struggled to make sense of this new monster, finding ironic contrasts in the complexity of persons within the bounds of simple communities, and the simplicity of individuals in the boundless complexity of modern society. Some scholars sought to piece the fragments of society together from individual up (J. S. Mill, Max Weber), others to resolve the whole structure into its components, from the top down (Comte, Marx). The middle ground between these poles was littered with bones of contention: what makes a social class, or a nation, or a city.

The assumption that free markets would "transform selfish individual behavior into benevolent social outcomes" is the basis of liberal economics as a policy science. "The leap from positive to normative economics is usually accomplished by a wave of the invisible-hand theorem" says Mueller.[58] The theorem has nurtured the economic profession for two hundred years, but public faith in economic science has been stretched very thin during the course of the twentieth century. The liberal theorist can only shrug: show us a better theory and we'll buy it. The Marxian objection is that markets are loaded with values which direct benefits towards the privileged few (the bourgeoisie) who organize markets in the first place. The socialist remedy is to change and control these values so that they actually do work democratically. To achieve this, however, the economy would have to be stripped down to its most basic social relations, and reassembled. As they developed during the nineteenth century the doctrines of liberalism and socialism, symbolically contrasted as Right and Left, formed different rationales about what was *natural* about progress. The socialist sees modern society as a perversion of nature (and God as the opiate of the masses) and yearns for the restoration of our simpler communitarian selves. Trusting in individual free will, the liberal is grateful for what little success we have had in taming nature. Modern society may not always seem so great, but unlike the socialist utopia it's *real*, and to the extent that it's the best of all possible worlds, it can only be "natural."

These new alliances between reason and nature pushed the passions into further disrepute. The Enlightenment scholars made a virtue of *sensibility* (the judicious use of sight, taste, touch) and excoriated the passions which were, in Kant's words, "without exception bad." They were "cancerous sores for pure practical reason" and thus the greatest threat to the freedom of will he so much admired.[59] For his near-contemporary Rousseau, the passions were somewhat ambiguously natural dispositions which rational adults should have outgrown and learned to control. For example, the enlightened educator could use the natural greed of little children to develop good taste, but adult gluttony was a failure to mature sensibly and reasonably – it was "the vice of feeble minds."[60]

While ordinary people have continued to use "greed" in much the same way as their medieval forebears to criticize much the same class of commercial upstarts, the word is banished from the vocabulary of Locke, Hume, Smith, Kant, and even Hobbes. Self-interest was smart, greed was dumb and retrograde, an unwelcome reminder of our brutish and unenlightened origins. And yet modern economics is still dogged by doubts about whether rationality has triumphed over greed, or whether this vice remains an ineradicable force in modern life. "Greed is always in the news," grumbles *Forbes Magazine* journalist Dan Seligman. "Let's deep-six the damned word. Its use on the religion page would possibly remain acceptable. On the business page it just muddles things." He mistrusts those cocky assertions that greed is good, urging that "it is time for the media to stop invoking greed as something that explains economic behavior." But very evidently the old vice remains behind its modern mask: "Face it: Self-interest is a universal human trait, a near-defining characteristic of Homo sapiens."[61]

The public has not been duped into imagining that "self-interest" has purged markets and money-making of old fashioned human vices. Mark Barton was not equivocating about self-interest when he murdered his wife and two children in 1999, then went on a rampage killing people in two day-trading establishments in Atlanta where he had lost a lot of money. His suicide note declared: "I don't plan to live very much longer, just long enough to kill as many of the people who greedily sought my destruction." To dismiss this ultimate act of self-recrimination as a tragic collapse of logic is to lose the moral significance of his final message. It is sobering to reflect that so much about the circumstances of Mark Barton's death now lies beyond the compass of the scholarly mind.

4

Disciplining Greed

While greed has kept its critical force by holding meaning and feeling together, scholarly explanations have been pulling them apart for centuries. Although modern scholars often say they don't take the mind–body split seriously, it is now set very deeply within academic structures. Disciplines have divided and subdivided along the major fissure, producing a mosaic of more detailed but increasingly divergent explanations of human life and behavior. A notable casualty has been the human body: although it is so evidently the center of our being, the disciplines have reduced it to different sorts of abstraction: a puppet for the gene, a sensory shell for the psyche, a symbolic machine for culture. Having lost track of the body in the making of meaning, biology, psychology, or anthropology can offer only fragmentary and conflicting impressions of something as ingenious as greed.

Everything a scholar does seems to affirm the imbalance between a superior and integral mind and a disintegrated and inherently meaningless body ("matter" is often the preferred pairing). "Since the seventeenth century," says Searle, "educated people in the West have come to accept an absolutely basic metaphysical presupposition: *reality is objective.*"[1] The program of scientific discovery is said to begin with the evidence of the scientist's own senses and some old-fashioned speculation, but the proof depends on rigorous objective procedures for verification. In this process, feelings must be suppressed, making them the *least* accessible phenomena for science. Scientific study of feeling, very important in, for example, the medical management of pain, is stuck with the problem of trying to define objectively something so utterly subjective. Efforts to deal with this have produced sub-disciplinary oddities like "psychophysics" and "sensorimetrics."[2] We approach the afflicted body through the mind, trying to make sense of what people *say* they feel. The result is a bizarre game in which the scientist tries to take his or her own mind out of itself, creating an objective third party which reduces the sufferer's sensations to case notes which can then be studied and compared. "We have the conviction that if something is real, it must be equally accessible to all competent observers," says Searle. The catch is that if a feeling is particularly difficult to objectify (foreboding, love, envy) we tend to think of it as "unreal." "The ultimate absurdity is to try to treat consciousness itself independently of consciousness."[3]

Greed and the psyche

These are basic problems for psychology, whose role in the scholarly division of labor has been to make objective sense of feelings. These are most usually treated as "emotions," a controversial label which reveals how widely and uneasily psychology is strung out between the natural sciences and the humanities.[4] In common with other universities my *alma mater*, Edinburgh, offered psychology degrees in two streams, one leading to a Bachelor in Science the other to a Bachelor in Arts. The schizophrenia appears in the many compound adjectives for "emerging fields" (psychoneural, psychophysical, psychosomatic . . .).

Finding physical analogs for mental states – the Cartesian "problem of representations" – is a practical dilemma for the scientist-psychologist trying to locate emotion as "a noncodified, prewired communication process" in the body.[5] The tendency for "anger," for example, to "light up" many different regions of the brain in electroencephalographic experiments indicates that it has little "domain specificity" – or that we do not really know what we mean by "anger" in the first place.[6] It is hard to imagine which part of the brain, if any, would be "lit up" by greed, partly because it is not "an emotion" in these reductive terms. Possibly gastric chemistry would provide a stronger clue. More than a raw motive, greed is a critical judgment, and its moral complexity suggests that, like other "emotions" such as guilt or shame, its meaning derives as much from what happens between people as from what goes on within their brains.

In Greek antiquity, *psyche* (like other aspects of being which we might translate as thought, consciousness or spirit) was a physical property of the living tissues, fluids, vapors, and processes (including reproduction) of the body.[7] It was also pictured as a sprite-like female figure who, in the myths, had some difficulty disengaging herself from sexual affairs. Because some ill-defined aspects of the psyche could survive death and decay it has been misleadingly translated as "soul" or "breath-soul." Later associations of "psyche" with consciousness and personal identity have given a little classical panache to the development of modern versions of "mind."

The psyche was captured as a scientific object in the nineteenth century, most notably in the work of Sigmund Freud (1856–1939). In his scheme, the individual psyche (Ego) is the active mediator between nature and culture. Its role is to "mentalize" as *"Id"* the energizing forces from bodily growth, and to "mentalize" as *"Superego"* the constraints emanating from social relations. It is important to understand that, for Freud, "Id" is not the "real" body but a psychic image of it, represented mainly as "drives" or "instincts"; and that "Superego" is not the "real" social domain, but a psychic image of it. The psyche is thus isolated as an integrated and integrating object, which may be explored clinically for malfunctions. Operating in and around the periphery of consciousness, the Ego provides access, mostly through talk, to experiences which are either too deeply rooted in the body or too dispersed in "culture" to be knowable without professional help. Needs and wants are strung out in a complicated process of communication between these three agents in Freudian psychology: bodily needs are translated as *"libido"* (Latin for "desire") by the Id and expressed socially via the Ego as *wants*. Healthy growth follows this path from nature to nurture, and unpleasant emotions like greed are libidinous frustrations (weaning, toilet-training) which linger into adulthood.

Disengaging the psyche from the "real" body (which, according to Freud, was the proper business of physiologists) and "real" societies (the proper business of historians and sociologists) was vital to the creation of a new discipline and profession of psychology. Freud himself could not resist the temptation to push psychology beyond the bounds of its own psychic constructs, offering the sweeping criticisms of *Civilization and its discontents*.[8] But Freudian analysis operates through a very limited set of metaphors which describe the negotiation of feeling and meaning *as if* they were in the hands of distinct agents (the feral Id, the conscientious Ego, the sociable Superego). The Ego is the analyst's ally in the struggle to get in touch with the other two, but the conversation is handicapped by the fact that they are all scholarly figments, not "real" objects with a role in history, economics, or politics. They certainly do not bring us any closer to the Cartesian grail of scientific proof that the mind exists.

Still, Freudian ideas have been very useful. While the public has been captivated by the idea of getting in touch with the inner beast, the link between the psyche and the social domain has had much influence on ideas of "culture." Psychologists on the humanist side of the fence reject the implication that "emotion is located in the bodily container" and look for cause in social influences rather than inner states.[9] In this reasoning, emotions are moral qualities rather than feelings: you have to know how to do them before they have any meaning for you. This has led to the view that emotions are essentially outside the body: they are, says Clifford Geertz bluntly, "cultural artifacts."[10] This view turns the attention of the psyche away from the Id and the libido, and focuses it almost exclusively on a quite different set of "needs": the preservation of order in the *collective* mind. Emotions are "constituted and prescribed in such a way as to sustain and endorse cultural systems of belief and value."[11] However, this new authoritative object is not the "Superego," which was just Freud's way of imagining how ideas from the outside world present themselves to the mind. The main hazard of thinking of culture as a communal "hyper-psyche" which shapes the individual psyche is the tautology of explaining one metaphor in terms of the already very complicated metaphoric extension of itself. "Culture," declared the anthropologist Leslie White, "must be explained in terms of culture."[12] There is no place in this closed loop for the meaning of something as sensuous as greed.

Greed and culture

"Culture," as it is variously understood in anthropology, history, and other interested disciplines (including the hybrid "cultural studies") exists outside our individual bodies as some sort of medium in which our minds are suspended. It is a system of ideas which gives meaning to all the physical and non-material things which are part of our lives. Culture tells us how to behave, but each of us has a tiny role in replenishing culture, because somehow messages about our actions filter back into the general pool for future collective reference. Exactly how this happens – how we do culture and how culture does us – is an old and unresolved question. The biggest puzzle is *how long* it takes (minutes? decades?) for actions to influence ideas, and vice versa.

The notion of culture as something separate from and bigger than the mind, and of sociology as quite distinct from psychology, owes much to the influence of Emile Durkheim (1858–1917), one of the "founding fathers" of professional social science. Trying to tidy up his ideas about "human nature" towards the end of his life, Durkheim embarked on a new level of conceptual splitting: if "man feels himself to be double," it is because "he actually is double." We have two entirely different sorts of consciousness, one tied to our bodies, the other to society as "something that surpasses us." This "dualism of human nature," Durkheim insists with breathtaking presumption, is "a belief that is universal and permanent . . . In every age, in fact, man has been intensely aware of this duality." It is only by communicating with others through this second sort of consciousness that we have any inkling about the first, which is locked up mutely within us. However, body-consciousness resists social-consciousness "and, in order to make it conform, we have to do some violence to it, we have to submit it to all sorts of laborious operations that alter it so that the mind can assimilate it." This Cartesian struggle, evocative of Freud's discipline of the savage Id by the refined Ego, is the making of civilization. To help us cope with this psycho-social "antinomy" we have religion, says Durkheim. And to help us deal with the objective analysis of it, we have the necessarily distinct professional disciplines of sociology and psychology.[13]

Our ideas of culture developed within the context of nineteenth-century natural science, and the image of society as a some sort of living "super-organism" has lingered in virtually every interpretation of culture. It is therefore ironic that the most important steps in the construction of culture as an object, and cultural anthropology as a discipline, were taken in direct opposition to biology. In America, Franz Boas based his challenge to racist elaborations of evolutionary theory on the assertion that every person "had" a culture, that cultures differed, that bodies – being inherently the same – had nothing to do with these differences, and that each culture therefore had to be understood and respected in its own terms. In this "highly reductionist project" the whole human world was seen as a mosaic of distinct cultures, each unit comparable with and morally on a par with the others.[14]

This appeal for the understanding of difference ("multiculturalism" as it is currently known) has greatly boosted anthropology's moral authority. And yet most anthropologists know very well that the "integrity" of culture is a myth, an assumption we make so we can get on with the analysis. In fieldwork the boundaries of culture are blurred or invisible, cultures nest within cultures, they mutate, merge, and disappear, and one individual can "have" many different cultures. Making "culture" into a scientific object of inquiry runs into a scaled-up version of the Cartesian problem of trying to know someone else's mind: if the idea of culture is actually a product of *our* culture, why should we assume that *other* people "have" culture, or even know what we are talking about?[15] When people distinguish themselves from others, they evoke many different sorts of symbol (language, dress, skin color, possibly even portmanteau words like "custom" or "tradition") but unless they have been talking to anthropologists they do not say "culture."[16] Confronted with this vortex of doubt, many anthropologists comfort themselves with the assurance that, however confusing culture may be, at least there is no risk of its being mistaken for biology.

The British anthropologist Bronislaw Malinowski (1884–1942) played a key role in extricating culture from nature and biology, and making it the center of gravity for a distinct academic discipline. The younger Malinowski reckoned that all human beings have physical needs which it is the function of "social institutions" to fulfil. "Kinship," for example, was organized in fascinatingly different ways around the world, but there could be no doubt that every society had to organize reproduction *somehow*. Conceptual difficulties began to appear when an institution (war, law, religion) in one society was either missing or did not appear to be doing quite the same job as "the same" institution in a different society. To complicate matters, the basic *human need* for food or sex is not the same as the *social necessity* for law. Institutions of "kinship," controlling sex and organizing reproduction, deal with both orders of need/necessity. To solve this, Malinowski moved his "*Scientific theory of culture*" across the line from materialism to idealism: institutions do not simply respond to basic human drives, they also *need to adjust to one another*.[17] To make up a coherent framework for action, ideas of kinship "need" to mesh with law, law with religion, religion with economics. With this organic metaphor of a self-regulating culture, anthropologists could give "scientific" assurances that if you meddled with land tenure, you could expect *some* sort of reaction in religion, or kinship. Of course, to know precisely what sort of reaction, you would have to pay an anthropologist to go out into "the field" to trace the connections.

The notion that culture (and language) add up to *one* thing and not many is modelled on the unity and integrity of the *mind*, in its bodily container, much as Descartes imagined it. But societies are not brains, and cultures are not minds. Exactly how and where cultural "thinking" occurs, and how such thoughts are contained, interconnect, and change, is the mystery which has kept anthropologists in business for so long. The main implication of Malinowski's or Boas's understandings of culture is that a great many of the ideas it contains (the Catholic mass, motorcycle maintenance) may never enter our individual minds (although some priests maintain motorcycles). Culture is much more than each of us needs to get through one life, and we become conscious of most meanings only when occasion demands (taking holy orders or trying to mend a carburetor).

Although culture does not have a "real" mind to contain it, its coherence is taken to be "obvious" or "logical." Language, the most obvious medium for moving ideas around within specific populations, is our basic model for the coherence and distinctiveness of culture. Language has grammatical and lexical rules which control meaning by restricting the ways in which you can put words together. Indeed, many scholars treat culture as just a more complicated and inclusive sort of language, in which everything from music and architecture to rolling a joint is part of the repertoire. Taking this a step further, many culturalists would agree with Wittgenstein that we cannot have thoughts which are *not* communicated to us through language. Without this coding even physical objects which we ourselves make (spoons, the Eiffel Tower) are meaningless. The implication is that it's actually culture and not our minds which does the thinking.[18]

Cultures are not self-conscious agents which set themselves up in opposition to people or nature, because cultures in that integral sense are inventions of scholars, notably anthropologists. Corralling cultures in their own self-contained fields of meaning makes it very difficult to explain what distinguishes one culture from another, or how and why they change. It's a problem of perception: to see the figures (cultures) you need a background which makes them apparent (some sort of "meta-culture" or universal pysche). The danger is that as an anthropologist you will unwittingly take your *own* culture to be transcendent, defining the terms ("kinship," "gender") in which *their* cultures are to be described and compared. But in what sense are (say) Eskimo ideas less effective than ours in coming to terms with Hindu cosmology? The only way out of this semantic traffic jam is to assert that all cultures share some common ground – that some meanings are universal, others not. But which? Marshall Sahlins, one of the high priests of American cultural relativism who has made passionate assaults on biological and economic determinism, tells us forthrightly that greed is "a cross cultural or human universal."[19] How does he know? He has neither a theory nor empirical evidence for this assertion, and other cultural anthropologists would be as likely to agree as to disagree with him. But Sahlins needs *some* universal background on which to set his distinct cultural figures. "Greed" is smuggled in to help explain culture, but by this gesture greed itself is culturally inexplicable.

Dissatisfaction with all this vagueness has turned increasing numbers of anthropologists to the search for generalizable, physical bases of culture. Curiously, one of the strongest influences in this trend has been the symbolic structural anthropology of Claude Lévi-Strauss. Raised in the Durkheimian tradition, he was fascinated by the integrity of culture, but as his career progressed he was drawn to the conclusion that the tendency to structure meaning was a general human propensity that could not come simply from within culture itself.

Earlier, Lévi-Strauss argued that each culture was held together by key ideas – not necessarily obvious to the people themselves – which could explain the whole assemblage of meaning. The basic need to find a mate led to rigorous coding of people into marriageable and non-marriageable categories, which formed the structure of "simple" societies like the Australian aborigines. Fascination with how symbols fitted together led Lévi-Strauss to the analysis of myths, in which a recurrent theme was the original separation of human society from nature – a question which also happened to be close to the heart of Western philosophy.[20] Lévi-Strauss concluded that the urge to make this sort of separation turned up in so many cultures that it could only come from the nature side of the gap. He found a timely ally in the linguist Noam Chomsky, who was looking for the "deep structures" of grammar which generated all languages and which were disguised by the more recent and superficial differences between languages.[21] In a reductionist leap which bypassed both body and psyche, Lévi-Strauss concluded that the tendency to split symbols into pairs (nature–culture, women–men, left–right, night–day) was a byproduct of the "electronic" processes of the brain. The idea was deeply seductive, captivating scholars far beyond the compass of anthropology: symbols do seem to pair off, in the manner of positive and negative charges. But what about the Holy Trinity, the Three Bears, or even the Magnificent Seven?[22] What is even less clear is why the pairs should *themselves* link up into strands (nature/female/left/night/) which weave the fabric of culture.[23]

The notion that we must necessarily have binary thoughts about our thoughts would seem to explain Cartesian dualism at a single, mind-numbing stroke. But humanists who have been entranced by Lévi-Strauss's speculations about "the binary oppositions which are basic to the structure of ordered thought," have been unable to accept the underlying biological premise that we must resort to the *brain* for an explanation of culture. In the work of Edmund Leach, who did much to spread Lévi-Strauss's theories in the English-speaking world, the *mind* which shapes language and culture is still serenely detached from the bodies which reproduce people. "Kinship," he insisted shortly before his death, is the ordering and naming of people and relationships which "has very little to do with biology." "Mating" and "marriage" are not complementary aspects of a single human process but are "as different as chalk and cheese," the one irrelevant to an understanding of the other.[24] Was this categoric distinction the mature judgment of a very experienced anthropologist, or was it, as Lévi-Strauss's structuralism would predict, just a primeval reflex of Leach's own brain?

Greed and the gene

Dissatisfaction with the "the ontologically vague, quasi-mystical notion of 'culture,'" which imagines the mind as an "empty vessel" to be filled with the ideas which float mysteriously around us in social space, has led to a regrouping of psychologists, anthropologists, neurologists, and others around the study of "cognition."[25] Ideas, private or public, must be suspended in some physical medium, and the only plausible mind-substance is the brain, without which ideas simply could not take place. And – so this logic goes – if the brain makes thoughts, it must have an active role in shaping the ideas we share as "culture." Inspired by computer analogies, cognitive scientists now seek to define "the architecture of the human mind," the ways in which brain structures dispose us to behave in some ways rather than in others. "Culture, to put the matter as succinctly as possible, is biological. Its elements are produced by individual cognition, which has a biological basis."[26] At the moment, however, the links between grey matter and even our simplest cultural constructions are almost entirely speculative, mainly because we still know so little about how the brain works.[27]

Ironically, culturalists are even more susceptible than biologists to the notion that we are all born equipped with some natural *potential* for culture. This is the basis of the supposed "psychic unity" of mankind, an idea which can be traced from contemporary textbooks back through the sermons of Bishop Butler in the eighteenth century, to Aristotle. Psychic unity is "a proposition for whose empirical validity the ethnographic and psychological evidence is altogether overwhelming," says Clifford Geertz, doyen of the American cultural anthropologists. It is "not seriously questioned by any reputable anthropologist," mainly because psychic *dis*-unity is a racist premise.[28] However, psychic unity is truly an "empty vessel," "the absolute zero of cultural development."[29] If we all have the same bodies and brains, they cannot explain why cultures differ, and it is cultural difference that keeps anthropologists in business. "How then does biology figure in culture?" asks Sahlins. "In the least interesting ways as a set of natural limits on human functioning. Most critically, human biology puts at the disposition of culture a set of means for the construction of a symbolic order."[30] This, of course still begs the question of what is doing the constructing. Most anthropologists are vague about this. "The term 'mind,'" says Geertz more cautiously, "refers to a certain set of dispositions of an organism. The ability to count is a mental characteristic; so is chronic cheerfulness; so also – though it has not been possible to discuss the problem of motivation here – is greed." This is a significant retreat from ground zero. But "the drawing of a line between what is natural, universal, and constant in man and what is conventional, local, and variable" is, Geertz admits, "extraordinarily difficult."[31]

This vagueness about our physiological potential for culture clears the way for the "naturalistic fallacy" that patterns of culture are biologically programmed. For more than a century this speculation has been driven by a powerful theory which unifies all branches of biology: evolution by natural selection. As a modern scholarly doctrine, evolutionism (or "Neo-Darwinism") is based on the microscopic processes by which life is regenerated. From fingernails to moral scruples, we are what we are because that is how our species prevailed in the war of adaptive fitness. If greed (whatever it may be) matters enough, it will stay with us from generation to generation as part of our survival kit. The meaningful question is whether our genes have any long-term use for it, not what we short-lived mortals think about it.

The modern baseline for the distinction between our nature (the material receptacle) and culture (the ideal contents) is the paleolithic, the period 50,000 to 100,000 years ago in which our physical evolution notionally "ended" and cultural development "began." This discontinuity is awkward: whatever physical capacity we may have to "do" culture – on which we are now so thoroughly dependent – must have been in place long before anything worth calling culture actually appeared.[32] This has prompted arguments that body and culture have "co-evolved" through to modern times.[33] But, say the geneticists, this is far too fast for any significant physical changes to have occurred. From the perspective of genes, the best we can say is that culture has lately become part of our environment, a possible constraint on *future* selection. But culture is a need which is encountered and dealt with today by our bodies, not by the genes themselves.

A great virtue of evolutionary theory is that it takes our meddling selves and all our fancy ideas out of the picture, connecting the microbiological (genes) to the macrohistorical (species), in one grand factual sweep. Messy middle-level things like greed only matter to the ephemeral beings we call ourselves, stuck as we are in our feeling-thinking bodies. The business of genes is not to make the organism happy or reveal life's mysteries: "Over generations, it is successful *traits* that 'survive,' not individuals, and this sort of long-term survival depends not only or even primarily upon the longevity of those carrying the trait, but upon the abundance of their progeny."[34] This "selection thinking"[35] regards the body as a sort of residue of species-making: "organisms are the sediments of contingencies which have passed the survival test."[36] The implication "is to leave the individual organism as a hermetically sealed bundle of innate dispositions" unconditioned by, and prior to, any social context.[37] August Weismann's separation of the "generative and immortal germ plasm" from the "transient, mortal somatoplasm which was effectively the adult organism" created the new science of genetics. This amounted to a reduction of life to molecular biology: "the organism as an entity structured by distinctive principles of order and organisation had disappeared." But geneticism – the doctrine which reduces the adult organism to information in the egg and sperm – is "as flawed as the claim that cookery books bake cakes."[38]

The division of gene and organism is reflected in the two disciplines, genetics and developmental biology, which have now become "damagingly separated one from the other."[39] Who we are depends not simply on genetic prescription, but on the contexts (material and ideal) in which that information develops into our bodies and selves; and the future of that information depends crucially on what we, as feeling-thinking beings, do with it.[40] Avoiding the body is a great convenience, but biologists bent on explaining the intricacies of human behavior are confronted with the extreme difficulty of arguing from microbiology through the many explanatory levels to a complete Beethoven symphony, the rise and fall of the Third Reich, or my preference for Bass ale.[41] Nevertheless, Wilson and Lumsden are confident that this is possible: "You can reduce the curves on a body-temperature chart, and the curves representing a mountainscape in a Japanese painting, apparently identical, by *reducing* the two expressions through the full complexity of levels of analysis and synthesis, to their biological bases."[42] Most biologists would wish to do nothing of the sort. But choosing to ignore culture altogether is, in the case of the human animal, to disregard the central ethological fact of its development.[43]

Since there is, as yet, no biological theory of ideas, or of desires, or morality, there can be no "natural" explanation of greed. Instead, explanation has moved in the opposite direction, culminating in Dawkins's well-known image of "the selfish gene," the greedy little meta-person who uses our bodies for his own sublime purposes, driving us willy-nilly to acts of evolution.[44] This is an image borrowed from Smithian economics, and it carries with it a similar false assurance that if genes are left properly to their own self-interested devices, all will be for the best in the best of all possible worlds. But in strict Darwinian logic, organisms are not "interested" in anything, nor do they "choose."[45] They are not evolving in any predetermined direction by design or intent, they are being selected by ecological mechanisms. Biologists are as much suckers for metaphor as the rest of us – witness the enthusiastic exchanges between biologists and economists about "altruism" (is the gene rational? Is self-interest natural?).[46] Another Dawkins invention is the "*meme*," a metaphoric shift of the gene into the domain of culture: memes are ideas and bits of behavior which mutate, select themselves, and direct our behavior, again without our knowledge.[47]

These grandiose claims about the gene have fostered the professionally empowering notion that it is "*biology*" (compare "anthropology" or "psychology") which directs our minds. Thus Richard Alexander in *The biology of moral systems* (1987) seeks to reduce the competitive interests of individuals to genetically programmed fitness strategies *and* to explain why idealist critics of biological theory do not know what they are talking about. "A theory of interests is a theory of lifetimes – how they are patterned and what they are designed (by evolution) to accomplish." These "ultimate interests" put humans on a par with other animals: "that is precisely what the science of biology is all about: finding out about the interests of nonhuman organisms and their manners and extents of realization."[48] Because the real bases of "interests" are beyond human consciousness, they are resistant to thought – especially to the thinking of cultural theorists. Our genes have no interest in letting us know what they are up to, which helps to explain why *we ourselves* have a built-in hostility (expressed in rudeness to biologists) to realistic explanations of the way we behave.[49]

Humanists who are content to let biologists define basic human nature should beware of what Oyama calls the "homunculoid gene" who inhabits our bodies and constructs our minds. This "animistic metaphor" is "a mischievous tautology": you can't have a gene "for" something (e.g. blue eyes, or cheating at cards) unless all sorts of other conditions, mostly to do with bodily development in a specific context, are fulfilled.[50] Steven Rose is appalled by the "neurogenetic determinism" which has taken such a grip on the public imagination. Among other things, it allows us to blame the wicked genetic homunculus for our sins – not the least of which is a belief that the "natural selection" of the liberal marketplace is politically and economically best for us. It is this sort of evasion which the moralizing device of greed disallows. Rose's solution is "to put the organism and its lifeline back at the core of biology, to counter the gene's eye view of the world."[51] This might allow us to understand the moral work of greed, but it implies an understanding of the body which may now have been lost to science.

Disembodiment

"Stiffened from long sleep in the background of scholarly life, the scholar's body yearns to exercise its muscles," says Stoller. But "a sensuous awakening is a very tall order in an academy where mind has long been separated from body, sense long severed from sensibility."[52] The privileged Cartesian mind has reduced our bodies to intellectual fragments. They have been dissected and reapportioned, claimed in material form by biologists, and in "ethereal" form by humanists.[53] "We now have discursive and material bodies . . . physical, communicative, consumer and medical bodies . . . individual and social bodies . . . medicalized, sexualized, disciplined and talking bodies." Little wonder that we have a deepening "crisis in our knowledge of bodies."[54] And little wonder that we have no coherent theoretical framework in which to account for greed.

The most promising effort to reclaim the body for modern scholarship has been the philosophical method known as phenomenology. Its modern pioneer, Edmund Husserl (1869–1938), proposed "an *all embracing self-investigation*" which took only the evidence of the senses as the basis for a universal "science of the factually existent." By a painstakingly subjective logical analysis of experience he sought to rebuild science which, in its obsession with objectivity, had become "lost in the world." This would be a bootstraps job, an "an egology of the primordially reduced ego" leading to an "intersubjective phenomenology" which would eventually stitch all our various individual awarenesses into some sort of human whole.[55] The tragedy of phenomenology has been its fixation on, and failure to resolve, the old Cartesian dilemma of trying to make sense of the body while actually inhabiting it.

Husserl's disciple, the French psychologist Maurice Merleau-Ponty, was persuaded that "The perceiving mind is an incarnated mind." He insisted that in phenomenology "the body is no longer merely *an object in the world*, under the purview of a separated spirit. It is on the side of the subject; it is our *point of view on the world*, the place where the spirit takes on a certain physical and historical situation."[56] Another Husserl disciple, Martin Heidegger, was likewise impressed by the *there-ness* of the body, its factual existence in time and space (*Dasein*), as a condition of our "Being-in-the-world." But in what possible form could the body, "understood as a thing among things, as a collection of physico-chemical processes," be admitted to the Cartesian mind, with its entirely different order of existence?[57] Only, it would seem, by reducing it to an abstraction of the same order.[58] This is bootstraps philosophy with a vengeance. For Heidegger "There-ness" is "ontic," an idea which must confront its *own* "There-ness" in a seemingly irreducible impasse: "the fact that in its Being this being is concerned *about* its very Being." Or, even more mysteriously: *"Understanding of Being is itself a determination of Being of Dasein"* (1977: 54).

Latterday phenomenology has been preoccupied with this agonizing business of " 'putting the body back into the mind,' " an inversion of Husserl's earlier goal.[59] The phenomenologized body has been obliged to part company with "the 'body' as a biological, material entity," and has been translated into a new metaphysical object, "an indeterminate methodological field defined by perceptual experience and mode of presence and engagement in the world."[60] This new abstraction is called *"embodiment"* (although a more accurate label would surely be *"enmindment"*) and has been turned into a psychic agent, "a mediator between the self and the world,"[61] "a hybrid looking both ways," subtly "transducing" and "transforming."[62] Despite the hope that this scholarly figment "collapses the duality of mind and body," it simply adds another doppelgänger to the old duo, and a new level of perplexity to the explanation of culture.[63]

Phenomenologically, there is no meaningful reality beyond the compass of our own senses. Antarctica or sheep's-eye stew exist in the very limited sense that I have heard you talk about them. On the other hand, the fact that we can tell each other about these things and find them marvellous points to *some* general sort of human perception. Merleau-Ponty was very excited about this: "The idea of a single history or of a logic of history is, in a sense, implied in the least human exchange, in the least social perception." Being able to "do" culture at all testifies to the ultimate irrelevance of cultural difference. "All human acts and all human creations constitute a single drama, and in this sense we are all saved or lost together. Our life is essentially universal."[64] But proving this version of psychic unity from first phenomenological principles was, Merleau-Ponty acknowledged, the most massively daunting task.

The reduction of the body to ideas produces interesting, and at first sight gratifying effects. Take, for example, Lakoff and Johnson's influential account of *Metaphors We Live By*, which starts with the phenomenological premise that we use personal experience of our physical selves to communicate things of general interest to others. From an awareness of our own coordinates (e.g. up:down) there "emerges" a consistent fabric of similarities (up/happy:down/sad) which we share with others as a *system* of metaphors. These in turn get parleyed into more complex notions, such as "objectivity": "The speaker puts ideas (objects) into words (containers) and sends them (along a conduit) to a hearer who takes the idea/object out of the word/container."[65] However, this raises tautological doubts about *where* these metaphors are doing their business: "out there" in social space, or "in here" in our embodied minds? Once it has served its metaphoric purpose, the body disappears. Lakoff and Johnson say that "each culture must define a social reality within which people have roles that make sense to them and in terms of which they can function socially."[66] Latching onto "culture," metaphors detach themselves from the body and acquire a mysterious life of their own, begetting *new* metaphors, which in turn shape our behavior. For example, the "entailments" of the metaphor "time is money" spin off influential similes like "investing in a relationship," which in turn affect the ways we do business with each other. In this shift from "nature" and the feeling-thinking body as a source of metaphor, to the metaphors as a self-regulating mass which influence our feelings and thoughts, the causal progression degenerates into "an indefinitely analyzable gestalt of naturally cooccurring properties." In this chicken-and-egg conundrum we are left even further from an understanding *why*, for example, we should imagine that "ideas are food."[67]

The problem for Lakoff and Johnson is that the "culture" to which they attach their body-metaphors has for long been thoroughly disembodied. Defined by Geertz as "extragenetic, outside-the-skin control mechanisms," the idea of culture cannot accommodate the feelings which earlier generations of philosophers knew to be the link between our ideas and our physical being.[68] "Instead, the body is viewed simply as a "blank screen" or "sign receiving system" ever open to being constructed by external texts or discourses."[69] Students of culture have come to imagine the body as an array of members, surfaces, interiors and connecting orifices whose purpose is to organize and communicate meaning (the queen is head of state, I foot the bill). For example, the mouth, deconstructed as a piece of symbolic equipment, becomes a topological object on the interface between an inside and outside.[70] However, cultural analysis has not been able to resolve a basic conundrum in body-symbolism: is the body merely a handy framework upon which any sort of meaning can be mapped, or is it a source of meanings which are projected out onto social categories? I can use bits of my body to register meaning (English is my mother tongue) or to express it (I can stick my tongue out at my mother), but it is easy to lose track of the direction in which the symbols are moving: "flesh both *inscribes* and *incorporates* cultural memory and history" declares Stoller.[71] Little wonder that the "real" body and its functions tend to get lost in this symbolic cross-traffic, while argument gets bogged down in ambiguity or in closed loops of cause and effect.

Many scholars today seem satisfied with this intellectual closure. A case in point is Pierre Bourdieu's assertion that "Taste, a class culture turned into nature, that is, *embodied*, helps to shape the class body." The argument begins with the idea that the taste for food depends, like much else, on "the idea each class has of the body." From this it follows that "the body is the most indisputable materialization of class taste." In fact there is no "material" here in any biochemical or neurological sense, for taste has been converted into a political metaphor, merging guilelessly with "taste" in the sense of preferences for clothes or art. The body is likewise put to work in the metaphoric loop, shedding its physical attributes and "shaping" another metaphor, the collective "body" of a social class. This in turn shapes taste . . .[72] These speculations draw on Bourdieu's influential "theory of practice" (which was in turn inspired by Heidegger) in which bodies are the physical agents in the "reproduction" of culture.[73] In this interpretation the body works like an electronic capacitor, accumulating, holding, and discharging bits of information and behavior (posture, gesture), mostly without the person being aware of what is going on.[74] The body is a repository for habits and routines, a machine for mimicking behavior, but not itself creating anything of any significance. The mass of our individual "performances" simultaneously realize and remake culture. These images of embodiment are attractive because they tell how culture actively persists in space and reorganizes itself in time. But in this representation of the body as symbolic agent, the living, growing organism, as any biologist might recognize it, is absent. "The embodiment of culture leads to nothing less that the disembodiment of the organism!" protests Ingold (1998: 27).[75]

Historians in particular have been entranced by the notion that the body itself is "unfinished," and that meanings must be "inscribed"

Gluttony and good taste

It is curious that taste, the bluntest of the senses, should have become such a strong metaphor for aesthetic judgment and social distinction. Our taste buds only discern bitter, sour, sweet, and salt. Our perception of flavor depends heavily on the subtleties of smell, but we do not usually esteem people for their good smell.

The authority of taste has some primeval, visceral roots, but it also measures the distance between our feral and our civilized selves, between our beastly guts and our refined minds. "Hunger is hunger," declared Marx, who undoubtedly enjoyed a good dinner, "but the hunger gratified by cooked meat eaten with a knife and fork is a different hunger from that which bolts down raw meat with the aid of a hand, nail and tooth" (Marx 1973: 92). Rousseau regarded taste as the foundational sense, the most important in child-rearing, and the one most in need of control in adulthood. He was disgusted by adult gluttons – "men who describe their dinner with as much detail as Polybius describes a combat . . . I have found these so-called men were only children of forty, without strength or vigour" (Rousseau *Emile* [1762] 1911: 117).

The guilty pleasure of luxurious consumption has been an intellectual neurosis since the early stages of modernity. In the sixth century Pope Gregory defined gluttony five ways: as eating ravenously, sumptuously, fastidiously, unneccesarily, or just plain too much. Gluttony was a serious, "capital" vice because it generated five "daughter" sins: "unseemly joy, scurrility, garrulousness, uncleanness, and dullness of sense in understanding." Thomas Aquinas agreed that if you stuff yourself you can't think straight, but like Aristotle he felt that indiscriminate engorging indulged the sense of *touch* rather than taste. On these grounds, there was nothing very vicious about wine-tasting, "for the inordinateness of that pleasure pertains more to curiosity than to gluttony" (1995: 421–3). Kant dignified this "rationalizing taste" with the Latin moniker *gustus reflectens*. He lectured copiously on how to run a good dinner-party, his menu picking its way from soup to dessert via "three stages of 1) narration, 2) reasoning, and 3) jesting" (1978: 142, 188–91). Thus we arrive at the class-based judgments of taste described by Bourdieu: "whereas the working classes . . . tend to go for products that are both cheap and nutritious, the professions prefer products that are tasty, health-giving, light and not fattening" (1984: 190).

upon it to make it civilized, or docile, or inferior. Michel Foucault has been the "founding father and guiding light" in this line of analysis.[76] Originally bent on reclaiming bodily feeling through an "archaeology of the human mind," he rejected phenomenological views of the subject and insisted that we are "an invention of recent date," objects on which the "fundamental codes of a culture" are inscribed.[77] Although his writing on the "immanence" of power in sexuality and penal discipline is very sensuous, "Foucault's body has no flesh" and its "desires" come not from the viscera but from public power-talk.[78] The result is a chaotic involution of the meanings which Foucault hopes to reveal. In one of his most famous images, the body is captured and incarcerated by a monstrous metaphor of itself, an "entire social body."[79]

Pasí Falk's assertion that "The mystery of the body is not solved by any biological or physiological knowledge – which is in fact only one mode of objectivising the body in a certain epistemic discourse" is of course a calculated provocation to natural scientists.[80] The latter insist that dispelling this sort of mysticism is what science is all about. And yet scientists who try to move from the empirical certainty of the human body into the realm of ideas and meanings, are soon confronted by the Cartesian gap. In the phenomenological spirit, the neurologist Thomas Damasio sets out on a quest for "the truly embodied mind" – but this time in resolutely *anti*-Cartesian mode. Damasio laments "the abyssal separation between body and mind, between the sizable, dimensional, mechanically operated, infinitely divisible body stuff," and "the unsizable, undimensioned, un-pushpullable, non-divisible mind-stuff." His solution is to reverse the proposition – "I am therefore I think" – and to regard thoughts and emotions as bodily products. This brings the "nonphysical cogitum" into "the realm of biological tissue."[81] This is an up-to-date version of what that staunch defender of dualism, Arthur Lovejoy, labelled "Hypodermic Philosophy."[82]

Clinical observation tells Damasio that rationality is not based on some disembodied logic but on the feelings and emotions which each of us experience. These in turn are generated not by ideas, but by the physical constitution of our brains, which are in turn genetically defined by processes of evolutionary adaptation – "Nature, with its tinkerish knack for economy." "I am not attempting to reduce social phenomena to biological phenomena," protests Damasio, "but rather to discuss the powerful connection between them."[83] The book jacket is more candid: Damasio's exposition of "Descartes' Error" is a triumph for science over the unreliability of ideas. It "leads us to conclude that human organisms are endowed from the very beginning with a spirited passion for making choices, which the social mind can use to build rational behavior."[84] The ideological agenda of Smithian liberalism stands revealed once again.

Three decades ago John Blacking made a stirring appeal for "an anthropology of the body," to be understood as "a total physical system" inseparable from mind.[85] Alas, the subsequent spate of discourses on "the body" has produced nothing better than "disembodied representation, a bloodless prose that saps the body of its sensuousness."[86] As efforts to reclaim the body continue, the culturalists rail against the iniquities of "sociobiology," and the biologists against the self-absorbed decadence of "postmodernism."[87] Both sides are entrenched in centuries of disagreement. It seems that biology can tell us as little about the meaning of anatomy as the study of culture can tell us about the anatomy of meaning. Analytically, the bodies are lifeless: they are "states," or "texts," or "products," or (very commonly) "sites."

In becoming so clever about the mind, it seems we have become increasingly stupid about the body. ("Is a male body something one can use to create the impression of masculinity?" asks Harré, with evident gravity.[88]) Current efforts at "embodiment" have not closed the Cartesian gap, they have made it more mysterious.[89] Turner thinks that this amounts to "a crisis in the intellectual politics and epistemology of Western social thought." It is not just an intellectual failure, it is part of the ideological claptrap of the professional classes. It has the tendency to cripple social critique before it gets going. For example, the "antipathy of much contemporary social theory to flesh and all that goes with it" has had a particularly perverse effect on feminism. From the earlier predicament of being mindless bodies, arguments about the "embodiment" of women has reduced them to asexual schemata, "gendered" in highly localized and contingent ways, and thus politically fragmented.[90]

The "there-ness" of the body often eludes us, and yet as the earlier phenomenologists pointed out, being embodied prevents us from being in two places at once, exposes us to the scrutiny of others, forces us into interaction, and carries us in a relentless trajectory from micro-organism back to dust. Heidegger admitted only the most parsimonious definition of the body: we are simply "thrown into the world," make of our lives what we can, and quit. But "real" bodies do so much more than supply time-space coordinates for the mind, they make relations with *other* minds which in turn define the integrity, boundedness, persistence, and transformation of our own minds. This happens because real bodies *grow*. Mental abstractions or symbolic machines don't. *We* develop skills, knowledge, memory, "because of the brute fact of *being* bodies." No part of our psychic apparatus has a detachable existence. As the real body grows and decays "so particular skills, habits, capacities, strengths, as well as debilities and weaknesses, are enfolded into its very constitution – in its neurology, musculature, even its anatomy."[91] This is as true for being able to do philosophy as to ride a bike.

Husserl or Merleau-Ponty would probably have been very interested in such apparently trivial questions as why humans are more likely to use their right hands than their tongues or genitals to symbolize trust. Our multifarious, disciplined knowledge of the mind and body offers endless partial explanations, ranging from ancient convention to the hemispheric structure of the brain. But scholars can only disparage the idiotic explanation that a handshake simply *feels* right: the disarming closure of fingers and palms, like in like, the assurance of being with friends and brothers, a sense of well-being-in-the-world. These are the terms, far more interactive than merely existential, in which the critical device of greed works. Greed certainly does not defer to a mind which "inhabits" the body or claims to have possessed it. This is why it can expose anyone who hides behind symbolic images of themselves (monarchs, CEOs, superstars, respectable citizens), insisting that there is a more mundane reality in which they can be judged.

So – where did the real body go?

In one sense it fetched up in other subdivisions of the academic tract (the anatomist's slab, the physiology lab), where it could be constructed as an object stripped of inherent meaning or moral signification. But out there in modernizing society, the real, living, breathing, eating, shitting, dying body was locked up in that intimate domain we call "*The Family*." "Family" now draws an arbitrary line beyond which physical growth has been denied any meaning in the making of history. And today, the professional interests of natural science and the humanities work to ensure that the boundaries will not be transgressed. But meanwhile, the real body, with all its rude functions, remains where it has always been, embedded in the everyday lives of ordinary people, wherever they go. It is lived in and maintained by them, and is used as a critical measure for the wider, disembodied, and unsympathetic world in which we live, work, and play.

For a great many centuries the merchant ideologues have been driving a wedge deeply into the heart of "the family" in order to release the imaginative powers of the desiring mind from the constraints of the needy body. They were also concerned to insulate the business enterprise from flesh and blood – the perennial problem of keeping family fingers out of the till. There was a time when the "natural" sociality of the family was a model for public order.[92] Aristotle admired the affective bonds of the household, in whose management (*oikonomicos*) the selfish, mercenary interests of the market (*chrematistika*) had no place. He visualized growth as an outward extension of physical and moral relationships, from body to family to community to *polis*. The marketplace could infect the family with greed, but only through the unmoderated behavior of its individual members. The passionate desire for more, *pleonexia*, was in men's souls, the marketplace released it, and it was the obligation of the *polis* to contain it.

The Enlightenment scholars were much affected by these images. Hume's idea of "confined generosity" matches the ideal of the family as a political unit, with the paterfamilias as the public voice and agent of the private domain. But if the family was the natural node of altruism, it was also the unit on behalf of which one could be legitimately selfish. If the family does not *consist of* self-interested individuals, it must in effect *be* a self-interested individual. Accordingly, utilitarian economics has assembled "the household" into one thinking-acting-choosing persona with a single schedule of preferences: an ageless, presumptively male, pseudo-self which has been the object of much critical attention, mostly from feminists, over the last few decades. Modern talk is now thoroughly confused about the differences between altruism in the "natural" domestic frame, and the sorts of trust which businessmen need to pursue their own interests in the marketplace.[93] The denatured "family" is the metaphor with which business corporations try to stitch together personal loyalty. Election rhetoric in the Western democracies also makes it clear that many people firmly believe that greed is not something which happens *in* families. On the contrary, "family values" are the best antidote to the public vice of greed.

From the eighteenth century onwards, individual bodies were overwhelmed by the transformations of social scale – the multiplication of people, energy, power, into ever-larger concentrations. To explain this new multitude, persons with real lives were split up into static, interchangeable functional identities: the new individual was a citizen, a worker, a worshiper, a shopper, a voter. These fragments ("roles" or "statuses") were in turn recombined into new meta-bodies: the church, the business corporation, the political super-body of the nation state. However, these were bodies in an unnatural form, purged of copulation, decay, and death. Output was construed as "commodities," "wealth," or "energy," not shit. A problem arising is that in public arenas (insurance offices, lawcourts) the value of "real" bodies is now almost impossible to determine, most notably in legal settlements for personal injury.[94]

The body has lingered on in the public domain – but as an extended metaphor which has duped many scholars. Bodily functions provided the political economists with essential images of circulation, input and output, functional specialization, integration, and, above all, healthy growth.[95] While the new body, metaphorically transformed, reached out to draw the ramifying fabric of public and republic into recognizable shapes, necessary acts of reproduction and physical growth were consigned to the privacy of "the family," the proper container for all natural business, and for its main agents – women. But while the "real" body no longer had any historically recognizable functions, it has continued to provide ordinary people with juicy private imagery for the disgusting aspects of public life. Dragging an over-extended metaphor back to its point of origin in the guts and genitals can be shockingly effective.

5

Scholars and Idiots

The small Minnesota town of New York Mills (population 972) plays host each year to "The Great American Think-Off," which culminates in a debate on a hot moral issue. In 1995 a 66-year-old retired stenographer, seconded by a 16-year-old boy scout, lost the motion that Americans value morality more than money. The topic for 1998: "Is honesty *always* the best policy?" Contestants are invited to submit an essay of less than 750 words, which must be *"free of academic language and references."*[1]

The gap between scholars and the public has never been larger. Ordinary people depend more on common sense than disciplined reasoning in understanding the world. We don't deal with everyday life by separating how we feel and what we mean, and our accusations of greed don't depend on a thoughtful weighing up of wants and needs. A minority of scholars have always been aware of this, arguing against the prevailing separation of mind from body, with all its philosophical ramifications. But dualism still prevails. Between the meaningless body of the biological sciences and the disembodied meaning of the humanities we cannot explain how and why the meaning of greed is freighted with visceral feeling. Between universalizing science and particularizing humanism we cannot agree on what is general about greed and what is specific to certain times, places, or peoples. Between the temporalities of evolution and history we cannot explain whether greed makes us or we make it, and if there's anything we can do about it. Between physiology and economics we can say nothing about why the meaning of greed should stretch from eating and copulating to the accumulation of material goods. And we have no scholarly basis for judging when and why it can be *good* to be greedy.

However, everybody – even the off-duty scholar – continues to talk about greed because it "works." It's a matter of common sense: it is sensible in that it is based on feelings and experience, and it is common in that we believe all humans are susceptible to it and can thus know its essentials. As part of our understanding of human nature it is useful in our ordinary assessments of the people around us, and around the world. But scholars mistrust it for this very reason.[2] So who is right about greed – the scholars or the idiots?

Common sense

From Aristotle through to the seventeenth century, common sense was a bodily reality, a sixth master-sense which was, in Robert Burton's words, the "judge and moderator" of the other five.[3] Hobbes believed that meaning was firmly attached to our physical experience of the real world, but his contemporary Descartes shifted it from our bodily sensations and interactions to the privacy of the mind. Scholars who subsequently resisted this maneuver (Condillac, Helvétius, Diderot, La Mettrie) were called "Sensationalists," but in arguing that everything must enter our minds through our senses they had already fallen victim to the Cartesian discourse. Thomas Reid's *Inquiry into the human mind on the principles of common sense* (1764) was a vigorous and influential effort to sustain the integrity of feeling and meaning. He challenged the basic idea of Descartes and Locke, and of his own contemporary David Hume, that the immediate object of perception is merely a mental image. Reid insisted that it is not our minds but our senses which tell us what is out there. We must trust them morally and scientifically, partly because we can agree easily enough that we all feel things in basically the same way, and partly because we simply have no other means of knowing about the real world. No sense (reason, consciousness) is more reliable than any other (touch, smell), so we have to trust all of them or none of them. But senses are equal in the further respect that nobody's sense is necessarily more privileged than anyone else's. As both leveller and moral arbiter Reid's interpretation of common sense meshed with liberal democratic ideas, and was strongly defended right through the twentieth century.[4]

Just as everybody right or left is now a democrat, few would doubt the virtues of common sense. By the late eighteenth century even the idealists were reclaiming it, but as a function of the rational mind rather than the sentient body. For Rousseau, common sense was the intuition that particular ideas are right. Education involved "the training of a sort of sixth sense, called common sense, not so much because it is common to all men, but because it results from a well-regulated use of the other five." This psychic super-sense "has no special organ, it has its seat in the brain, and its sensations which are purely internal are called precepts or ideas. The number of these ideas is the measure of our knowledge; exactness of thought depends on their clearness and precision; the art of comparing them with one another is called human reason."[5] Around the same time Kant was proposing that the "sensibility" (*Sinnlichkeit*) of the mind, its innate capacity to organize what the senses conveyed to it, was the basis of the logic by which we come to understand things. But because our minds, not the external world, did the organizing, our capacity to rationalize gave us the freedom to think creatively, and to obey or disregard the laws of the universe. The scholarly mind took common sense a step further, advancing it from everyday practical or "concrete" judgment to the "abstract" and self-critical reasoning of *science*.[6]

The ideas of Rousseau and Kant, full of redemptive promise, were an inspiration to those intellectuals who were appalled by the effects of the industrial revolution but fascinated by the prospects for individual liberty in the new society. For philosophers and writers like Herder, Coleridge, Blake, and Zola, common sense wove feeling into meaning in ways which were intensely personal, and required aesthetic skills for their communication. The main challenge to this Romantic mood came from science, the mindset of modern industrial man.[7] The version of common sense to which scientists appealed was more disciplined and ascetic in its claims to truth, universal in both the logical and biological senses, and thus mistrustful of the personal, introspective and intuitive styles of the Romantics, especially their enthusiasm for mysteries and fictions.

The new generation of scientists took the Aristotelian view that "nature" is "out there," orderly and meaningful, waiting for us to grasp it. Meaning, for Thomas Huxley, was in the logic of matter rather than in our minds, and science was essentially *disciplined common sense.*[8] Science systematizes and tidies up what ordinary people believe: lay persons think on their feet, not in libraries or laboratories. They move pragmatically from one assumption (the world is flat) to another (take care not to fall off the edge). The great scientific breakthrough may begin with naive speculation, but good science puts it through the mill of consistency, linking other assumptions and observations to useful effect, and convincing colleagues and the public (relax, the world is round). In this formulation "truth" is a goal, not an actuality. Enthusiasts for scientific discovery tend to forget the distance between exciting speculation and proof, which is supposed to involve the meticulous and methodical exercise of doubt.

A further interpretation of Huxley's aphorism emerges from cognitive science: our sense is common because that is how our brains are structured. "Quite simply, common sense lights a world for all to see – a world that is, in its fundamental contours, much the same for scientist, layman and bushman."[9] But lurking behind the cognitive scientists' rediscovery of common sense is the doubt that just because we all think the same way about something doesn't make it true. Bigger and better brains might explain things quite differently.[10] "Daily practical living is naïve," warned the phenomenologist Husserl. "Nor is it otherwise in the positive sciences. They are naïvetés of a higher level."[11]

Once again, it is psychology that bears the brunt of these anxieties.[12] *Can* ordinary people really know what they think? And in what sense can science improve our consciousness of consciousness, or understanding of understanding? Those who are skeptical about "folk" psychology worry about its concepts and their lack of coherence: it pulls fuzzy ideas like " 'believe,' 'remember,' 'feel,' 'desire,' 'prefer,' 'imagine,' 'fear,' " into "a loose knit network of largely tacit principles, platitudes, and paradigms."[13] The puzzle for the cognitive scientist is that if we are "hard-wired" to think in this naive way, what possible (evolutionary) advantage could it give us, and how might this interfere with science? Sometimes common sense just doesn't make sense – at least in Cartesian terms. As "folk" psychologists we have a pathetic tendency to attach meanings to "real" things like apples and refrigerators, kidding ourselves that how things seem is how they really are.[14] Such "beliefs" are just not good enough for science. They are too vague and context-sensitive, especially when it comes to trying to explain "the cognitive states of relatively exotic subjects such as young children, 'primitive' folk, and people suffering from various brain injuries and mental illnesses."[15]

The most passionate opponents of common sense were the behaviorists, led by B. F. Skinner, who sought rigorously objective explanations on the grounds that we ourselves, left to our own devices, are the worst judges of what we think and what might be wrong with us. Skinner's view of the psyche as "conditioned" by the world around it, and treatable in much the same terms, was deemed too authoritarian. Although cognitive scientists today still doubt that ordinary people can have reliable knowledge about knowing, they are uneasy about a version of common sense which leaves little scope for individual imagination and free will. Daniel Dennett intuits that "folk" psychology cannot be objective, yet he agonizes about the hazards of excluding living persons and their moral concerns from the domain of psychology.[16]

"Folk" psychology fails the test of objectivity. If it had a voice, "folk" psychology might retort that science cannot account for feelings, which are the bases of intuition – the supposed wellspring of science. To ordinary "folk," scholarship looks over-cautious, introverted, normative, closed, dogmatic, boring. To sympathetic scholars, especially anthropologists, "folk" theories look action-oriented, pragmatic, evaluative, instrumental, fluid, extrovert and *plural*. It is the business of anthropologists to reckon with the fact that "ordinary people" in different places have very uncommon understandings of the world: they claim general knowledge (the world sits on the back of a giant turtle) which others would with equal certainty reject. Sympathetic anthropologists learn to suspend disbelief – to the point at which they too begin to believe in turtles ("My People, right or wrong").[17] From these exotic perspectives, cultural anthropologists look back "objectively" at the particular naiveties of science. It is "just" another idea system, distinguished mainly by its arrogant, self-justifying obsession with universal truth, powerful only because it has been nurtured by mercantile and industrial capitalism, by privileged education systems and the mass media. Scientists are bewildered by this leveling assumption that *any* notion may be as valid as any other. Liberal-minded scientists find other peoples' theories of fire or blood interesting or suggestive, as images of how the objects of scientific interest look to other logical systems. But the idea that "folk" ontologies will cut science down to size looks like a stubborn refusal to recognize that "science *works*" in the real world, and magic doesn't. To which the anthropologist replies, with a populist flourish: "In *their* world, magic or turtle-theory works just fine."

It is not the variability of "folk" theories which makes them more or less commonsensical than science. Science and "folk" theories both

---

The Copernican shift

It is reported that Wittgenstein once asked a colleague "why do people always say it was *natural* for men to assume that the sun went round the earth?" To the assurance that "it just *looks*" that way, Wittgenstein retorted "Well, what would it have looked like if it had looked as if the earth was rotating?" (Lockwood 1989: 15; told by Elizabeth Anscombe).

The "truth" about the earth going round the sun was known to Ptolemy in the second century, and probably long before, but common sense, backed up by religious authority, doggedly resisted it. Copernicus is famous for the shift in perspective, but not for his explanation, which imagined the planets pasted onto concentric rotating spheres, with the stars clinging to the outermost layer. It took Galileo, Newton, and a sequence of philosophers well into modern times to work out the very considerable subtleties of celestial mechanics.

Now that scientists vouch for heliocentricity, the puzzle is why the evidence of our senses should have misled us on such a fundamental cosmic fact. The truth is that for common and sensible purposes *it simply doesn't matter* which goes round what. Science cares, common sense doesn't. During his travels in Africa towards the end of the eighteenth century, the explorer Mungo Park "frequently enquired of the negroes what became of the sun during the night, and whether we should see the same sun, or a different one, in the morning; but I found that they considered the question very childish. The subject appeared to them as placed beyond the reach of human investigation; they had never indulged in a conjecture, nor formed any hypothesis, about the matter" (*Travels in the interior of Africa* (1799) vol. 1, p. 265). For the Victorian anthropologist and scientist Sir John Lubbock, this was scandalous. For him, Park's noble but indifferent savage was a primitive moron. "Such ideas are, in fact beyond the mental range of the lower savages, whose extreme mental inferiority we have much difficulty in realising" (Lubbock 1875: vol. 1, 265).

No doubt Lubbock would be pained to know that civilization has made little impression on this piece of idiocy. At the end of the twentieth century barely a third of Britons knew that the Earth goes round the sun, and takes a year to do so. One-fifth thought it took a day (Bogdan 1991: 2). Most, probably, didn't give a damn, and may even have resented the prick with the clipboard trying to make them look stupid.

pursue singular truths, and both thrive on contrary hypotheses and arguments. It is the sense which is presumed to be common, not the various derived meanings. The troublesome implication is that if we are looking for a general definition of common sense, we are unlikely to find it in the various meanings people attach to it ("culture"). This is how it slips out of the anthropologist's grip. Either we dismiss "common sense" as a notion specific to our culture and meaningless in everyone else's, or we declare that it is "*pre*-cultural," part of the "psychic unity" which is as irrelevant to the differences in meaning systems as weeping, talking, or having two legs. Either way, the views of the native are pre-empted: we have no way of knowing whether people in another culture have anything that matches our understanding of common sense, and the science-turtle issue can't be resolved. Likewise, we are as likely to believe (like Sahlins) that greed is universal to the species or that it is culturally specific, for any or for no particular reason. The basic reason for our indecision is of course the ambiguity of greed and common sense (and love, and anger, and many other interesting things) in relation to our cardinal separation of mind and body.

One of the tragedies of anthropology is that we have brought this radical assumption about knowledge to bear on nearly all our explanations of *other* ways of knowing. If anthropologists take the mind–body split as so absolutely commonsensical, so pre-cultural, they will "find" it in other meaning systems, even where no such epistemological distinctions are made. We simply have no ethnographic testimony as to whether monism, dualism, or neither is the human rule, and it seems very late in the ethnographic day to start asking such fundamental questions. The proposition that dualism must be universal is as strongly defended as it is denied. Andrew Strathern concludes that "the kinds of ideas about the body that are found in cultures of the Pacific – and in many other parts of the world – are closer to a 'psychosomatic' model also than they are to a Cartesian dualistic scheme."[18] Word-pairings which superficially resemble the mind–body distinction may have been too readily translated as such. Lambek, on the other hand, argues that something "roughly equivalent" to the mind–body split *must* exist everywhere, because certain "fundamental tensions of human experience" are universal: "connection to and separation from others, the boundary between the subjective and the objective, the relation of concepts to objects, or reason to sensation, experiences of the voluntary and the involuntary, morality and desire, being and becoming, active and passive, male and

---

Lirima in Bugisu

In an illuminating account of "the making of men" in Bugisu (East Africa) Heald approaches male circumcision ritual through an interpretation of the "vernacular psychology," rather than its Western counterparts. She found the key concept of *lirima* virtually impossible to translate, because of "the lack of a one-to-one correlation between 'emotion' and physiological stimulus." "The Gisu do not rigidly distinguish between qualities of mind or character and those of body." For them, "The key feature of *lirima* is the intensity of the emotion experienced." To get into and through the trial of initiation (slitting the foreskin and stripping subcutaneous flesh from around the *glans penis*) the 18–25-year-olds have to whip up *lirima*: "As the ordeal gets closer it is *lirima* which drives him on and dominates his thoughts and feelings." *Lirima* is passionate, wild, assertive, danger-ous. It has physical symptoms (like having a lump in the throat) and "it is also tied to the negative emotions – hatred, anger, vengeance." It is linked to ancestral power, and is all about manhood; it is related to yeasty fer-mentation and sexual potency. But it is also ambivalent, because a good man must *control* it – it is a test of volition, of responsible maturation to adulthood and parenthood. In one episode, Gisu feared that a particularly passionate, troublesome 16-year-old pre-initiate could not cope with the added charge of *lirima*, and that he should therefore be killed now.

Heald 1982: 18–33.

---

female, the transient and the enduring, culture and nature, life and death."[19] But this is not ethnography: it is a characteristically Western form of logic-chopping.

If "the mind–body problem" is so glaringly obvious, asks Matson, why were the ancient philosophers unaware of it? Though they did not lack a concept of mind *(nous)*, "mind–body identity was taken for granted." From Homer to Aristotle, if the distinction was made at all, the line was drawn to put our perceptions "on the body side," where they didn't bother the mind. To make a problem of the mind–body relationship, "one must theorize mightily about Mind," in the manner I have discussed in chapter 3.[20] Anthropologists have rarely considered whether, and why, other people *don't* theorize about the mind as we do. In his classic study of *Divinity and experience*, Lienhardt tells us that the Dinka of southern Sudan "have no con-ception which at all closely corresponds to our popular modern con-ception of the 'mind,'" no interior entity reflecting on, mediating, or storing up experiences of the "self," no consciousness, no "distinction between the psyche and the world." They do, however, have ways of imagining actions and experience which Lienhardt would like to translate as *passions* – if scholarly decorum would allow him.[21]

It is ironic that anthropologists, who dread the disparaging suggestion that "primitive" people lack our sort of "minds," have always fallen back on the body and on common sense as our way of arguing the common bases of humanity. We use the idea of "emotion" to argue our basic humanity with people in very different social worlds, even though it has proved impossible to find a match for this thoroughly ambivalent idea in other cultures.[22] Ethnography, the principal method of anthropology, is often criticized as "unscientific" because of its openness to how people feel about things. According to John Leavitt, "good ethnography" plays "on one's own and one's reader's emotions to attempt to convey those of the people under study, not only in their meanings but also in their feelings."[23] Here, the implication of common *sense* is that we can base our judgments on what people in other cultures say or think, on certain shared *feelings*. The idiocy from which all social life proceeds, and without which such generalized notions as biology or culture are impossible, is that we all have bodies, and that we all feel things in basically the same way. This vindication of common sense emanates from the generality of our bodies, not the random specificities of "culture." It would make good sense to Thomas Reid.

Our authority for this intuition does not come from textbooks on genetics or anthropology, but from the experience of growing within and around human bodies. Each of our lives is a personal excursion from the smallest microbiological fragments of existence, through the episode of consciousness of self and others which we call life, to the dispersing molecules of bodily decay. In this short span we try to make sense of where we came from and where we are going, and to prolong our existence in time by leaving traces of ourselves in the lives of others. We may even dream of making an impression on the grand human scale we call history. It is this life process which sustains the local fabric of ideas about ourselves, commonsensical in their own terms, which anthropologists have called culture.

Exotic greed

As I have dissected it in chapter 2, greed is a critical interpretation of people's behavior based on common sense – that is, senses which are reckoned to be common. With gut feelings and bodily growth as its prime indices, greed is a measure for everybody, everywhere. Cultural anthropologists, devoted to the discovery of difference, have no such sense of assurance. Whether or not "primitive" people share our vices is a persistent and tantalizing question, but not one for which anthropology (or any other modern discipline) has a coherent answer.

The Cartesian way of spotting greed in other cultures would be to see whether they compare needs and wants in the way we do. If I *presume* that they do, I can go ahead and measure off the excessive desires of my brother and an Australian aborigine with equal ease. This is the opposite of moral relativism: *my* interpretation depends on how extravagant *I* think the aborigine's desires – which he has not actually expressed – "really" are. Anthropologists shrink from this, mainly because accusing an aborigine of greed does not take account of the fact that he and my brother most probably *want* very

---

Aboriginal gluttony

"It is hardly necessary to remind the reader that with the Australian, as with other savages, quantity is considered rather than quality. A full grown 'boomah' kangaroo will, when standing upright, in its usual attitude of defence, measure nearly six feet in height, and is of very considerable weight. And, when an Australian kills a kangaroo, he performs feats of gluttony to which the rest of the world can scarcely find parallel, and certainly not a superior. Give an Australian a kangaroo and he will eat until he is nearly dead from repletion; and he will go on eating, with short intervals of rest, until he has finished the entire kangaroo. Like other savage creatures, whether human or otherwise, he is capable of bearing deprivation of food to a wonderful extent; and his patient endurance of starvation, when food is not to be obtained, is only excelled by his gluttony when it is plentiful. This curious capacity for alternate gluttony and starvation is fostered by the innately lazy disposition of the Australian savage, and his utter disregard for the future. The animal that ought to serve him and his family for a week is consumed in a few hours; and, so long as he does not feel the pain of absolute hunger, nothing can compel the man to leave his rude couch and go off on a hunting expedition."

Rev. J. G. Wood, *The natural history of man: Being an account of the manners and customs of the uncivilized races of men.*
George Routledge, London, volume 2, 1870, p. 27.

Plate 3   Negro gluttony; from the frontispiece to the Rev. J. G. Wood's
The natural history of man volume 1: *Africa* (1868)

different sorts of things. This is why it is useful to have "culture" as a third set of ideas to interpose between those of my brother and the aborigine. But this does not address the need side of the calculus, nor whether aborigines attach the same meanings to bodily feelings as we do. If they do not share our understanding of need, moral judgment as *we* see it cannot be completed – unless we, as observers, complete it for them. This sleight of hand is often detectable in anthropological attitudes to primitive vice.

Three brief examples will help to reveal the troublesome gap between "culture" and the assumption of "psychic unity" on which it covertly depends. In the first, the ethnographer sees his subjects as hopelessly overwhelmed by greed; in the second, they are blissfully innocent of it; and in the third they struggle manfully to keep it at bay.

In his well-known book *The mountain people* Turnbull describes a small nomadic population in northern Uganda whose already precarious livelihood had been demolished mainly by the intrusion of a national game reserve into their territory. According to Turnbull the Ik, scavenging for survival near a government post, had lost the communal bases of their morality, even among close kin, to the extent that acts of gross selfishness were viewed without censure, and even with glee. Although Turnbull's account of the Ik as "a people without life, without passion, beyond humanity" has been much debated, their predicament has become an allegory for our alienated times: when we can no longer discriminate greed we have lost the protection of social values.[24] The shock of Turnbull's tale was not simply that in dire straits people could turn so nasty. The Ik, as he represented them, lacked not only food but also that central object of anthropological attention: culture. Meaning had, quite literally, gone out of their lives. In the process, the Ik had become meaningless. Cultural comparison has always been the central device in anthropological explanation, but without morals and manners the Ik were comparable with nothing. "There is no goodness left for the Ik, only a full stomach, and that only for those whose stomachs are already full. But if there is no goodness, stop to think, there is no badness, and if there is no love, neither is there any hate. Perhaps that, after all, is progress; but it is also emptiness" (Turnbull 1972: 286).

Turnbull paints a gloomily terminal picture – better dead than Ik. It has often been remarked that the counterpoint was with Turnbull's earlier fable of *The forest people*, an ethnographic idyll of happy, caring, musical pygmies.[25] But subsequent inquiry has made it evident that the morality of the Ik – the nature of their culture – has been ethnographically in question for a very long time. It transpires that these people have a history and an identity, as well as a territory, which goes far beyond their immediate plight (stranded on a Ugandan mountaintop in 1967). They are, however, one of those peoples who are destined to appear marginal to others, very much like gypsies in the European context. Otherwise known as the Teuso or the Dorobo, their livelihood as hunting and gathering people, operating in the gaps between more affluent and photogenic pastoral peoples like the Masai, has demanded great pragmatism. If people like the Ik do not actually exist, says another anthropologist, we invent them as an embodiment of dangerous, amoral, fearful tendencies in our own societies.[26]

Turnbull's account of the Ik may look like bad judgment, but the more familiar, but no more plausible problematic in anthropology has been why exotic people are *not* greedy. This is inspired by a mixture of dismay about what we have become and nostalgia for what we once supposedly were. The populist assumption is that in "simple, small-scale societies" people "know" how to keep greed in check – until modernity besieges them with corrupting desires. The implication, universal in its own terms, is that *we* are greedy because we are modern. In his account of the Tupi-Guarani Indians of Amazonia, Clastres argues that the cultures of small-scale, relatively isolated populations form a benign moral circle which counteracts the desire to accumulate wealth and power. The essence of primitive society is its totalitarian closure, "its exercise of absolute and complete power over all the elements of which it is composed." The ideologies of Amazonian hunter-gatherers are not simply egalitarian, says Clastres, they are anti-hierarchical: "it is not possible for the state to arise from within primitive society."[27]

Clastres candidly admires the way these cultures reject modern vices, and his argument has had a lasting populist appeal. The moral antibody possessed by people like the Tupi-Guarani is "the refusal of a useless *excess*, the determination to make productive activity agree with the satisfaction of needs." However, on closer inspection it appears that the barrier posited by Clastres is not the product of concerted moral force, but of some sort of hyper-psychic tension. The Tupi-Guarani are not innocent of greed so much as neurotic about it: "Indian cultures are cultures anxious to reject a power that fascinates them: the affluence of the chief is the group's daydream."[28] The argument has fallen victim to the metaphorical trap of ascribing a mind to culture, which can then start contemplating its own moral premises. But cultures, as figments of the anthropologist's imagination, do not think (or feel, or worry, or dream) although they may include the symbols which are handy for people to think (or feel, or worry, or dream) *with*. If we reckon that Amazonian Indians actually think for themselves, and if it is they rather than their culture who experience anxiety about excess, then they do not look so very different from the rest of us.

All this then brings the Tupi-Guarani more into line with other ethnographic reports of peoples who see social order as fragile, and in need of persistent and rigorous maintenance – "ritual" for the anthropologist. According to Errington, meaningful order in the tiny Melanesian island of Karavar does not emanate from disembodied "customs" or "traditions" but from continual efforts to keep at bay the forces of *Momboto*, "an image of antisociety," "the anarchic energy underlying human behavior." Momboto was a time when men looked and behaved like wild animals, fighting each other for women and eating even close relatives. Momboto is "a statement of the Karavaran view of basic human nature, a nature of greed and violence, characterized by the untrammeled exercise of individual interest. The expression of unrestrained human nature is seen as a chaos of conflicting desires and activities." To counter "their disruptive and selfish natures" Karavarans work to create orderly exchanges of kinship, marriage, and politics through a strenuous discipline of rituals. These escort each individual through a sequence of hazardous life stages towards death, diverting the energy of the Momboto to more constructive social ends.[29]

Although drawing different sorts of conclusion, these three studies posit *culture* as the antidote for greed. For Turnbull, the Ik lapse into selfishness for lack of culture; for Clastres, a generic hunter-gatherer culture protects the Tupi-Guarani from incipient nastiness; while for Errington, the people of Karavar struggle endlessly to construct cultural bastions against their natural depravity. But the contrast here is essentially exotic: it pits the healing force of the anthropological construct "culture" against depravities lurking in human "psychic unity" – which is also an anthropological construct. Greed, in this calculus, is *pre*-cultural, which snuffs out any serious anthropological questions about what people in different cultures might actually think it is.

To know how other people around the world think about greed, and whether they think about it the same way we do, we will have to break out of the framework of exotic nature/culture mind/body contrasts. I propose that we go instead to the feelingful core of greed as I have interpreted it, and consider whether and how other people use visceral sensations to make moral judgments about persons.

Witchcraft

If I tried to explain my interpretation of greed to people in Africa, in a few localities in which I have worked as an anthropologist, the chances are that they would recognize it as part of a syndrome which they could readily name: *mangu, obulogo, itonga, ubulosi.*[30] Groping, in my turn, for a translation back into English, I would probably settle, like so many anthropologists before me, on an English word which (like "greed") is deeply rooted in our northern European languages: *witchcraft.*

My English dictionary will remind me that "witchcraft" attributes trouble to the outrageous desires and monstrous capacities of certain individuals. Compared with other sorts of practical knowledge (cooking supper, building a truck) it is extremely difficult to find out how witchcraft works, mainly because the technical processes are not visible – we call them "supernatural" or "magical." If we could get under the skin of a witch we might have a better idea of what they are up to. I shall come as close to that as I dare in the following account of the internal aspects of witchcraft and its bearing on how people judge each other's behavior. While such theories have been reported from all over the world, in what follows I shall stick to eastern Africa as a broad ethnographic frame of reference.[31]

Like greed, witchcraft is a theory, touched by paranoia, about what other people (or the darker side of ourselves) feel. It is a means of bringing these less accessible aspects of human beings out into the world of talk, action, and real objects, forcing people to justify what is going on within themselves and if necessary to purge themselves of antisocial malice. When things go wrong in the real world (crops fail, people die) witchcraft stands by with an explanation. It rationalizes suspicion and demands self-control, imagining a contest between our inner lives and the indignation of the community.

The witch is adept at breaking the "normal" connections between motives and actions, and reassembling them in perverse ways. A malicious feeling may be translated into physical harm without any observable action. The problem for the moral majority is how to make sense of this. No matter how vigorously you torment your suspects, they are unlikely to give a coherent explanation, ultimately because witches operate with a sort of "anti-knowledge." Trying to explain something whose business is to be inexplicable is uphill work for the anthropologist's informant. People are witches because that is what they need to be – it is their nature. Being a witch is not a "choice" under any conception of rationality: nobody "wants" to be a witch, and people "profess" witchcraft only under the greatest duress.

This unknowable and involuntary character of witchcraft makes it a threat to everyone who imagines that their intentions are honorable and their thoughts healthy. Dreadful urges may bypass their consciousness, sallying forth under cover of darkness and invisibility to wreak physical harm on others. Conventional alibis will not suffice, because witches are usually physically asleep while they are mystically "at work": body and malice are in different places. The only subjective clue one may have that this horror is going on is a feeling of guilt, or anxiety, or anger, and the traces these nocturnal maneuvers leave in dreams.

However, one thing is certain: witches have bodies. The fact that they flit around at night causing trouble only means that their bodies are in some respects peculiar. The Nyakyusa witch "leaves his skin *(ungobo)* on his sleeping-mat and goes naked."[32] (If this notion of an embodied body seems alien, consider the invitation of a Californian gym to *"Feel Good in Your Body,"* or the various body-inhabiting homunculi described in chapter 4.) Like everyone else who has a body, witches have physical needs. For most of the time, witches eat, shit, and have sex like the rest of us. The critical difference is that they have certain hideous needs, and the capacities to fulfill them, which the moral majority do not have. It is not that they lack physical substance, but that they are excessively vital. Most fundamentally they are possessed of a corrupt appetite. What witches do is *consume*. That they are ravenous for food is bad enough in hungry African villages, but what makes them greedy in a preternatural, superhuman sense is their appetite for human flesh. Witches *need to eat people*.[33] Nyakyusa witches borrow their victims' own teeth for this purpose. If you are attacked in this way it is unwise to scream until you are sure that your teeth are safely restored to your mouth.[34]

To revert briefly to greed as we know it: advances in modern medicine have stimulated a trade in body parts which conjures up fearful images of cannibalism. "The lack of available organs arouses desperation and rewards greed."[35] Nothing is more unsettling, more evocative of witchcraft, than for me to imagine that you *need my insides* so badly that you will go to almost any lengths to get them. Tabloid newspapers take a special interest in the victims of those who steal or buy body parts: desperate Indian peasants who part with their kidneys, or the seduced and sedated tourist who wakes up with a clumsily sutured belly. In these lurid tales, "greed" has its most awful resonance, matched only by accounts of the market in whole bodies

---

Ki'yem

Among the Kuku of southern Sudan, *ngula* is a passion with many of our qualities of greed, envy, and avarice. To the extent that it is rooted in the body and exerts malign effects on others, it is greatly feared. Mothers watch for, and deter, signs of *ngula* in their children, because the greedy person may be a *ka'yemanit*, harboring in their hearts the much more serious, hereditary malignity *ki'yem*.

Ki'yem is aroused specifically by envy for *food*. Kuku are always on the watch for gluttons. Even if a *ka'yemanit* has just dined, the sight of other people eating arouses envious thoughts, and when she swallows her saliva (women are most susceptible to this weakness) it catalyses her *ki'yem*. At this stage, a *ka'yemanit* who intends no malice should spit, not swallow. The activated *ki'yem* then seeks out the objects of envy and afflicts them with vomiting and diarrhea, eventually death. They may have to consult a medical specialist (*'bunit*) to relieve the symptoms. When you are eating, if you catch sight of someone you believe to be a *ka'yemanit* the best tactic is to offer them a share, but without seeming suspicious, and thus insulting. If they are socially responsible people they should accept at least a token morsel.

Although it is unlikely that anyone would admit to having *ki'yem*, Ka'yemak (pl.) are known persons: the malignity is a congenital condition acquired from either parent. At marriage, it is important to know that your prospective partner's family is "clean," for the malignity is dangerous and although your spouse may not "infect" you with *ki'yem*, she can pass the "gene" on to your children. In a recent case, a Kuku living in the US got a fax from Germany warning her that her fiancé came from a tainted family.

Based on conversations with Dr Sikopasi Poggo in Santa Barbara, California, October–December 1997.

(slavery, or Thai babies hawked on the adoption market, or errant English or American teenagers sold to Middle Eastern sex fiends). These matters say something about morality and the marketplace: if you need something as priceless as my body, my blood, or my viscera, let me *give* them to you.

East African witches embody evil. Whatever worldly interest may activate their malice (getting rich, or hanging onto chiefly office) they work by mobilizing forces inherent in their own bodies to attack the bodies of others. There is a relentless logic about these physical associations of witchcraft: anything *without* an ordinary human body, and thus without basic human appetites, cannot be a witch. Devils, were-animals or malicious spirits form quite distinct categories of mischief-maker. Witches certainly cannot be *dead people* (ghosts) of any sort, although witches may try to make use of corpses for their own wicked purposes. Again, while ancestors or other deceased relatives cannot operate as witches, the propensity to witchcraft can be *inherited* from them, along with other physical traits. By genetic association with "known" cases, an entire lineage may bear the stigma as one aspect of long-standing hostilities within a particular locality.[36]

Witches can pass so easily among us because they have bodies (deceptively) like ours. Your closest friend may be a witch: "you eat with him," a Lovedu proverb runs, "but actually he's eating you."[37] Cunning witches keep the physical sources of their malice hidden under their skin. These deformities are usually visceral: a python coiled up in the belly, a cancer on the heart, a ball of hair with sharp teeth in the spleen, or poisonous bile. These can be treated physically, excised and exorcised by specialists, reducing if not altogether eliminating the source of the mischief. It is part of the logic that such abnormalities *grow* in and with the body. The witchcraft of children is too small to cause much harm, but since any propensity to be a witch increases physically with age, the older you are the more culpable you become.[38] The privileged innocence of children may sometimes be used in the process of witch-finding, but on the other hand, a child who is a proven witch is something truly dreadful. One further detail of witch physiology should not pass without mention: they shit. They signal their evil presence by leaving their feces in people's farms and gardens, on the threshold of their houses, in the middle of the floor. The horror of their residue turns on what, in all senses, they have consumed.

In his classic account of *Witchcraft, oracles and magic among the Azande*, Evans-Pritchard made the highly influential observation that however bizarre magical ideas might seem to us, what is significant is their *logic*, their intellectual coherence as a social theory of causation. "They reason excellently in the idiom of their beliefs, but they cannot reason outside, or against, their beliefs because they have no other idiom in which to express their thoughts."[39] Azande witchcraft ideas not only meshed with one another, they were part of the self-reinforcing fabric of culture which covered every aspect of social existence. While this classic study of the integrity of African thought helped to picture our own intellectual closure (McCarthyism in the

US, Soviet totalitarian ideology, the logic of science, etc.), it was less eloquent on how ideas about witchcraft struggle to come to terms with fearful and largely incoherent *feelings*.

Truth in any knowledge system depends on consistency, and cultural comparison tells us how diverse internally consistent explanations of "the same" phenomenon (wind, blood) can be. But all knowledge systems are simultaneously coping with *in*consistency, the problems of partial understandings or rival explanations, the gaps between what we know and what we witness and experience. Knowledge of witchcraft is in a double bind because witches actually subvert knowledge. Explanations of their behavior are preoccupied with doubt and incoherence, and have to be argued with a strong sense of conviction. On closer consideration it seems that what the Azande were good at was not so much expounding the orthodoxies as rationalizing the inconsistencies of witchcraft beliefs, such as why many, if not all, "witch-doctors" were known to be frauds. Middleton, writing of the nearby Lugbara people, took the view that witchcraft rationales were inevitably inconsistent, if only because they were speculating about something so empirically elusive.[40]

The main difference between anthropological and "folk" explanations is that the scholars have regarded witchcraft as an explicit theory of social actions and interactions, whereas for the people themselves it is much more a matter of feelings, which are inevitably less accessible to words. "Witchcraft" is the ordinary, moral, law-abiding person's best effort to figure out what is going on, to bring bad feelings out into the open, to make fine judgments about what is intentional and involuntary. But the explanation is complicated by the fact that knowledge of witchcraft is in itself suspect: only witches really know what they are up to, and avoid offering detailed explanations. How, then, are we, as anthropological observers, to write about something which defies normal categories, and which "natives" themselves find so difficult to put into words? In trying to describe witches ordinary people usually fall back on the idiom of reversals: witches walk upside down on their hands, or gnaw their food with their anuses. We wear clothes, they go naked. We bury corpses, witches dig them up. If we are black, they are white. They are virtually anything which moral persons are not – sufficient warning to anyone with a mind to act deviously. The convolutions of suspicion are boundless: Lugbara in Uganda are suspicious of loners, but anyone who acts as though he is trying to convince people that he is *not* a loner is surely a witch.[41] This is the best normal people can do to picture what witches are like, but everyone knows that they are much smarter and more complicated, and that ordinary language will always be insufficient to contain them. Only extraordinary words (spells, incantations) can stand a chance. Reversals are pretty predictable, but the syndrome thrives on the ambiguity and uncertainty which are so much a part of anxiety and fear; and there can be nothing more fearful than the utter familiarity of the witch who happens to be your father. Incest, which anthropologists have interpreted as the horrendous cosmic vice marking the separation of culture from nature, is the play of witches.

Anthropological attention to the "techniques" of witchcraft (a nice extension of Cartesian empiricism) has been a source of some confusion. For example, much has been made of Evans-Pritchard's distinction between witches, whose actions are inherently invisible, and *sorcerers*, who "do" black magic with physical substances (medicines) and procedures (spells, rituals). This has proved useful in translating a distinction made by some East African peoples about who is suspected of what: in-laws or strangers, for example, are likely to be accused of the crass manipulative art of sorcery (often indistinguishable from poisoning), while kinsfolk are associated with the more subtle and dreadful hereditary force of witchcraft.[42] However, the witchcraft–sorcery dichotomy is clouded by the fact that both forms of malice "exist" essentially at the level of suspicion, that both are "caused" by envy, and that both assume *some* sort of substance abuse.

Anthropologists have studied witchcraft not as it is practiced, but as it is expressed in accusations, diagnoses, confessions, and treatment. Attention has therefore focused on the specialists ("witch-doctors") who mediate and explicate cases of witchcraft, on the oracles they use, the interpretations they make, and the remedies they propose. These people know about witchcraft in much the same terms as an anthropologist wishes to understand it, and are often treated with collegial respect. They do not, of course, "profess" witchcraft – these "doctors" could not afford to allow their skills, however mysterious, to be confused with the "practice" of witchcraft itself (just as we might not welcome treatment from a schizophrenic psychiatrist). But like modern medical specialists they do have special powers, including an ambiguous capacity to punish, require stern tests (poison oracles, psycho-active drugs) and prescribe harsh remedies (sacrifices, strait-jackets).[43] Although suspects may be quizzed, the investigation of the inner states of witchcraft have not been well reported. "Witch-doctors" are inextricably involved in the witchcraft syndrome, and may be masters of its rationales, but like psychiatrists they necessarily operate at some distance from the feelings of the victim, and at even greater distance from the sensations of the supposed perpetrators.

Accounts of the diviner's or witch-doctor's work usually note their capacity to sense malaise – the envy, spite, or anger which turns one person against another. *Doing* something malicious, overtly and intentionally (stabbing you, insulting you, or torching your crops), does not make me a witch – there are civil mechanisms for dealing with such crimes. Witchcraft is the link between your spleen and my misfortune, and since your actions are assumed to be covert, even to your own consciousness, simple prudence dictates that you will take any accusation of witchcraft very seriously. Many, if not all, people have the *capacity* for witchcraft (just as anybody might be greedy); what matters is whether this capacity is activated. It is usually in everyone's interest to reckon on the *involuntary* nature of the offence, and for suspects to submit promptly to the proper remedies. Many of these treatments are couched in body-language which symbolically sheds any mischief: spitting, blowing, vomiting, sometimes shaving. The test of poison is a more drastic, intrusive method which parallels the damage which is supposed to have been inflicted. Cures may likewise involve fasting or sexual abstinence. The ultimate treatment is to get rid of the witch, body and all (in Europe, by burning). Witchcraft prevention is the basis of numerous cults throughout Africa, conspicuously in periods and places where the material forces of modernization have roused envy.[44]

Witchcraft thrives in troubled times, and while victims should seek redress in normal, moral ways (asking the chief to intervene) counteraccusations can rapidly escalate into an epidemic. To counteract this there are, very commonly, harsh penalties for false accusation, because invoking witchcraft at any level is extremely dangerous. Chronic cases overwhelm life in a neurotic, all-pervasive suspicion of the most trivial acts.[45] Accusation and confession are seen as ways of clearing the air, of relieving the pressures in dense relationships by ventilating anxieties in public. Frustratingly, there are very few documented accounts of this social psychotherapy. Most of what anthropologists know about witchcraft is derived from fragmentary traces in ritual and gossip, from talking to people after a crisis, and engaging in long conversations with ritual specialists. But the evidence we have indicates that the therapeutic process is concerned not with the insider-as-outsider so much as with *the insider's insides*. Anthropological interpretations of witchcraft fix on malice as a social disorder of the person, although "folk" theories insist that it is a disorder of the body. If it is impractical to scrutinize the suspect's viscera, a chicken's entrails must suffice. Restoring the accused's social relationship with the complainant plays a remarkably small part in the actual therapeutic proceedings. The Zande "witch" blows water on a chicken's wing, he does not shake hands with (or blow water on) his supposed victim. The Safwa "witch" (not the victim) is dosed with medicines to bring his *itonga* back into kilter.[46]

For these reasons, anthropologists have often remarked on the functions of witchcraft in social control. It is given the appearance of a village policeman, a flat-footed but fearful embodiment of the moral sensitivity of the community.[47] It hangs over people's heads like our apprehension of parental knowledge of our nastier inner selves, producing "altruism" in the same sort of roundabout way which Hobbes ascribed to selfishness, and Adam Smith to "self-interest." This interpretation helps to account for the colonial administrations' tolerance of the cycles of witch-finding and witch-curing in so many parts of Africa. It is always helpful when people police themselves (the British called it "Indirect Rule"), although colonial authorities were clearly embarrassed to find themselves endorsing "primitive" theories which they could not have condoned "at home."

Although anthropological attention has focused much more on symptoms, diagnoses, and cures, it is *sensations* which are the subjective reality of witchcraft for ordinary people. If fear is a vital element, its reflexive element – fear of oneself – is the most intimidating: "even I could be a witch." This is one of the liabilities of human existence, of having a body. As a responsible person I must do my best to calm and control my inner beastliness. It can lie dormant within me throughout my life, along with all the other propensities, good and bad, which make me human: the capacity to be afraid, to get angry, to feel disgusted. It is my dealings with other people which arouse these sensations, and in the case of witchcraft *envy* is the principal instigator. Middleton translates the *"ole"* of the Lugbara witch as "indignation," noting that people feel *ole* when they see people eating and are not asked to join, or someone enjoying the admiration of others, or the wealth, fertility, or success of a neighbor. "Or a man who wishes to seduce the wives and daughters of other men, may feel *ole* against their guardians who prevent his doing so."[48] I want something, with a grudging passion, and the internalized figures of guilt or shame begin to cluster around me. My feelings may explode either in fearful confession, or in outraged accusation: "Your envy is eating me up!" Explanations of the social or cultural construction of witchcraft say so little about the internal anguish. I can only testify to the shocking appearance of the victims I have seen myself.[49]

The importance of subjective sensation does not dissolve when the witchcraft shifts from the individual to the categoric level: "why *us*, and why *them?*" Anthropologists have been much concerned with witchcraft in relation to social boundaries: it does not "work" for strangers but it makes outsiders of insiders. The true nastiness of witchcraft is that it "works" to most devastating effect at the closest social range – between siblings, or parent and child. Anthropologists have explained this as part of the agony of growth in tribal societies, the alienating fault-lines which cause families to divide into new lineal groups. This long-term process of subdivision creates tensions among categories of person – families, clans, communities, ethnic groups, women, old people. But just because larger numbers of people come under suspicion does not diminish its visceral awfulness. In subjective experience it is not the social classifications but the bad feelings which come first, emanating from the intense and largely unspoken interactions of bodies in close proximity. My own limited observations in Africa assure me that people do not need to talk about or even comprehend witchcraft for its emotional force to be communicated very effectively.

Our scholarly reluctance to explain witchcraft as in the human body as well as in social relations has left many interesting questions unanswered. A classic problem is why it should be women rather than men who are accused of witchcraft – not just in Africa, but wherever and whenever such phenomena have been identified. It has been suggested that women's greater affinity with "nature" in patriarchal societies makes them prime suspects in antisocial activities like witchcraft, but this is laying our own cultural categories on people for whom they may have no significance.[50] Explanations in terms of cultural constructions of *gender* can make few inroads into the stark generality of *sexual* discrimination. The peculiar susceptibility of women is emphasized if we add the factor of generation: again, older people generally are more likely to be identified as witches, with older women (spinsters, widows, divorcees) being favorite targets.

Anthropologists' preoccupation with witchcraft as culture has done little to explain the generality of the phenomenon. Witchcraft is ubiquitous and tenacious because understanding of it is rooted in the body. Like greed, witchcraft has kept pace with modernity, adapting to the material development of our world, extending the moral index from outrageous consumption to the abominations of accumulation (the big farmer buying out his poorer neighbors). We might imagine witchcraft as a set of "traditional" beliefs which must yield to modern rationales about medicine, economics, and so on, but modern Azande might have little faith in the power of such exotic logics to dislodge the malign, hairy growth in someone's belly. They may indeed be ("logically") more likely to attribute nasty aspects of modernity to a multiplication of these visceral tumors. By contrast, the dialectic of needs and wants in which we struggle to rationalize the function of greed either in human progress or in impending catastrophe, looks trite.

Greed and witchcraft are critical explanations of behavior which differ from scholarly theories by incorporating feeling. Because they are locked into our understandings about our lives within the fabric of human relations, they are very persistent. As part of the communication on which humans depend, we talk about greed or witchcraft – accusing, excusing, explaining, translating – but words are no adequate substitute for those basic feelings. If we can intuit what bothers the Azande or the Lugbara, it must be because something common and sensible bridges the gap between us. But is this common sense, or is it mere idiocy?

In defense of idiocy

Once upon a time is was quite respectable to be an idiot. In Greece around the fifth to fourth centuries BC, *idiotes* were private persons who held no public office and claimed no specialist, professional knowledge. The basic, morally unobjectionable connotations of private, personal, peculiar, distinct, linger in our contemporary word "idiom." The worst that could be said about an idiot was that he did not voice his political opinions. For a scholar like Aristotle this was a failure of democratic duty. Our traditions of *scholarship* can be traced back to the professionalization of knowledge by the Sophists, the fee-earning tutors and explainers of ancient Greece, of whom we are the heirs. Their task was to make better-qualified democrats, teaching rhetoric to scions of the elite, thereby separating the articulate, the politically responsible, and thus the respectable, from the *idiota*. Of course, distinguishing ordinary citizens from the specialists, especially the clever professionals, put the term on a slippery slope. When the word *idiota* became current in Latin, it denoted a simpleton, and by the time the French had passed it on to the English, *idiot* had come to mean "a person so defective in mind from birth as to be unable to protect himself against ordinary physical dangers."[51]

Because of this change, "idiotic" seems to me a useful, if rather violent, symbol of the historic gap to which I want to draw attention between ordinary and professional intellectual understandings. Words like "common," or "lay," or "popular" seem to me too comfortable in their scholarly condescension. "Idiocy" evokes the passion which rational minds abhor but which is vital to ordinary understandings. I use it to make *myself* uncomfortable, because it is those of us who claim monopolies of knowledge, and who have blackened the idiot's reputation down the centuries, who are most in dread of appearing idiotic.[52]

Scholars, in their everyday idiotic roles, are as likely to refer to greed (or human nature, or luck) as anyone. Isn't this cheating? Thanks to dualism, the absent-minded professor can discard his body like an overcoat at the door of his study, but common-sense notions like greed remind us that what we think and how we feel are inseparable. It seems that we can make such comfortable, "naturalizing" references to greed *because* we are confident that it is safely outside the domain of scholarly meanings (rather as we imagine that poetic references to the heart do not obtrude on cardiology). But obtrusion is how greed works, jabbing critically at our bodies, reminding us that no meaning, however scholarly, is isolated from feeling.

Thinking about modernity is a professional task on which many of us now depend for a living. We may like to believe that our disciplines are simply a practical sharing-out of subject matter, but as our academic enterprises have expanded we have differentiated our various theoretical products, put up barriers and charged tariffs, just like the businesspersons we now often disparage.[53] Scholars have made knowledge-making in many ways more efficient, but not without costs. Boundaries exclude as well as include, encouraging dogmatism, extravagant deterministic claims, territorial wars, over-specialization, private languages, the preservation of ideas which have long outlived their usefulness, and the abandonment of others which do not seem to "fit." Disciplines become locked into their own rhetoric, posing orthodox questions and getting answers in the same coin which often look to outsiders like elaborate evasions of the obvious. Meanwhile, unattended gaps open up, not just between the disciplinary cells but within them. Every discipline has its "black boxes" on which basic arguments depend, but whose contents we either take for granted or believe, mistakenly, to be in the safe custody of some other discipline. One discipline's "fact" becomes a misplaced metaphor in another: a notorious example is the application of "natural selection" to everything from unemployment to the design of teapots, and even to the "fitness" of theory itself.[54]

Up to the nineteenth century it was still possible for most scholars in greater Europe to talk intelligibly to one another about most things. The days of the polymath are over, and the integrity of the intellectual quest is a thing of the past. As perspectives have narrowed, we see only aspects of things, while beyond our vision the areas of darkness multiply. One of the ironies of today's surfeit of communication is that it promotes detailed knowledge at the expense of the general. We may hope – in vain – that it is somebody else's job to pull it all together. Efforts to do so usually end up looking like academic imperialism.[55] Intrepid scholars always hope to make discoveries in the gaps between disciplines, or by playing up side-effects in their own. In the latter half of the twentieth century feelings of intellectual constraint encouraged "interdisciplinarity," and with the establishment of new "Centers" for this and that, some of the old disciplines have begun to look peripheral. With a dozen disciplines studying gender, or globalism, or Africa, the diseconomies of resources and effort multiply outrageously, suggesting that some reinvention of the structure of the academy is long overdue. But the disciplines are deeply entrenched professionally, and challenges to the established division of labor usually end up reinforcing it. Without sound credentials in one discipline, you cannot intrude on others.

If "Simple-mindedness consists in having too few thoughts and feelings to match the world as it really is," then scholarship is increasingly simple-minded.[56] "Good theory" modestly recognizes its limitations and the need for articulation to other theories, and the "best" theorizing takes pains to explain what these interconnections might be. This is hard work, and the best the ordinary academic foot-soldier may hope is that he may cut a different path through the fragmented fiefdoms of the modern academy.

If greed appears crudely "simple-minded" it is because, for our own scholarly reasons, we have ruled common sense out of our definitions of it. To recapture the feelings which are embedded in our understandings of greed we must return to the body, and imagine how meaning emerges sensuously within it as we make our way through life.

How Greed Grows

6

Feeling and Meaning

Greed has a history. Dictionaries tell us that over the centuries its meaning has grown from ravenous appetite to include the lust for money. But greed also has a "natural history." Its meaning grows within each of us as we make our way from gluttonous infancy to teenage lust, and by way of the expansive responsibilities of parenthood towards avaricious old age. Here in the bosom of the family is a living portfolio of characters, known to us through our own unfolding experience, to whom we can refer in our critical judgments of the people around us.

Having disconnected human life-history from the history of human life, modern scholarship can no longer trace how meaning moves from our molecules and guts, through thought and conversation, to the widening circles of community, society, and "culture." If we think of the mind as a disembodied state we will understand little about how meaning is made, or how thoughts and the things they refer to merge in the long-term practical process of "coming to know." And if we imagine the body as a passive object we will have no means of grasping its agency in history.

Growth is a provocative agent of change, producing new people and killing the old, placing relentless demands on how we organize our world and how we explain and evaluate ourselves. Time itself does not distinguish between history and the processes of human growth: both "take" the same spans of time – years, decades, centuries. Nor are there barriers in time or space between feeling and history. These are just words which we, as we have grown, have found to cut the single seamless process of human growth down to thinkable components. But if we insist that growth is irrelevant to culture and history, we risk losing track of the sensual components of meaning. We also lose a vital element of moral criticism – something the visceral notion of greed will not allow.

Growing bodies

In cosmic time-space coordinates we are creatures living within the span of 2 meters and 100 years. In the context of our fellow animals on this crowded planet we are a late-developing, bigger-brained, chattering, symbolizing, gregarious, hardy, omnivorous, bipedal, tool-wielding super-predator.

If we roll out a conventional anatomical chart we will see an image of ourselves at one instant in the time-space progression we call life. It will almost certainly show us at our fullest physical extent and near the middle (around thirty years) of our normal life course. The chart will probably offer us *two* specimens of *Homo sapiens*, their subtly different body forms expressing the sexual dimorphism by which our species, like most others, is regenerated. With segments of skin peeled away to show muscle, bone, and internal organs, these pictures help us to see how our many component parts are assembled into a supple and adaptable whole, centered on our most distinctively developed organ, the brain. With the help of some arrows and explanatory notes, these drawings might tell us something about the processes which hold all these parts together: nerve activity and muscle movement, blood circulation and digestion, glandular secretions and tissue repair. We might even be able to draw up a budget of inputs and outputs needed to keep each of these two specimens alive, measuring in calories the solids, liquids, and gases required. We would seem to be well on our way to defining a basic index for greed, a schedule of needs and capacities which would give us an authoritative basis for judging superfluous wants.

Were it all so simple it is unlikely that greed would ever have become such an interesting moral issue. The two-dimensional representation of our "perfected," mature bodies on the chart tells us almost nothing about growth, our transformation from microscopic organic matter back to dust. We do not have one physiology but many, as we make our way from infancy through adulthood to old age. The simple male–female contrast is also misleading, because that too is a process. Sexual differentiation builds up to puberty and diminishes after the female menopause.[1] "Femaleness" is most pronounced between about 10 and 40 years of age, the reproductive period which now accounts for only about a third of an American or Japanese woman's life. Development, variation, and adaptability are the bases of life in general, and human life in particular. Our physical plasticity has allowed us to disperse as a species around the globe, through the millennia. Depending on where and when they are, people are fatter or thinner, taller or shorter, darker or lighter, stronger or weaker.

The normal adult humans in our anatomical diagram have a remarkable go-anywhere, do-anything physique. Our simian cousins may be more clever with their feet, but the structure of our hands gives us a powerful and precise grip which, coupled with our brain-power, allows us to extend our physical capacities by the use of tools and to develop intricate and specific skills. Our flexible capacity for *work* is matched by the ability of humans to eat almost anything. We have an array of teeth which can bite, tear, and chew, and a phenomenally long gut which can break down fibers, metabolize proteins, and emulsify fats. "No other mammals, with the possible exception of the rats and mice that live in human settlements, possess the same ability to adapt themselves to a variety of conditions."[2] Human omnivorousness means we have to be able to discriminate accurately by taste, color, smell, texture, etc. to avoid poisoning ourselves. While creatures with more specialized diets may do this instinctively, we depend on our enlarged brains to evaluate whatever foods the environment offers, to store and reorder information, and, by sharing knowledge, to *learn* which meals are more nutritious. The same talents have allowed us to extend our menus by devising production and processing techniques (farming, cooking). This versatility opens up to us almost every environment from the freezing Arctic to the scorching Equator, and to resist blights, droughts, and other disasters. We can postpone our needs (go hungry) or accelerate our capacities (work harder) as occasion demands.

Sex and death are two vital and closely related aspects of our physical adaptability. Our genetic structure is reshuffled every generation by the sexual conjunction of woman and man. We are born, mate, and die, and our offspring get off to a fresh start in the battle for survival against the micro-organisms which mutate so rapidly within our bodies. Unlike fish and other creatures which depend on copious production of progeny to hedge their bets against predators and other selective effects, humans take care of a small number of offspring to ensure that a larger proportion of them survive into adulthood. As with other mammals, development begins in the controlled environment of the mother's body. For her, this is a costly, hazardous, and protracted business, subject to the long-term regulation of estrus, lactation, menopause, etc. Sexual relations are profoundly inequitable, but although the male may enjoy his vast capacity to fertilize, he also has some long-term selfish interests in being an attentive spouse and parent.

In the survival game, the *way we grow* is the most important distinction between ourselves and other animals. The numerous "clocks" governing our diverse bodily parts and processes are set in a way which makes some aspects of our growth take longer than it would in other animals. A much larger proportion of our development takes place outside the womb: by the clocks of our mammalian relatives, we are walking fetuses, or sexually precocious infants. Biologists have linked this *neoteny* to various other aspects of our evolution, most usually to the expansion of our brains, which outgrew the pelvic capacity of our mothers and now have to achieve more than three-quarters of their size outside her body. In its first year after birth the brain doubles in weight, sopping up half the body's available energy, and continues to grow throughout the first two decades of life. Our growth is so retarded that our juvenile curiosity and neurological capacities to learn last well into mature adulthood. During this protracted period, body, brain, and social being develop, each at their own pace but locked in profound interdependence. Although they eventually give us remarkable freedom of movement, our bodies have become utterly dependent on the basic social relations which make and sustain life.

However, it has always been nature's privilege to kill us off. A set of "atrophic changes" in different parts of the bodily system cumulatively afflict and eliminate us. Bits of us wear out, and how long we live depends on how slowly and how concertedly the various components of our bodies decline (some are still growing after "we" die). Neither nature nor biologists care how we die, so long as we eventually do so, for without death there need be no *re*production, no renewed growth.[3]

Images of growth

Stuck within the time-space confines of our own bodies, creeping our way through the physiological program towards death, each of us is in a poor position to see the broad picture of human growth. The agony of trying to understand our own lives is that it takes a lifetime. We never really know what it was all about until it's too late, and even then the picture is biased by age and failing memory.

Imagining time, especially a process as long as our own lives, is a big challenge for our poor human brains. To talk about how an egg turns into an eagle, or how a bird's wings keep it up in the air, we usually reduce the seamless process of change to a sequence of static pictures, like movie footage. Family photo albums do this, helping us to visualize the passage of our own lives by comparing one snapshot with another. But like the anatomist's chart of the healthy young adult, photo albums oversimplify our lives, memorializing the good times rather than the bad, the family in bloom rather than in decay. The closer we get to the end of our own lives the more urgently we want time to stand still, preferably back when the kids were young and life was sweet. Our own yellowing albums are superseded by those of our children, new glossy perspectives on the not-so-same old faces.

To talk about growth we have to reduce it to simpler metaphoric images. Like many people, the Gnau of Papua New Guinea refer to trees or plants, which do their growing visibly, rooted in one place.[4] A cruder, and characteristically modern image is the individual life-line or life-course, extending between the clinical boundaries of birth and death. Our tendency to think of ourselves as independent, mobile agents "leading" this linear life is a cheerful denial of the tendency of life to lead us, our absolute dependence on others, and the brevity of our existence. While we think of our interdependence in terms of "relationships" between separate bounded units, people in other times and places have imagined life as extending beyond the threshold of birth and death, merging with others, especially our parents and children, in a family circle. In such understandings, people seem more "dividual" than individual: their lives absorb and disperse aspects of other people, they do not (as we seem to) simply build up and express to the world a single proprietary identity.[5]

In medieval Japan individual lives were thought of as a gradual "thickening or densification of being," and death as "thinning"

rather than a single terminal event. Childhood was a progressive dis-
engagement from, and aging a progressive re-engagement with, the
world of gods and Buddhas. From an adult perspective this helped
to account for the often unintelligible behavior of the very young and
very old.[6] In many societies a small child is not enough of a person
to need a full-scale funeral, and sanctimonious treatment of the fetus
would be regarded as bizarre. This is not to say the child is nothing,
only that it has not yet emerged and distinguished itself in the world
as *we* know it. Entering life, it is physically merged with its mother,
but other aspects of its being are elsewhere, invisible to the living.[7]
In such continuous understandings of life it is less startling to think
of an individual, in sleep or illness, moving back and forth across the
physical margins of life, or even for a funeral to be conducted for
someone we would not think of as "dead."[8]

   In the understanding of peoples like the Wolof of West Africa,
growth occurs *between* lives as well as within them – life grows us
up. Much attention is paid to the continuity and health of these long-
term connections, and it is not so strange, when one life is seen as a
function of others, that child and grandparent should share one identity and personality.[9] This image of the integrity of life contrasts with
the desolate modern vision of extension from past into unknowable
future. In many cosmologies the progression into and out of individual consciousness is explained as a movement round the arc, with
adulthood as the period in which we are, ironically, most self-aware
but least conscious of the "dark" side of the circle; most responsible
for our actions but most at the mercy of fate and fortune; most
knowledgeable about immediate material things but least informed
about the cosmos. Middle age is a time of doubt, speculation, and
analysis, of the Cartesian sort.

   In biology, the dominant image of growth is neither the family
circle nor the individual life-line, but a repetitive oscillation, the cyclical rhythm of reproduction. Von Kondratowitz has traced the development of this model in a comparison of entries in two German
encyclopedias, one published in 1732, the other in 1848. The first
explained growth as a "path of life" for each organism, arranged
"like the ascent and descent of a staircase, a series of stages." The
later version represented human life as a cycle, concerned with
"keeping movement stabilized by insisting that a periodicity repeated
itself."[10] This was in tune with evolutionary interests which were, at
that time, narrowing the biological view of life to the sexual role
of the organism in sustaining and developing the species. The

reproductive cycle focuses on a recurrent event, the fertile union of two organisms and the fertile union of their progeny some years later. This narrow image has pervaded science: the closed parent–child dyad has become, for example, the basic image of Freudian psychology, an introversion which obscures the importance of relations between grandparents and grandchildren.[11] From the perspective of ourselves – feeling, thinking, imagining, ego-centered beings – this biological model, focused on the individual organism's duty to the species, is distressingly narrow. It does not, like the Wolof or Japanese circles, take account of the number, duration, or "density" of the relationships which sustain human reproduction, even though these social features have been essential to the later stages of our evolution as a species.

The biological cycle, tracking one pregnancy to the next, is not concerned with what happens to the organism after it has performed its reproductive tasks. But if our genes appear to have little "interest" in our survival past middle age, *we* as human individuals assuredly do. We have put our slower, neotenous growth and our expanded brainpower to work in assuring our *own* welfare, not just that of our progeny. For biologists "senescence" is the period – too short in most of the animal kingdom to be very interesting – of declining sexual capacity ending in death.[12] But genetics alone cannot explain how "senescence" has come to occupy such a conspicuously large part of human lives. Agricultural, industrial, and other quite recent historical developments have allowed us to live much closer to our "natural" (i.e. genetically endowed) limit of around 100 years than did our paleolithic ancestors, most of whom probably died in their thirties. Our lives are drawing increasingly long threads through historical time, extending the range of memory and knowledge, as well as complicating our political and economic life. While we have been complaining that "the family" is being stripped down to almost nothing, the relations of reproduction have been creeping up to four, even five living generations.[13] To the extent that "becoming a person is a matter of gathering those relations into the structures of consciousness" we differ significantly from our immediate ancestors.[14] There is probably no period in history in which our understanding of the world has been *more* influenced by old people.

Biologists interested in human evolution from the perspective of the life of the organism *(ontogeny)* rather than simply the development of species *(phylogeny)* are seeking broader views of the contexts within which human growth unfolds.[15] Between the microscopic parts of which we are individually composed, and the societies into which we have over the millennia assembled ourselves, there is a process of regeneration which is not mechanical, but creative in complex ways.[16] Growth is a journey through many levels of composition, the folding-together of molecules into cells into organisms into communities into societies, which we might imagine as a process "worming" its way through many levels of space-time. Our idiotic consciousness is stuck in "this isthmus of a middle state,"[17] our eyes neither large enough nor small enough to observe the wider continuum in which we are suspended.

As a compromise among these various images of growth, I propose another simple geometrical image to assist our basic thinking about the fusion of feeling and meaning (see figure 6.1). It imagines growth as occurring not within a single lifespan but between – minimally – three consecutive generations. It makes more sense to imagine feeling/meaning as an emergent property of this triad, rather than of an isolated individual, where it can only appear, deceptively, as the formation and dissolution of "a body" and "a mind." This model takes some account of the more circular images in which children "produce" their own parents and grandparents, and form, transfer, merge, and shed personal identities. But it is also intended to suggest a historic progression rather than cyclical closure. Growth in this matrix is a long-term, cumulative process of making people and communities, in which exchanges are never directly balanced (mother's milk is not repaid in kind) but are rolled forward into the future.

Meaningful growth

"The mind is born with the body, grows with it, and likewise grows old with it," said Lucretius two thousand years ago.[18] As we come into physical existence, our neural processes do not set up an opposition between feeling and thinking. This is a piece of imagining which occurs later in our growth (especially in our societies, where we talk about such things), in which the made-up mind encounters the ready-made body as a stranger, naively unaware of their common origins. Like any other thought, self-awareness is not one definitive object, but a complex of *feeling about feelings*, often experienced as the shock of reflection, of consciousness becoming aware of itself. We are struck by the two-sidedness of this encounter

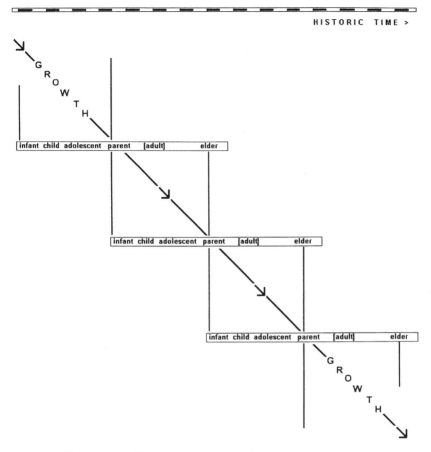

Figure 6.1 The trans-generational structure of growth

and – being only human – imagine it as distinct and opposed primeval states, rather than a fragment of the huge and continuous complex of interactions (mitosis and meiosis, infection and antibody, food and saliva) by which we have grown. Having separated itself from the processes of growth, the Cartesian mind is the ultimate unreality – integral, detached, eternally adult. It came from nowhere and "exists" nowhere.

In biological terms, feelings are feedback processes in the body's nervous system, contacts between organs distributed about the body and collated in the brain. Stereoscopic perception is an example of a complex, interactive process which assembles stimuli (light frequencies) into new and useful sensations (visual distance).[19] The "feeling" media are both electrical (fast, insubstantial) and chemical (slow, substantial), providing a versatile response system with a perceptual range of tiny fractions of a second (e.g. sounds up to about 20,000 cycles per second) to many hours (adrenal secretions). All these media (not just the electrical) are at work in thinking and communicating – which is one reason why computers with their binary logic provide such poor models. These multimedia processes also *take time*: the faculty of "memory," essential for conscious thought, is an obvious manifestation of this. Feelings are processes which extend from microseconds to whole lifetimes, and their meaningful interconnection and elaboration is sustained within the complex process of bodily growth.

Viewed this way, consciousness "is as much a part of our biological life as digestion, growth, or photosynthesis."[20] We perceive consciousness as "within" us, but as an elaborate compound of feelings-about-feelings it is part of the construction and maintenance of the relations with others on which human life depends. The puzzle of consciousness captivates us because it lurks at the level where "internal" reflections are folded into the reflections of other people around us.[21] What we call mind becomes evident to us at this level of flickering reflections about the "otherness" of ourselves. As we grow, the apparently "extrasomatic" or social connections of our feelings (which tend to take more time) are an inextricable part of the feedback process: they can cause or quell pain, stimulate appetite, or make us feel greedy. It is my subjective facility for coming to terms with the sentiments of others, and my dealings with others over time that are my best assurance that their feelings are pretty much like my own. Hit your thumb with a hammer and I will wince.[22]

Mercifully, nearly all our elaborate feedback activities, from digestion to keyboard work, take place (as we say) "sub" consciously. The body develops a large repertoire of signals, some simple (pain) some complicated (puzzlement) to bring feelings to consciousness and, if necessary, to the attention of other people. "Paying attention" is a process of perceptual *exclusion*, as in the visual shift from wide-angle to pinpoint concentration, accomplished with no apparent adjustment of the eyes. This enables us to simplify and scrutinize a sight, sound, smell, or whatever, but also to compare and analyze it with reference to our stored experiences – putting our expanded brains to constructive use. Most life functions are too important and too

> ## Apple trip
>
> In a nice reflection on how food passes into and out of our consciousness, Leder traces the progress of an apple. First, "a slight gnawing in my stomach, a longing, seemingly emanating from the mouth, for something to eat. My limbs are growing heavy, my mind a bit dull." He heads for the cafeteria, where "my gaze fastens on a particularly appetizing apple." He buys it, cuts it up, bites. "I revel in its sweetness for a moment, but soon I am lost in the newspaper . . . I absentmindedly chew and swallow . . . I have a slight sensation of the apple piece sliding down the back of my throat. Past a certain point this fades away . . . After a few minutes I burp and feel a bit of acid burning in my throat . . . a sense of fullness in the mid-section . . . renewed energy flooding through my limbs . . . I can occasionally, and perhaps unpleasantly, hear or smell evidence of diges-tive activity . . . many hours after eating, I grad-ually become aware of a new project: the need to find a bathroom . . . I allow what remains of the apple, and all else I ate, to reemerge in its mysteriously transformed state."
>
> Leder 1990: 38–9.

intricate to entrust to this last-resort level of conscious attention. I would fare better trying to fly a jumbo jet than operate my own liver.[23] Internal processes like heartbeat or peristalsis proceed unconsciously until they declare their presence by alarming sensations. Their feedback apparatus is neurologically simpler than the sensual apparatus of the skin and are represented (as physicians know to their cost) with smaller vocabulary, but their signals are no less blunt and forceful. Gut feelings do not simply ring a little bell in the brain, they rouse all of us: "hunger is not just in my stomach but pervades my mouth, my muscles, my mood . . . The world itself shifts with a shift in the visceral."[24] Greed links the inner compulsion of hunger (eat!) to the external options of taste (soup or salad?). The "must," "can," and "may" of greed threads its way between pang and desire, compulsion and restraint, sympathy and disapproval, savory anticipation and the sour memory of vomit. Greed (or envy, or anger) invades consciousness, and our thoughts track this mischief back to its visceral origins in the belly, the spleen, the heart.

It is activity of this sort which psychologists have sought to capture in the concept of *emotion*. The word connotes movement, imagined as a shift from one internal state to another and, in Cartesian logic, between feeling and idea (*"affect"* and *"cognition"*). Feelings can be fleeting (pangs of hunger, twinges of remorse) but in the context of reflection and interaction, emotions take more time. We talk of "states" or "moods" – someone whose emotions change too rapidly is "moody." The duration of emotions, along with their range and frequency, are important components of what we call personality, which is a summary of the ways in which our feelings and behavior are interpreted by those around us and thus, on reflection, by ourselves.

Psychologists consider our capacity to experience and express emotions to be a vital part of other aspects of growth. Their emergence in due order, and our ability to balance and control them, have been objects of much speculation. Did we evolve "anger" before "guilt," or "disgust" before "anxiety," and any of these before "consciousness"?[25] Figuring out which are more likely to be "hard-wired" and which are shaped by social action and reaction has been a perennial issue in developmental psychology.[26] Those who see emotions as developing in social experience regard the process as more variable and continuing well into adulthood, with adolescence as a particularly stressful period.[27] A child does not add "guilt" as a fully formed emotion to her repertoire one day. What she and other people identify as "guilt" is a complex of continually developing feeling-meanings, which they and she associate with the recurrence of certain sorts of events. In these terms, emotions are "epigenetic" – we build them up progressively. "Doing" guilt "properly" is a matter of experience, the cumulative result of personal episodes, the earliest of which are deposits of feeling far beyond the reach of consciousness. The prickle of fear you experience when you steal somebody's pen was probably built into your understanding of guilt a long time ago.

The fast-moving sensations at play in greed seem to have similar epigenetic roots. A snapshot of a situation in which a judgment of greed arises (you take a second slice of cake) may say quite a lot (it is a big slice, the cake is pricey, beggars are watching). But in the event, you and your judges make references forward and backward in time (the slice you just ate, how little of the cake will remain). Reckoning whether you should have more cake puts you into a wider time frame (it is your birthday, you are a calorie-starved adolescent). And in the few seconds occupied by the incident (your hand hovering over the last slice) observers have fleeting feelings-about-feelings (hunger, satiety, disgust, guilt, anger, amusement, etc.). These are powerful elements in what we think of as "greed," but we do not have to go through the actual experience of hunger and glut to reach the judgment (you do not have to gorge, vomit, and distress the onlookers – childhood memories are probably sufficient). Unseen in the snapshot, everyone's memory and imagination are selectively at work, pulling the long term and the short term, the past and the future, together to give meaning to this particular incident.

"When push comes to shove," says Tony Hendra, "there's only one person who can have your experiences, and that's you."[28] The catch, however, is that the "you" who thinks you are one person is a fiction because the experiences you are having are changing "you" all the time. But if you did not *create* some sense of a stable self, by telling yourself stories about who you are, you would be a disordered and difficult person to live with. This fixity is the assurance of the made-up Cartesian mind, the stable center of our being and our identity. However, what we know about the body suggests that "mind" is contained in a very fluid medium. In the "thick custard" of our brains, neural interconnections multiply at a staggering pace in childhood, rearranging themselves to deal not only with routine growth but even with major damage.[29] Although these connections are pruned at the rate of thousands per second after puberty, the chopping and changing continues well into old age. "Hard-wiring" is an absurd image of this medium, and seeking to distinguish between internal feeling and external experience as they converge in this hectic neural activity seems pointless.

The marvel, about which we know so little, is how the apparently copious neural resources of the body adjust to the elaborate process of assembling consciousness of context, self, and other selves. However, the need for the young human to be able "to discriminate himself as an object in a world of objects other than himself" is painfully evident.[30] To survive in society we have to be able to "do" relationships in thoughtful ways. For psychologists, detaching ourselves from our mothers is the most essential step towards this objective imaging of ourselves.[31] It brings an uncomfortable discovery of the shame, jealousy, envy, rage which underlie our dealings with others throughout our lives. Guilt, a favorite emotion among psychologists, takes time to develop, since it involves observing how other people react to your behavior. Kagan reckons that because choices are involved you have to be about 4 years old before you can "do" guilt properly.[32] On the positive side, most children discover early the rewards of "empathy," recognizing how someone else feels, and making sympathetic responses. The learning process involves observing and communicating through "body language," "a bodily awareness of the other in oneself" ("mimesis").[33] In its advanced adult forms, empathy is knowing more about others than they do about themselves – the talent developed by spiritualists, fortune tellers, priests, and others with special gifts of "understanding."

In these early stages of growth, the senses are working overtime. "Kinesthetic learning" is fundamental to what we call "skills": the "hands-on" interaction with materials and objects, the manipulation of fabric and needle, the physical coordination of making music, the complex sensuousness of turning wet clay into a pot.[34] Pain and humiliation in the form of corporal punishment is a common part of the bodily conditioning of morality, and loom large in initiation rituals around the world. All of us know the potency of smells in these elaborations: they symbolize and affect in ways which are truly beyond words, and are perhaps the aspect of meaning which is most easily lost in communication.[35] Music, too, is an emotional vehicle strongly connected to growth. Feeling and meaning are seamless, and the idea-actions associated with them can defy our best efforts to tease them out into words. If the process is mysterious, it is because it is so pervasive but gradual to the point of imperceptibility.[36]

Bloch reminds us that "language is not essential for conceptual thought." We build up our understanding of things as networks of association, not like dictionary definitions, and feelings are essential to these associations. If "Children have the concept 'house' before they can say the word" it is because they have crawled around it, tasted it, fallen off it, got lost in it. This in turn helps to explain why body symbols are so important in describing dwellings in many parts of the world.[37] Houses are objectively perceptible, material structures: substantially and coherently "there" with – it would seem – one shape and a single story to tell. The paterfamilias, with all his social authority, may tell that story, but enveloping as they do the relentless life processes of several human beings, the meanings houses contain are multiple. It is interesting to reflect that such a basic grouping as the household, which brings persons at different stages of development into the most intimate conjunction, are likely to contain the most differentiated understandings. A wall, a room, the location of a piece of furniture, are freighted with quite different significances and sentiments for a girl or boy, a child or adult, a grandparent or grandchild; and, developmentally, for a child as she turns into an adult. Later, when we build or furnish a house of our own, the meaning will change again. Though we all depend on the word "house" to make ourselves understood, and although there is a basic sameness about how you and I discovered the "house," your significations will always be at variance with mine.

Meaning is the process by which our feelings are put into communicable order, most notably through shared symbols (words, gestures, signs), but at the same time "Feeling is the catalyst that transforms acquired knowledge into understanding."[38] This two-way development connects the collective stock of *knowledge* with the emergent *understanding* of individuals. Human growth merges "*autopoiesis*," the process in which each organism must make its own life, and in the process by which each of us contributes to the making of the social life on which we depend.[39] In this sense, growth is simultaneously psychic and historic, in that the development of our understanding depends on the knowledge other people have accumulated, and that our shared knowledge is the product of numerous *developing* understandings. This dynamic aspect is lost in images of culture as a disembodied, self-regulating abstraction. According to Geertz, "A child counts on his fingers before he counts 'in his head'; he feels love on his skin before he feels it 'in his heart.'" True enough, but the next sentence doesn't follow: "Not only ideas, but emotions too, are cultural artifacts in man."[40] The child's sensation of love on his skin has nothing – *yet* – to do with culture, but the sensation will undoubtedly merge with the various understandings of love which social relationships may subsequently convey to him. Love is not a state, ascribed by culture in some generalized terms. It is the name we give to various sorts of gratification as our own lives intertwine with others – parents, peers, mates, children. In recent years our failure to understand the relationship, so basic to the organization of human growth, between the eros of conjugality and the eros of parenthood, has created nightmarish confusions (fathers who dare not touch their children). Geertz's formulation rules out the possibility that the *child* has a hand in defining the (adult) definition of "love." Culture, in his terms, is an adult affair – a mistake which adults everywhere are very prone to make.

Explicit meanings build up within the intergenerational structure of human growth through an active process of questioning, speculation, and efforts to resolve the inconsistencies between what we know and what we experience. There is "a developmental pattern in belief": we do not hold all our ideas with the same degree of conviction throughout our lives.[41] Our practical understanding of "deep culture" (an important ritual, reciting a myth) is likely to change quite drastically as we grow older, and as we move from the status of juvenile observer to active participant to venerable orchestrator of the event. These differential understandings make the idea of a fixed, objectively defined belief or practice, or a homogeneous culture which constructs meaning for all individuals, look less convincing. Over time, each performance, deploying changing actors, will alter – imperceptibly or quite drastically – the meaning of the ritual, the telling of the myth. For the anthropologist, knowing the myth without understanding how and why it grows can be thoroughly misleading.

Meanings which look pretty rigid from the morally "dense" perspective of adults can look incoherent to children as they struggle to learn the rules of life's games. Meaning is not something which adults dump, ready-made, into the brains of children. Indeed, it seems more logical to reverse the argument, and think of meaning as something which children dump in their own adult minds.[42] Children are notorious skeptics, and if adolescents seem scary and unintelligible it is largely because, as Margaret Mead noted, they are being subjected to the elaborate process of adult mystification – "culture."[43] A byproduct of this (conspicuous in modern thinking) is the isolation of childhood as a mentally fantastic form of life categorically distinct from adulthood.

Much knowledge is ephemeral, plastic, serving a particular life-stage, but also anticipating the next.[44] The early stages of life are most concerned with its formation, the middle stages with its consolidation in social experience, the later stages with the formal definition and transfer of knowledge. In this regard, our ability to *forget*, so conspicuous in our infancy, may be one of our most useful adaptations.[45] The phenomenon of "infantile amnesia" has its senile parallel, expressed in a greater ease in retrieving older, more thoroughly reinforced memories, and a tendency to lay these on younger generations as absolute moral truths.[46] "Culture" speaks to children with many voices, not one, and whatever integrity culture *does* have is largely a product of the hard, constructive work of growing up. Culturally, we are all pluralists. Imbibing uncritically everything your mother told you is a recipe for disaster – certainly in the brutally critical society of children. Despite what adults preach, the skill of "being yourself" involves developing a highly versatile, multifaceted persona which meshes unobtrusively with all the other personae with whom you relate. Woe betide the child who behaves to aged Aunt Mary and to the other kids in the playground in exactly the same way. Meanings and personal identities are very fluid among friends *within* younger generations (we tend to call these "*sub*-cultures"), but organizing reproduction is a *trans*-generational process locking individual meaning-making into collective understandings of social history.[47]

It is ironic that our most passionate and rigid moral ideas are focused on families, the social groups which are *most* disturbed by growth and by the motley understandings it produces. It is, of course, parents who enforce "family values," often pushing grandparents and grandchildren into furtive coalitions.[48] Sandwiched between generations, surrounded with responsibilities for young and old dependents, people in the middle stages of growth receive less sympathy than they may feel they deserve.[49] As they put their shoulders to the wheel of life, Wolof parents have to make sure their children quit the spirit world, "get real" and grow up, and must be patient as their aging parents gradually return to the spiritual domain. The ultimate frustration of living is never knowing enough to take full command of the middle ground.

Shared knowledge is an essential, static fiction which is at odds with the relentless dynamics of growth. To "do" social life we need to believe that other people ascribe meanings in much the same way as we do, but this is always at odds with the fact that knowledge must grow. An infant and its mother commune by intense feelings, but *know* very different things. We have to ascribe some general, objective meaning to being a mother, because maternity keeps happening and is hugely important. But like everything in life, being a "mother" is a process not a state, an unfolding sequence of events, duties, rights, sensations. Writing and other symbolic codes help us to standardize meaning in this way, but general knowledge is impoverished mainly by its loss of feeling, strung out as it is between the people whose changing experiences make it. Each of us may experience many understandings of each fragment of collective knowledge

Cake and culture

Culture, in the form which anthropologists communicate it, is a feeling-eradicator.

Cake, on the other hand, is a feeling amplifier.* We apply our skills, labor, techniques, imagination, and much else to making cake, playing with flavor, texture, temperature, to combine basic ingredients into more intense experiences. Trying to reduce cake to something we might all recognize if we were deprived of everything but the capacity to read, is a sorry task. "Cake," says the *Oxford English dictionary*, is "a comparatively small, flattened sort of bread, round, oval or otherwise regularly shaped." With the briefest digression to butter, sugar, currants, and childish tastes, the *OED* pursues cake to Scotland ("a thin hard-baked brittle species of oaten-bread"), and thence to the generality of "a mass or concretion of any solidified or compressed substance."

Little wonder that successive editions of Chambers' excellent dictionary have preferred to define *éclair* as "a cake, long in shape but short in duration." This lexicographical lapse flips us back to the lip-smacking delights of the real thing.

*I am grateful to Ramon Guardans for this fine perception.

during our lifetime. Imagining that knowledge can be encompassed by a single mind – some wise old bird like Solomon – is obvious nonsense, but helps to make it feel more durable and consistent. Hence the notion, entrenched in anthropology, that culture somehow *is* a mind.

"Culture," at least as anthropologists have perceived it, is essentially a geriatric phenomenon. The tidy authorized version is found in the resolved mind of the experienced adult, not in the tentative, experimental imaginings of youth. But the imaginary consensus of culture disguises the vital plurality of meaning as it is constructed, sustained, and altered in its passage through the various under-standings of the young and the old, women and men. Justifying the urgent need to record customs in the Torres Straits (Melanesia) a century ago, Haddon declared: "When I began to question the natives I discovered that the young men had a very imperfect acquaintance with the old habits and beliefs, and that only from older men was reliable information to be obtained."[50] Like many anthropologists after him Haddon assumed that the inability of young men to pon-tificate about culture meant that traditions were about to die out, and should be "saved" by urgent ethnographic attention to the "reliable" elders. Psychologists have speculated about the need for retrospec-tive order, to place self in wider time-space coordinates, which increases with age.[51] This "crystallized intelligence" is the repository of publicly valuable information, increasingly important as human lives have lengthened. But to compensate for dwindling physical powers, increasing dependency, and a need to retain access to ma-terial resources to assure survival, elders may claim far more knowl-edge than they actually possess, and profess supernatural powers to boost their credibility.[52] There is some strategic purpose in nourish-ing the doubts and anxieties of the middle generation.

Growth and the meanings of greed

> And because the constitution of a mans Body, is in con-tinuall mutation; it is impossible that all the same things should alwayes cause in him the same Appetites, and Aver-sions: much less can all men consent, in the Desire of almost any one and the same Object.
>
> Thomas Hobbes[53]

Bodily development presents a perpetual moral challenge. It forces on us a shifting scale of needs (food, sex, capital, care) and a paral-lel set of capacities (strength, skills, fertility) against which those around us measure off what we deserve. Greed is a critical monitor of how we grow, but the meaning of greed itself shifts as it tracks the relationships among our growing bodies through time.

In figure 6.2 I have arranged the meanings of greed along a continuum of growth, suggesting a cumulative development from the "earlier" and more "internal" gluttony to the "later" and more

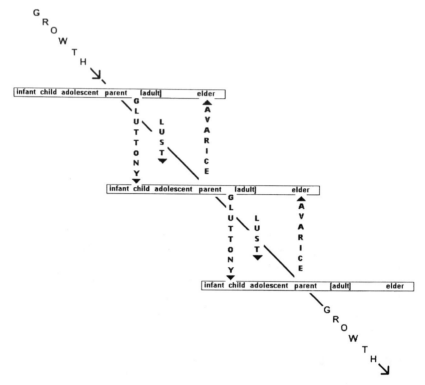

Figure 6.2 The development of the meanings of greed

"social" avarice. This breaks up the meanings into a pattern in which individuals are considered more, and less, susceptible to greediness. The process tracks material relationships, from consumption, through reproduction and accumulation, to savings and a renewed concern with consumption in the "second childhood" of old age.

It is one of the oldest and most basic ironies of human life that vices like greed are nurtured at home, in the bosom of the family.[54] Growth perpetually disrupts domestic harmony, shifting the balance of needs and capacities, wants and entitlements. But ultimately it is within the long-term fabric of reproductive relationships that the inequities of growth must be in some fashion resolved. Altruistic pictures of family life, from Aristotle, Locke, and Marx, through to the present day, have dwelt on the resolution of conflict, rather than on the conflict itself. The reality of this balancing act is competition between the sexes and the generations for access to scarce resources – including such intangible things as authority. Families have to hang together to do the business of reproduction, despite the incipient rivalries between spouses, siblings, and the generations. In human growth there can be no short-term trade-off of need and capacity. Capacities develop from zero and decline to zero, slowly, or abruptly at the moment of death. That many people look after themselves for much of their lives does not alter one of the central facts of human existence: no individual has the autonomous capacity to satisfy all his or her own needs – that's what families (and, more recently, public welfare systems) are for. Viewed narrowly, and in the short term, the infant epitomizes selfish greed, the mother selfless altruism. But we do not abominate "greed" at this stage because infants are un-socialized, without conscience, and utterly dependent: they have neither the physical capacity to satisfy their own needs nor the mental capacity to articulate their wants. Thus, if she thinks about it at all, a mother may set the inconvenience of child-raising against the prospect of support in her old age, drawing pleasure in the meantime from infant smiles.

The vigor of my accusations of greed reach deeply into my past experience to the layer of disgust which, psychologists tell us, is one of our oldest emotions. Disgust is epitomized by two substances: feces (food-that-was) and putrid flesh (body-that-was). "What a shit," I cry, contemplating the greedy capitalist. Or: "that makes me want to puke." Gorging, the bloated hunger-to-bust sensation at the core of greed, evokes the same vomit response as toxicity (eating a particu-lar delicacy to excess can put you off it for years). Disgust is conta-gious, and we readily make associations between one nasty substance and another, so that the very idea of something unpalatable can make us retch. Pork is repulsive to my Muslim friends, but it is futile to ask them whether it is the thought or the feeling which repels them – it is, of course, both. Nurture is in our nature: just the mention of dinner can give me pangs of hunger, and the very suggestion of excess can evoke the grimace, the shudder, the hand gestures (covering the mouth, clutching the stomach) of empathic disgust.[55]

Getting to know your gastric limits is one of the challenges of growing up. Infants seem able to adjust the input–output balance without too much discomfort or inhibition, but the shift from a single food (breast milk) towards the adult repertoire is stressful. The sepa-ration of the gluttonous infant from the bounty of the breast may indeed, as Melanie Klein insisted, be the beginning of greed. Consider

---

The poisonous breast

In Melanie Klein's psychology, "the retaliating, devouring, and poisonous breast" becomes the object of our deepest alienation, a frustrated desire which fixes on other persons and objects for the rest of our lives. "Greed is an impetuous and insatiable craving, exceeding what the subject needs and what the object is able and willing to give. At the unconscious level, greed aims primarily at completely scooping out, sucking dry, and devouring the breast." Envy goes further, seeking "to put badness, primarily bad excrements and bad parts of the self, into the mother, and first of all into her breast, in order to spoil and destroy her. In the deepest sense this means destroying her creativeness."

Klein 1975: 231, 181, 251.

---

the agony of hunger and disgust caused by the common motherly practice of putting bitter substances on the nipples to encourage weaning. The breast is where infant incapacity meets adult capacity, and we must be grateful that the scheduling of human reproduction tends to bring the two together in a timely fashion. Thereafter, dependency relations within the family create tensions about competing needs and wants: the grown son who eats at the family table and will not make shift for himself; the aged parent who monopolizes the comfy chair and will not yield control of the purse-strings.

After their period of indulgence at the breast, children are subjected to quite painful repression and constraint. Sherbro children in Sierra Leone "are considered proto-social, egotistically greedy and wilful. They are analogous to spider who, in folk tales, has human appetites untempered by rule bound decency."[56] In Japan, the child who does not soon learn to moderate its appetite is *Ga ki*, literally "starve devil": eating too much, too fast is a ridiculous and disgusting childish trait, and Japanese apply the phrase to adults who are overbearing and ambitious.[57] Children everywhere have to learn the arts of give-and-take, largely through interaction with peers but always within a context of their dependence on adults. In many societies, ranging from hunter-gatherers to our own, children do not become net producers of food until their late teens.[58] Piro children in Peru enter a world in which "The production, circulation and consumption of food is the central drama of village life and sexual relationships are the primary topic of everyday conversation." Production and consumption of food (game and plantains) are organized around sex and generation relations, converging on marriage, and are rich in humorous metaphoric allusion – especially the relationships between desired food items and sexual substances. Low on sexual desire, children are always hungry, and often baffled by the intricate web of meanings their seniors have woven around "good taste." The piece of childish behavior that bothers Piro adults most is eating earth. Such children are *viciosos* or "perverts" – gratifying themselves with "food" they immediately and without mediation acquire for themselves. "Earth, the supreme antithesis of real food, is produced and consumed in a perverse caricature of the subsistence economy."[59]

The Roman philosopher Seneca declared that "A stomach firmly under control marks a considerable step towards independence."[60] The balance is persistently disturbed by time, in the sense of both daily rhythm and bodily growth. The same grandmother who condemned snacking between meals stacked my dinner plate to meet the awesome demands of adolescence. During this "growth spurt" (around 10–11 years old for girls, 12–14 for boys) we may need as many as 10,000 calories per day, three or four times as much as an adult man. "This can result in almost continuous eating in an attempt to meet energy needs."[61] The prodigious fortitude of bodies at this stage is a good match for the colossal adjustment to adult life (sexuality, responsibility for livelihood and parenthood) that is taking place.

Balanced growth depends not just on the sheer quantity of consumption but on ideas and rules about the *right* foods, grown in the right places in the right manner, prepared for consumption in the right way, and eaten correctly. Likewise, consuming the *wrong* substance at the wrong time can jeopardize growth, and evoke moral judgments. In my childhood in the 1950s, cigarette smoking was not advised because, like masturbation, it stunted your growth. Grownups were therefore not at risk – cancer was not yet considered a significant threat. Lewis describes the developmental aspects of diet among the Gnau of Papua New Guinea, who see growing as a progression from softness and wetness at birth through to toughness and dryness in old age, with concomitant dietary rules and therapeutic procedures. While a baby, for example, normally eats wet foods, adjustments may be made by sweating it by a fire or in the sun to toughen it; and "It is not until the end of life approaches that men or women see themselves as fit to eat those birds associated with the dead or death."[62] Such changes in diet with age are a mixture of

The nightmare of the palm-wine drinkard's gluttonous son Zurrjir – a synopsis

One day the Drinkard's wife's thumb swelled up. It touched a palm-tree thorn, and burst to reveal a child who at once began to talk like a ten year old. An hour later he had grown to more than three feet, was swigging palmwine furiously, and told his parents his name, Zurrjir, which means "a son who would change himself into another thing very soon." While the Drinkard, ashamed about the unorthodox birth, was contemplating how to abandon his son, the latter marched off to where the Drinkard was living, introduced himself to the people there, and proceeded to guzzle all the food he could find. Asked to leave, he responded by smashing everything in sight, including the domestic animals. The Drinkard and his wife cooked more food, but Zurrjir gobbled it hot from the pot. "Now he became our ruler in the house," denying his parents food, driving them out of the house for hours on end, and making them prostrate themselves before him. When he started burning down the townspeople's houses they complained to the Drinkard, who contrived to burn his monstrous offspring to death in his hut. As they were moving on from the town, the Drinkard's wife remembered she had left a gold trinket in the hut. Against his advice she returned to the town, fished in the ashes with a stick and up rose "a half-bodied baby" who "was talking with a lower voice like a telephone." When the Drinkard and his wife refused to take him with them he struck them blind. Still they pressed on, so he made them stop breathing. They relented and went back to fetch him. He insisted on riding on the Drinkard's wife's head, "whistling as if he was forty persons." They paused in a village for some food, but the half-bodied baby prevented his parents eating, and swallowed everything in sight. They were driven out of that village, but everywhere they went the same thing happened. Everyone feared the Drinkard and his wife would abandon their voracious half-bodied baby in their village. Still perched on her head, the half-bodied baby's belly had "swelled out like a very large tube," but still "he could eat the whole food in this world without satisfaction." The Drinkard's brief attempt to relieve his wife of her burden reduced him to sweaty exhaustion. Then they chanced on a trio of creatures, "Drum, Song and Dance" whose irresistible entertainment induced them all to dance and sing for five days "without eating or stopping once." The half-bodied baby took off with the trio, never to be seen again. The Drinkard and his wife "set out on a fresh journey."

Amos Tutuola 1962 [1952] *The palm-wine drinkard and his dead palm-wine tapster in Dead's Town*. Faber & Faber, London (1962), pp. 31–9.

meaningful privilege and physical preference. Older people may eat less, but compensate by preferring tastier, less chewy foods which may also be scarcer and more fattening – "greedier."[63]

Specific foods in particular quantities are eaten not simply to enhance tissue growth and body weight, but to develop personality and morality. Green reports that the Pogoro in Tanzania have special dietary supplements for this purpose, and also apply growth-enhancing substances in poultices or with the aid of incisions, or sometimes by wearing amulets. Pogoro think of these as essential material treatments for personal growth: "There is no break between being and becoming, or between representation and experience, because practice involving the body continually seeks to change it." Green reckons that such practices, widely reported in other parts of the world, are not just symbolic gestures, as anthropologists generally suppose, but "can perhaps be explained in terms of the universal experience of growth and biological process which being a person in all cultures entails."[64]

Childhood is a journey of the unwary innocent into the jungle of adult constructions. But as naive *viciosos* they focus the thoughts of adults, challenging them to "make" structure by haranguing their juniors about the peculiar meanings of life. Advising American parents on how to "combat children's inclination toward greed," Deborah Wood insists that there should be no room for parental guilt in "Coping with the 'Gimmes,'" because "A child's value system is very different from an adult's."[65] The imposition of guilt and shame tells children that the eccentricity is in them, not in the adult machinations of Piro, Pogoro, or American "culture." And yet in so many societies childish innocence is perversely equated with some sort of natural truth in the face of adult doubt and confusion. A vivid example is the case of children who "find," or confess to being, witches. Among the Bangwa of West Africa these are "sky children" who "confirm in a clear, matter-of-fact fashion the vague beliefs of adults."[66] They provide lots of lurid details, the more way-out the better, but with an amusingly juvenile twist:

The confessions of the Bangwa sky children are always very meaty. The orgies of the witch-bush are orgies of eating. The meat is human, but it is not described as disgusting either by the witch or by the accusers. The plump are preferred to the skinny, and the young to the old ... it is, therefore, significant that a confession of witchcraft usually leads to a good meal: chickens are brought by relatives and given to the child as part of the ritual of bringing him back from the sky.[67]

At around twenty years calorie demand steadies and declines slowly for the rest of life. In economic terms, the disutility of over- and under-consumption is very evident in societies where survival depends on physical exertion. In a long hot day of manual labor, obesity is as debilitating as emaciation, and the pain of both signals the extremities of greed. In our more sedentary lives a distinction has emerged between the failure to take proper control over body weight and the *disease* of obesity. More than half the adult American population is officially "overweight" and, despite efforts to blame genetics, or leptin, or the sofa, TV, and remote control, the cause is officially "just eating too much."[68] Body weight has become a national neurosis, appearing most cruelly in the starve–glut disorder of bulimia – so modern and so mysteriously associated with adolescent development in women.[69]

The turbulent passage to adulthood marks a shift in the meaning of greed, a confusion of the infantile vice of gluttony and adult lust. It also inaugurates the first serious episode of intergenerational conflict. The imperative of youthful growth excuses gluttony: as far as food is concerned, body-building legitimates the demand for more. The contradiction, which shifts the meaning of greed from consumption towards reproductive matters, is *sterile growth*. The will of the rising generation to release its sexual energies constructively in childrearing is a time bomb which will ultimately force the fission of the family. Containing the sexual appetite of the adolescent is a major preoccupation in many societies, especially where material resources are in short supply and restrictions on fertility are acute.[70] There are strict limits to the satisfaction of sexual urges *within* the family – for reproduction to proceed outsiders are necessarily implicated, with all the diplomatic hazards that entails.

Just as lust enters the dictionary definitions of greed as an afterthought to gluttony, these two feeling- and meaning-laden aspects of our existence, food and sex, are sequential in the growth process: we eat first (as infants and children) and have sex (as adults) afterwards. We can experience hunger in a matter of hours all by ourselves, but the experience of sex implies an inter-somatic relationship of some sort, with the expectation (or hazard) that its reproductive consequences will extend through much longer tranches of time than the production, consumption, and elimination of food, and will cause

social relations to ramify. The need to eat is not indefinitely post-
ponable, but the need to reproduce is. Especially where contracep-
tion has been unreliable, the threat is that sex would precipitate
reproduction with its potentially costly consequences.

The sting of greed at the post-adolescent stage is wanting sex
more than the commitment of reproduction. But raising a family
depends on material resources, especially access to productive capital.
What economists and demographers have called the "family life cycle
squeeze" provides a *long-term* pattern of economic motivation.[71] At
this stage, the urge to accumulate for family growth mitigates accusations of greed: decent people want more for their children. In
modern societies a married couple has only a few fleeting years to
meet the consumer demands of their children and then to insulate
themselves from the effects of their own (increasingly protracted)
physical decline. In their prime, parents must take a grip on productive processes, save and invest, take innovative risks, and pin their
faith on any institution (ranging from banks and educational trusts
to lotteries and religious cults) which can offer some assurance of
long-term security. Acquisitive zeal extends to dynastic planning for
grandchildren and further descendants.

The history of economic development owes much to this power-
house of material needs. Its force has been described in ideological
terms as "familism," selfishness raised to the level of the reproductive group. Accusations of greed may resurface at this corporate level
– one family "eating" an unfair share of community resources. Where
these are in short supply, reproductive relations (marriage) are commonly deferred, or prevented altogether: monasteries and nunneries
institutionalize sterility, requiring a lifetime commitment in which
bodily needs are supposedly transcended by spiritual desire. Bach-
elors and spinsters who accumulate to secure their own childless
future are most culpable of "sterile growth." These are the Scrooges
and witches on whom suspicion of avarice is most sharply focused.
If they have banked in material wealth rather than human relationships they stand isolated and critically vulnerable as they approach
the threshold of death.

Sandwiched between gluttonous youth and avaricious age, the
middle generation has a particularly critical eye for greed. The thoroughly middle-class, middle-aged "fear of falling," the loss of income,
respectability, property, has as its base the specter of *family* starvation.[72] Women, at the center of processes of reproduction and consumption, and commonly of production as well, are most heavily

implicated: "greedy institutions such as the family are hard task masters" say the Cosers, and the "housewife" bears an unfair share of the stigma.[73] Especially where families have contracted to late-modern sub-nuclear or "matrifocal" patterns, "familism" is, at heart, "maternalism." A woman informant told me that women were more susceptible than men to "fear of want," and thus "biologically" more disposed to greediness. Frugality is a housewifely virtue on which men may make apprehensive and malicious sexual play, especially when she controls the family purse.

Women's powers within the relations of reproduction have exposed them to every accusation of disorder, vice, and evil, not only from men but from the rising generation of women which threatens to displace them. Much has been written about the female identity of witches.[74] That they are so often *older* women raises again the notion of sterile growth: the woman who wants to secure her survival after her family duties are fulfilled is suspect. Women outlive men, nowadays by as much as 10 years, and in a patriarchal world women usually have to struggle harder than men against the notion that the elderly absorb resources needed by the younger and more vigorous.

There is a human tendency to see all the exchanges of growth in zero-sum terms: one generation saps the energy of the other. The Lusi of New Britain specifically attribute the weakness and senility of the very old to the fact that their vitality has been expended into their children.[75] The senior generation is expected to devolve power and wealth, but for their welfare they must depend on the attentions of their able-bodied juniors. Avarice, said Kant, "belongs chiefly to older persons (as a substitute for their natural impotence)."[76] The key to survival in old age is retaining some control over family assets in all forms – savings, land, movable capital, and the labor of the younger generations. This extends to sexual control, the planning and sanctioning of marriages which keeps the reins of growth in the hands of the senior generation.[77] This is the framework in which the last epigenetic stage of greed emerges – an invidious mixture of concern about hoarded wealth, the dwindling contribution to productive efforts, and the food consumed. Old people guzzling at the family table is second childhood without the promise of growth.

While scholarly images of consumption and growth have evacuated the body, "greed" has retained its center of gravity in the gut. As a truly embodied means for judging motives, greed has the power to drag distant persons, categories, and events down to familiar human proportions *because* its meaning is rooted in visceral feelings, in alimentary and genital processes, in the material and moral transactions of everyday life, and in the subjective experience of growth and reproductive relations.

To the scholar it may seem idiotic to measure the grand activities of multinational companies or super-states against something so frail and ephemeral as the human body. But our own bodies are, after all, the center of our being: we all acquire them, grow in them, and eventually lose them, and it is only through them that anything in the world matters to us. The managers and politicians who run big corporations and states are just people like us, but they have seized our idiotic understanding of growth for their own metaphoric purposes, using the idea to justify the expansion of sales, the development of capital, or imperial growth of all sorts – just as we might justify the appetite of the hungry adolescent. But greed, laden with visceral meaning, has the marvellous capacity to recapture the meaning of growth, flushing the individuals from their corporate cover, pulling their enterprises back to human scale, confronting their zealous accumulation with the old familiar images of gluttony or avarice.

The irony is that in talking about firms or states as if they were bodies, businessmen and politicians are referring to a truth which has been heavily disguised in modern scholarly thinking: the needs which drive our largest corporations are *the same* growth-driven needs which have animated family and community enterprise for millennia. Greed remains such a strong critical device not simply because everything in industrial societies has become so huge, but because all of us everywhere grow in much the same way as we have always done. Greed does not take its meaning from the economic excesses of the modern world, it marks those excesses with it own visceral power. We have industrial corporations because humans grow, not vice versa. Regardless of the metaphors we spin to make big things look good, greed insists on the priority of one meaning of growth over all the others.

7

Growth and history

Human history has been largely about getting more – out of nature, out of ourselves, out of other people. We need more because we grow, and growth is our justification for expansive acts – having kids, farming an extra acre, raising an army for imperial expansion. But by scrutinizing our bodies *greed* detects the metaphoric shift from physical need to political necessity. Aging, decline, and decay are essential to human growth, and it is here that the metaphor makes a telling departure from its bodily source. Greed insists that *boundless growth* is physically and morally monstrous.

In modern times we are acutely interested in how institutions, businesses, whole economies grow, and we evoke images of our bodies and our families to talk about it. "Money, like children, should develop and mature," says a recent bank advertisement.[1] There is something unsettling about such metaphors: in precisely what sense are children "like" money? Of course children are material assets (and liabilities) and any responsible American parent knows that the child and the college fund should grow together. But it is easier to sympathize with the proposition that money grows *for* children, than that it should lead an expansive life of its own in a bank or brokerage house.

The gap, detected by the idiotic notion of "greed," is obvious: that societies and our ideas about them have got bigger does not mean that the link with our growing bodies has been severed. Losing track of how needs have been a driving force in history has given us the chilling illusion that it is history which is driving us.[2] Insisting that behavior on the large scale (corporations, nations) is now qualitatively different from behavior on the intimate scale (persons, communities) is morally hazardous. It permits us to excuse excesses we would not tolerate among our friends and acquaintances.

The bodies with which we have made history also provide us with the means to grasp it. But much of this meaning is unspoken. Nationalism is a gut feeling. Mickey Mouse, the Internal Revenue Service and the Pasadena Rose Parade are also loaded with feelings, which are absolutely basic to what they mean. But having disconnected feeling from meaning, and biology from history, modern scholarship can no longer trace how meaning moves from the viscera to the widening domains of community and society. The main route, I have argued, is growth.

Need and necessity

"Luxury." Like greed, the word is thoroughly sensuous. It has also fascinated historians for millennia. In his scholarly essay on the subject, *The idea of luxury*, Christopher Berry strives to trace it to its roots in basic human feelings, but encounters an apparently unsurmountable obstacle: ideas can't be reduced to bodies, basically because history can't be reduced to biology.

Berry begins with "the seemingly obvious 'fact' that luxuries are not needed." He sees them as four distinct sorts of desire, each "corresponding to" and a "refinement" of the basic need for food, clothing, shelter, and leisure. The addition of leisure to the age-old triad immediately raises a doubt: is this really a basic human need, or just a modern sort of desire? If leisure, why not sex, a much older candidate for the list? Insisting that he does not wish to reduce needs to "social constructions" (i.e. to culture or history) Berry musters strong philosophical support for their universality, and defends "the naturalism that underlies my four categories."[3] "I want coffee, you want tea, he wants lemonade, she wants whisky. These differences nonetheless have a common focus because of their roots in common need: we all need a drink." The way in which desires stem from bodily needs makes them a formative influence in all cultures. Thus, "luxury can be understood as one of the basic categorizing components of a society's grammar."[4]

Berry is most at home in the historical parts of his argument, especially when he explains how, from the seventeenth century onwards, the bourgeoisie made luxury respectable. However, his universal (he calls it "conceptual") framework for needs is always in danger of slipping back to the historically relative side of the fence: "Human needs are never brute and are always, in principle, open to question."[5] As his analysis strives to discriminate which sorts of desire are more or less "necessary," or which sort of needs are more or less "instrumental," it tends to drift away from the four strands anchoring desires to needs, and thus from the "real" bodies which supposedly experience these needs. The idea of luxury as a universal meaning-maker in human societies looks a lot less convincing, as the dualistic framework reasserts itself.

Berry's book pivots on an intriguing and self-critical question: "In what sense, if any, can needs be said to have a history?"[6] The issue boils down to one of disciplinary domain: whether "nature" (alias "biology") is or is not the proper business of historians. Most historians would take it for granted that since our "animal nature" was defined many thousands of years before "history began," it is beyond the compass of their profession, best left to natural scientists (the "natural historians" of bygone days).[7] For their part, biologists think of history as the span of "evolution," something much grander than the historians' sliver of recorded time in which nothing significant in our *nature* can have changed. Contemplating this interruption in our understanding of human time raises a converse to Berry's question: "In what sense, if any, can history be said to have needs?" If the question is taken to imply something in our nature – hunger, thirst, sex – then the question will be meaningless to most historians. Most historians, like cultural anthropologists, are interested in the things which make people different (politics, architecture, technology), not the things we all have in common.

In the historian's non-biological world, needs are interesting only as ideas which get elaborated in different ways at different times.[8] However, this relativistic notion of "need-as-an-idea" is a very slippery one, especially when it comes to making arguments about cause and effect (ideas-making-ideas). Baudrillard, for example, attacks the "naive factuality" of a "naturalistic account of needs." They are, he says, what rich people think poor people deserve. Specifically, needs are what are left when you subtract the *luxuries* of the privileged: they are desires stripped down to a "survival threshold."[9] This formula (which looks something like "*need* equals *greed* minus *desire*") has an indignant, populist ring to it, but it makes the outrageous assumption that poor people themselves don't really know what they need – and that Baudrillard does. The argument that what I need is really a byproduct of somebody else's ideas is more than ludicrous, it is morally dangerous. But Baudrillard is much less interested in what poor people think than in grumbling about the claims of scientists to know more about the human condition than historians.

However, not even economics, "the master science of modernity," has a theory of need.[10] What the rival ideologies of modernity – liberalism and socialism – have to offer are different theories of *necessity*. While socialists would argue that history is necessarily moving in one particular direction (the demise of capitalism), liberals would say that it is necessarily moving only where our choices lead us. By allowing us to negotiate freely what we *want*, efficient markets assure us that we live in the best of all possible worlds. It's socialists who try to dictate what we need, which is why the Soviet Union collapsed in a surfeit of shoes, cabbages, and alcohol.[11] But liberal economics has no basis for explaining why, for example, "wanting" a baby is not quite the same thing as "wanting" an apple, an oil tanker, or a job. Taking wants at face value, says the socialist, is a fundamental moral failing of liberal notions of democracy, leading to environmental asset-stripping and the polarization of wealth and poverty. "Necessity" for the liberal is the freedom to pursue individual desires on the one hand and, on the other, for some sort of governmental order which will prevent that freedom from degenerating into competitive chaos. Precisely how the state should intervene in this delicate balance (prices-and-incomes policies in the UK, the endless cycles of regulation/deregulation in the US) remains at the heart of liberal debates.[12]

Engels insisted that "Naked greed has been the moving spirit of civilization from the first days of its existence to the present time; wealth, more wealth, and wealth again." The key word is "civilization": in the Marxian scheme greed is a historical, not a biological condition. In this rhetoric it is a particular sort of acquisitive passion, the *"unmanageable power"* of the "property fetish."[13] Marx's *"Bereicherungslust,"* often translated as 'greed,' is a "mania for possessions" which originates in money and the historical circumstances which define it.[14] But whether this mania has beastly origins is unclear, nor does Marx clarify the distinction between "historically developed 'natural' needs and 'wholly historic needs.' "[15] To make farms in the very early days we needed to take control of nature, specifically land, and as one technical advance led to another the need to accumulate capital increased. Smaller numbers of people own more wealth not because they "want" to, but because that is what the material laws of history dictate. In this variant of the natural science of modernity, what "began" in an imagined agrarian context as the increasingly unequal possession of productive resources ("primitive accumulation"), acquires its own momentum. While plainly a vice, greed in this scheme is not associated with physical sensations or bodily requirements: it is an abstract historical force, and we have to purge it from our political-economic systems by suffering the epoch of capitalism. When capitalism has been blown apart or has burned itself out, a new form of society will emerge in which property and money have no meaning, and *Bereicherungslust* no function. Automation, the blessed legacy of capitalism, will mean that there will be plenty of leisure for everyone to share.[16] The fear that capitalism will keep popping up has led Marxists to reckon that communist society will have to live in a state of perpetual revolutionary alert. But is this still the work of a historical mechanism, or of our greedy human nature?

It is a basic Marxian tenet that our ideas derive from our material circumstances and not vice versa, but the extent to which our *bodies* enter the material scheme is far from clear. Accumulation is an abstract force in the relations of production, involving classes of people whose personalities have little relevance. In the Marxian scheme, bodies and their reproduction become an abstract component in the economic process, principally in the supply of labor.[17] What is of interest is how productive power is extracted from bodies and converted into capital owned by others – Marx's central diagnostic idea of *surplus-value*. In primitive society surplus production had no value because nobody needed it. Where people produce only what they need for immediate consumption, anything extra is literally useless. With the historic transition through feudalism to capitalism, need and capacity are not balanced among individuals in small communities, but are split up among unequal and opposed classes of people: the factory owner needs and therefore appropriates ("owns") the workers' capacity. Commodities are exchanged not for other immediately useful commodities but for money, which allows the profit from a sale to be transferred, saved, or invested at will. "Valorized" in this way, money is the means by which a minority can accumulate resources, and thus control production in the system as a whole. "Surplus" here is the exploitation of the *capacity* of one class of people (the workers, who supply labor power) and the transfer of the value they create to the class which rules them (the owners of capital). The laborers are separated ("alienated") from their own, over-stretched capacities. They do not *want* to produce more, and do not benefit from doing so. They are forced to produce more by the class which owns the essential productive resources, and thereby controls the coercive powers of the state (the police, the army). The capitalist, for his part, does not "want" economic monopoly; he is impelled to accumulate by historic forces which have created the class in which he and all his thoughts and actions are embedded.

Marx's most basic point was that the bourgeois himself, with the best will in the world, could tell you nothing reliable about his own motives and interests. This was tough on his victims, since it was the bourgeois who controlled schools, libraries, and all the other official apparatus of knowledge-making. The task for an honest and objective science was to put the bourgeois into historical perspective, explain how capital worked on him and on others, and communicate this new knowledge (through political parties) to history's victims.

The Marxian scheme is only indirectly concerned with wants, which are the theoretical fixation of liberal economists. The Marxian economy is driven by two opposed sorts of "need": the worker's struggle for physical survival on the one hand and the abstract accumulative force of capital on the other. Marx, like Ricardo before him, understood very well that capitalists need a *needy* proletariat: the labor supply must be kept alive and breeding as close to the basic level of subsistence as possible, and the maximum value of labor extracted from them at the minimum cost. All surplus energy should be absorbed by the growth of capital, not by any sort of mischievous political activity. When a group of laborers protests that they *need* more – almost invariably drawing attention to the physical stress under which they and their families are living – their demands must be portrayed by the opposing class as mere *wants*, and as a symptom of brutish greed and envy. If the pressure mounts, they must be bought off with bonuses, overtime, and other petty consolations. In a parallel ideological trick, the surplus-value extracted from workers is represented as a "need" of capital, often dressed up as a national interest which the powers of the state can be called upon to protect. The disembodied energies of capital must be freed: people no longer produce what people need, *capital* produces what *it* needs. This "need," of course, has very little to do with physical sensation or bodily survival: a theory of need in this sense is what Soper calls "the absent centre of Marxism."[18] Instead, we have the *necessity* of abstract historical law, just as freedom and constraint are "necessities" in Smithian liberalism. While Marxian theory builds elaborate constructions around this metaphor, it takes the "real" needs of the worker, the physical deprivation which drives the proletariat to the despair of revolutionary action, for granted.

The failure to distinguish need and necessity, and to explain their interrelationship in the transition *out of* capitalism, is a fundamental flaw in Marx's theory of history. It is evident in the shift in the prophecies of the "young" visceral, choleric Marx and the "old" cerebral, phlegmatic Marx. While the former believed that the proletariat will be moved to collective revolutionary rage, the latter saw capitalism eventually collapsing under the weight of its own monopolies. The earlier Marxism has a perennial, visceral appeal to youth, the "more mature" Marxism has a more logical, dispassionate, geriatric appeal. We have Marx's failure as an editor to thank for the visibility of this confusion – other famous philosophers have managed to cover the traces of their intellectual growth more successfully. For Marx, the most intriguing question of all was why people believed what they believed. But ironically, why we have two interpretations of progress, why he changed his mind, why it would not be in the nature of the older Marx to advocate revolutionary violence, in short, how Marx's growing body affected Marxism, are all questions which this stupendous all-embracing theory of history and knowledge cannot, in its own terms, begin to explain.

Instants, lives, and epochs

Modernity has put our knowledge of the fundamental coordinates of time and space into disarray, dramatically extending the horizons of human relations and making us starkly aware of the contrast between past and present. Each academic discipline has developed its own understandings of time and scale, but for all our mastery of nanoseconds and the mapping of the universe in light years, we have no clear conception of the time frames within which human lives matter to history, or to evolution, nor how to argue up through the various levels between the intimate social space of the household and the massive political domain of the modern state. The failure is astonishing, since the best reason we can have for taking an interest in any process in the cosmos is the manner and extent to which it dovetails with our own personal existence.

Evolution and history have become mutually exclusive constructions of time. The development of the species is irrelevant to the causes of the French Revolution, and vice versa, mainly because they are regarded as two distinct sorts of event. Those who wish to argue that there *is* a connection, that genes affect political events, have (amongst other intellectual difficulties) to argue across two seemingly incompatible meanings of time. On the other hand, those who wish to argue historical causes for history have to invent a super-historical timespan of their own, such as the epoch-making span of Braudel's *"longue durée."*[19] There, where the importance of individual heroes, wars, and civilizations recedes, the historian finds himself uncomfortably close to those very general aspects of human being which concern the natural scientist.

In modern theory, the body, its feelings, growth, and reproduction, has been assigned a temporal niche of its own, often referred to as *"substantive"*: a repetitive, cyclical sort of duration which is time*less* from both a historical and an evolutionary point of view. Substantive time is isolated from the *epoch* of (Marxist) historical materialism (archaic society, feudalism, capitalism), and also from the *instant* of neoclassical economic analysis, a "world of prudent calculators in a timeless bargaining situation."[20] From these two ideological perspectives, human growth is a historically inert, technically invariable, "natural" process which does little more than provide the raw material (population) for economy, society, and history to work on.

The trans-generational process of human growth is slower and vaster than any agricultural or industrial process we know. The effects on human growth of major economic events like a boom or slump can be hard to define because they take many decades to play out.[21] Likewise, changes in reproductive patterns happen so slowly and pervasively that their influence on economic choices and institutions can be extremely difficult to detect. Conventional economic reckoning can more easily explain how setting up a factory changes the lives of people in the surrounding community, but we need a much broader and more inclusive sense of the meanings of time to spell out how the social organization of reproduction in a particular region affects the establishment and operation of a factory.[22]

Efforts to reduce human growth to the "instantaneous" economics of the liberal marketplace have had small success. The analytical problem is that reproductive decisions are neither short-term nor simply matters of individual choice. Individuals do not produce *themselves*, they *reproduce* others, with costs and benefits dissolving into the relationship between generations. This may have little obvious relevance to a decision to buy oranges, but it strikes at the heart of long-term interests like saving, investing, or pensioning. We do not "choose" to be born or die, and our major reproductive transactions operate largely beyond the range of everyday economic or political reckoning. Our behavior is qualified by the accumulating demands made on us over long periods of time by our relatives, and by their obligations to us as we grow. The meaning of these is largely lost in any short-term material calculus. This is painfully evident in economists' efforts to model fertility decisions, which fix on positive discount rates – "giving greater weight to near term costs and benefits than to more distant streams."[23] For example, it is generally presumed that the alternative uses of a mother's labor (its *current* opportunity costs) structure the demand for children: a woman simply "decides" whether to have a career or a baby. The presence or absence of a baby testify to her "choice." Her complicated feelings or the lengthy agony of *indecision* are simply unaccountable.[24]

If they have taken any interest at all in physical growth, Marxists have concluded that since its "techniques" don't change or develop, in the manner of agricultural or industrial technology, they can have little effect on human history.[25] "To speak of reproduction is to show the processes which permit what exists to go on existing," says Aglietta. This is not history, whose dynamism "*means rupture, qualitative change.*"[26] Accordingly, reproduction has become a political metaphor in Marxist analysis, recurring in such phrases as "social reproduction," or "the reproduction of labor power," or of "ideology," or of the "conditions of production." In recent years Marxist anthropologists have struggled to put human growth back into historical perspective. This has involved separating reproduction from the historically more interesting processes of production. While the new abstract force of capital set about "reproducing" *itself*, the reproduction of people still went on at home, under the management of women.[27] The problem is how to explain how these two sorts of reproduction – the one historically new, the other very old – are "articulated." For example, in most "developing" regions of the world, industrial enterprises in "the capitalist sector" depend on drawing labor out of "traditional" or "precapitalist" households, free-riding on the reproductive work of women in the process.[28] The trouble with this line of argument is that it violates Marxian notions of what history is and where it is headed. Two historical epochs, the capitalist and the precapitalist, appear to be linked in space rather than time. More fundamentally, this ignores the persisting function of human growth not just in keeping social systems going, but also in transforming them.

Liberal sociologists like Giddens and Bourdieu take the view that meaning-making is a continuous transaction between individual agents and social organization.[29] In this "dualistic" view, structure is "the medium and the outcome of the conduct it recursively organizes."[30] Both scholars recognize that, though continuous, this "structuration" cannot be instantaneous: the transaction of meaning and its diffusion through society at the level of historical time must depend on interceding processes longer than the fleeting action or encounter, and that human bodies are somehow implicated. Although both imply that active bodies make historical meaning, neither explains how this dynamism relates to human growth. The fault is less in their intentions than in the intellectual traditions which insist that ideas as we represent them in history or "social structure" must be held apart from the physical processes of life.

In a world of immortals, free of the agony and ecstasy of growth, there would be no history. History is ontogenetic: as our predecessors have made it, it informs us, and we inform and re-form history through the process of our lives. It is easy to lose track of the connections. An editorial on the 1997 Los Angeles mayoral race declared that "We need to restore '60s idealism, not enshrine '80s greed."[31] But as Callinicos points out, the 1960s idealists and the greedies of the 1980s were the *same people*. The difference was a matter of growth – radicalized middle-class youth "settling down" in families and rewarding jobs.[32]

Why we wanted more

Growth means more: more body tissue, more progeny, more material sustenance, more communication with more people, more needs, and more wants. Less obviously, it also means less: aging, declining capacity, disinvestment, death. These are facts of life, but they are also facts of human history. Bodily growth is a provocation, a cause:

it dictates the order of certain events, it changes materials and meanings, it creates new needs against which expanding wants must be judged. But with several billion of us all growing slowly and differentially, it is not easy to observe the implications. Demographers tell us about the gross effects: the increases and decreases in population, changing age and sex pyramids, rates of urbanization, etc. Changes at the margins (a 2 percent annual growth in the Indian population) distract our attention from the massive internal dynamism of growth within any population (four Indians became parents and two died in the time it took to read this paragraph).

We would be forced to take a lot more notice if we all grew simultaneously rather than differentially: imagine millions of babies arriving one morning – our quota for twenty-five years – and the clinical services which would be needed to cope with the flood. The tidal wave would make its way through history, causing a gigantic boom and slump in diapers, the opening and closure of thousands of schools. Then, as one generation braced itself for the collective arrival of the next, the urge to accumulate would incinerate every national economy. The fuzzy category we call "generations" would be very visible cohorts, and the conflicts between them would assume massive proportions. Eventually the funeral industry would have its cyclical binge until the dust settled and business was once again reduced to a trickle of fatal accidents.

In short, human society would be entirely different, and the connection between growth and history would be starkly evident. The "Baby Boom" of the 1950s has presented us with a "cohort effect" of this sort, evident in a progression of historic changes ranging from welfare policies to voting patterns, and from the demand for children's books to the sales of rock music. Mercifully, the differential organization of human fertility softens the historical impact of growth: marginal changes in its effects are reduced (students come and go fairly steadily, and the demand for college places stays roughly constant). If we were born in 25-year cohorts, there would be long gaps in knowledge of baby care, or how to deal with acne or incontinence, or how to do bar mitzvahs, or how to talk and read. Our continuous style of breeding allows us to maintain "culture" in inconspicuous ways, but it also disguises the general effect of growth in organizing and transmitting culture, and the fact that social institutions (colleges, mortuaries) cater in particular ways for specific stages. Indeed *all* institutions (banks, parliaments, bowling clubs) are in some ways and in some degree structured by the motive force of human growth. Social theory is simply not geared to specifying how and why.

In a real sense it is all beyond us. What deceives us is the sheer scale of human relations in the modern world which has made our individual growth seem historically irrelevant. Two centuries ago our forebears made the most spectacular piece of history: the industrial transformation of northwestern Europe. The contagion was rapid, and modern social theory struggled to make sense of it; we have still not fully come to terms with the vastly expanded coordinates of time and space. But Enlightenment scholarship made one thing seem quite certain: it was all an invention, a product of the supple mind rather than the historically inert body. Life is now very different, and the haunting question is whether our ancient bodies, which must include our pre-paleolithic brains, can deal with it. In cities, nation states, and ultimately the world, we have become involved in relationships on a scale hitherto unimaginable. Modern sociology has told us that a life lived in the personal fabric of community relations has become one defined by increasing mobility, simpler categoric relations with strangers, and new identities of race, region, and economic class. These changes have also expanded our awareness of human time: no longer a mere handful of millennia since the Creation, but origins many millions of years ago, and (witness the breakneck pace of innovation) the prospect of further radical transformations *within* our lifetimes. Little wonder that many of the founding fathers of social science imagined that we had been taken over by forces greater than ourselves – that modernity had perpetrated us, rather than we it.

Life is growth, and growth inflicts on us needs, the fulfillment of which is the main driving force in human affairs. Once upon a time, the inequity of needs and capacities was both generated and resolved within the intimate circle of household and community, and within the compass of material resources which did not change much from one generation to the next. Arriving as infants with numerous needs and few capacities, we are acutely dependent on the credit which others (conspicuously our mothers) can extend to us. In old age we recall the loan: we may once again become very dependent, this time on a generation which we ourselves have raised. The basic groups within which these transactions occur are perpetually disturbed by the entries, maturations, and exits of individuals.

The reproductive pressures within families or households can be relieved within the wider and *durable* fabric of the community. For example, in European villages before the industrial epoch, "over-population" in one household could be adjusted by transferring people (as apprentices, servants, or lodgers) to an "underpopulated" or richer household. Likewise shortages of land or movable capital could be relieved by loans and contracts of various sorts.[33] Such exchanges depend on the long-term "banking" relationships in extended families or neighborhoods. Today, human needs are still generated within families, but are now satisfied within much wider political and economic processes. We count on a very much broader range of institutions to transact our variable needs and wants. In modern society people have been "grossed up" into larger groups, and their activities into larger organizations.

We are so awed by the variety and power of modern social institutions that we forget that they are all there because of the relentless process of human reproduction. While factories, colleges, or television have done so much to change our lives, they are as much consequences as causes of the way we grow. One story about the industrial revolution tells us that the mercantile capitalists wanted more, and that they had the intellectual capacity and the funds to break through the technical barrier, bringing new machines and new sources of power into dynamic conjunction. This was certainly the version of history preferred by the new ruling class, but it has always been open to question: why it had not happened before, why it did not happen elsewhere, and so on. For the working-class victims of capitalism, it is easier to believe that the industrial epoch was launched by the greedy dreams of the privileged, rather than by the will of an afflicted mass of ordinary people to survive. The clearest evidence that something broader was afoot is that the key technical innovations of the industrial revolution came from the laboring class, the impoverished spinners and weavers squeezed beyond endurance by the merchants who "put out" work to them, not from those who were raking in the profits in the towns of northern Europe.[34]

In recent years historical demographers and economic historians have been making longer and more intricate studies of the relationships between family life on the small scale and historical change on the large scale. Elaborate, computer-assisted studies of parish records have put gross statistics of births, marriages, and deaths into the context of unfolding family tactics and community relationships, which are subverting our assumptions about how industrial society developed.[35] The theory of "demographic transition" has been challenged by the discovery that fertility rates were rising *before* the industrial transformation, and that for many centuries English households were working to make ends meet by delaying marriage, breaking up into smaller units, or reaggregating into larger ones.[36] "The long-recognized effect of the economy on the family has too often obscured the converse – that the family may have important consequences for the economic system," says Furstenberg. "To understand the complicated relationship between the economy and the family, we cannot simply view the family as the dependent variable in the relationship."[37] To assume that physical growth invariably yields to political-economic forces ignores the extent to which reproduction itself must be *organized*, purposively and prospectively: to secure our lives we have to make the economy responsive to our wills in the long term. For this we cannot depend on today's markets, we need the assurance of durable social relations and institutions, backed up by dependable political power.

Such stability and durability as our political and economic institutions have owes much to the fact that our lives depend on them. Large rural households of a bygone era could generate sufficient internal scale economies to ride out the ups and downs of physical growth, but the characteristically small, mobile, and volatile "nuclear" household of industrial societies is chronically dependent on external support. Classic studies by Le Play and Rowntree a century ago showed how the modern industrial family was not, and could not be, "self-sufficient."[38] That is why we have state welfare systems, banks, insurance and pensioning corporations, and the other apparatus of modern public life.

Meaning is invested in durable social institutions, but through growing humans, not through genetic magic, nor through some psychically transcendent process – ideas sustaining and mutating ideas, economies bowling along under their own momentum, culture sustaining culture. Meaning is planted in *all* social institutions (households, banks, political parties) through the human life processes which they contain. Business firms are not simply structured by the political economy of the market, but also by the fact that they are inhabited and operated by growing people – young fathers and mothers bringing up children, grandparents planning their retirement. Max Weber and the modern sociologists have explained how the ideology of bureaucracy struggles perpetually and unsuccessfully to exclude these very personal interests from the structures of business and government. Nor is it just the urge of disembodied "capital" which produces social classes, it is also the urge of people, through the appropriation of social powers, to produce more people. Imagining that modern institutions have outgrown growth is a lethal delusion, weakening our capacity to make them serve our lives more efficiently and equitably.

While modern social theory has not found bodily growth very interesting, it is at the heart of our obsession with greed. Greed is not transmuted into something finer and nicer when it makes its appearance in governments or in business corporations. Suasive images of "corporate growth" or "national development" do very little to mitigate accusations of greed, because greed addresses growth in its bodily, not its modern metaphoric senses. Greed refuses to be intimidated by the scale of modern social operations. It is a tell-tale, pointing to the presence of our bodies in contexts where we might wish to ignore or deny their relevance. When it is evoked in criticism of the institutions which seem to have overwhelmed us, greed seeks out those same busy bodies which set human history in motion so long ago, and holds them accountable.

Three Bio-histories

8

The Gluttonous Peasant

Peasants play diabolical tricks on the historian: reactionary one moment, revolutionary the next. They are a category of humanity trapped in the ambiguity of our modern meanings of "growth" – the biological *versus* the historical. They are civilization's paragons of idiocy, mindless bodies. Our best hopes for this vast, yeasty bulk of humanity is that they will grow up and become progressive citizens leading profitable lives in developed societies. And yet popular sentiment keeps returning to the peasantry as a moral reference for simplicity, truth, and other virtues we have lost. Their ambiguous closeness to nature and to our civilized selves fascinates us. Confined within families and villages, victim to every petty vice, their propensity to grow is fearful, squeezing the political, economic, and intellectual boundaries we have set to contain them. They seem impervious to history, and yet the growth of the people we call peasants has been the main impetus in the making of our modern world.

It is one of the great ironies of modernity that while "peasants" have no meaning without reference to ourselves, we have never really understood them. In A. L. Kroeber's classic phrase, they "constitute part-societies with part-cultures" – they need us to complete them.[1] Although these people, who are the close ancestors of most of us, are so massively a part of our modern world, they stand, in our reckoning, apart from it. They are at best the raw material of modernity, a vast "transitional" category between savagery and civilization. They live beyond the pale of history as we tell it, cohering and persisting

Plate 4   Glutted peasants: detail from Pieter Brueghel the Elder (c.1525–1569), *The land of Cockaygne* (Alte Pinakothek, Munich)

by inertial processes of "tradition" (quaint myths and legends, fancy dress, unintelligible dialects).[2]

Using peasants to mark out the margins of our own lives and histories, we have inflicted on them the full force of our dualist thinking. Our feelings about them are therefore entirely ambivalent: they are our embodiment of the lazy, slow-witted, petty, unprogressive life we hope we have left behind; and yet we envy their simplicity, honesty, and the closeness to nature which we think we have lost. We are fearful that their vast, yeasty bulk will overwhelm us with more people, more needs, more wants. Greed voices these fears: we are guiltily aware of their poverty, and that through the centuries the wealth of modernity has been squeezed from them. But we also believe that peasants are themselves venal and envious not just of us, but of each other: their small-scale, meager societies are a Hobbesian compromise of the desire of every peasant to be a czar.

In modern theory, right or left, "the problem *of* the peasantry" is their ghastly propensity to grow without evidently progressing – that is, becoming more like us. So often peasants appear to defy the maxim that modernity is an inevitable, natural, evolutionary improvement of the human condition. Peasant greed is childishly obtuse: they do not want the right things (profits, investable wealth) with enough fervor, and are constrained by their own conservative "traditional" knowledge to want the wrong things (leisure, feasts, immediate gratification). "Progressive" peasants who want the "right" things fall victim to the narrow-minded levelling of their peers, and to accusations of venality. In the face of such lack of imagination, history is made for them, not by them.

The problem *for* the peasantry themselves is frustrated growth. What peasants do above all else is *grow* – crops, herds, people, communities – which is why others who are definitively *not* peasants have made a business of living off them. This, in a nutshell, is the political-economic history of the world – "social evolution" as it was once called. Peasants in this view mark an advance on tribal peoples and isolated "subsistence" farmers, and are defined by the larger power structures (feudal domains, states, empires, markets) which contain their lives. Once a dependent peasantry has been established, the trick is to contain their propensity to grow, and divert it to fuel the growth (in all senses) of their masters. Hunger has always been the basic controlling device: the capacity of various sorts of ruling class to skim off whatever peasants produce beyond what they need to survive. Here is the kernel of the peasant's reputation for gluttony: he *should* always be clamoring for "more," because the needy peasant is a productive peasant.

In these circumstances, maintaining a certain idiotic distance from the metropolis is a survival tactic for peasants. They are understandably wary of the money, laws, and other processes which link them to their rulers. Pushed too far, peasants revolt, and the history of modernizing societies is punctuated by sullen standoffs between the expansive demands of competing lords and the foot-dragging under-production of hungry serfs.[3] This reactionary idiocy, which has persisted among the "new" peasants incorporated within modern capitalism, is infuriating to the classes who write history. And yet peasants have repeatedly startled the modern world with the ferocity of their wars, the revolutionary consequences of which have been at the heart of twentieth-century history.[4]

Peasants and growth

In the early days of modernity Thomas Malthus gave scientific voice to fears which the more privileged classes have always had about the peasants: their massive, potent, and threatening propensity to grow.[5]

According to Malthus, breeding would always outstrip feeding: the "natural" geometric expansion of population would be thwarted by its merely arithmetic capacity to increase food supply. As the pressure mounted, dearth, disease, and war would cull the population, and the dismal cycle would begin again.

The gradual penetration of industrial capitalism into farming proved some aspects of Malthus's thesis wrong. He had taken too little account of human inventiveness, the capacity of farmers under the pressures of growth to make technical advances which would sustain larger numbers of people.[6] However, neo-Malthusians fear that this simply ratchets up the problem: a "Green Revolution" produces more food for the peasants, more opportunities for demographic growth, more "surplus" for landlords or tax collectors to grab, more misery for larger numbers of peasants, and greater risk of rebellion.

Because modern theory has chopped up our understanding of biological, economic, and historical time into irreconcilable pieces, we have not succeeded in allaying these fears about growth. Farming also takes time, the discipline of waiting months or years for an investment to bear its uncertain fruit. It involves taking possession of nature, the interseasonal and intergenerational attachment to the soil for which peasants are so well known. Farmers are the pioneers of property relationships, and working the land exposes farmers themselves to the threat of appropriation. They depend on physical and legal protection – this is the classic story of state formation. Growth for farmers is a political condition, because more land, more food, more labor, more technical improvements are also expanding liabilities.

"The family" is the social organism which organizes and animates the peasant farm, and intergenerational powers and privileges are its managerial structure. The lock between human and other biological systems is evident to the farmer in the years of labor involved in developing capital – "putting heart" into the fields. For the townee it can be demonstrated most clearly where the life of the crop extends through many years, as in the orchard or the herd. This dynamism is largely lost in our vision of the peasantry as a vast, undifferentiated human mass. From the perspective of the peasant family, the "efficiency" of the farm is its ability to adapt to changing needs and capacities, and thus secure lives in the long term. Only microscopic, long-term observation of individual households will reveal the basic dynamic of the peasantry: their propensity to accumulate capital and produce more under the pressure of human growth. This can entail radical changes in crops and techniques, and large differences in yields from one stage of family development to another.[7]

Peasants do not need some historic lesson on how to produce more: they make this surge every generation. The key question is whether there is any utility in pushing production beyond what the household itself needs. With repressive landlords, depressed or capricious markets, and no other external opportunities, family farm productivity will slacken until a new generation boosts demand. Rather than operating with the steadily improving profitability of the idealized business firm, family farm productivity ebbs and flows according to the family growth cycle – the fluctuating ratio of hands to mouths. Taken as an average, the performance of farms in a community inevitably drops below what an economist, using markets as an index of profitability, would regard as "efficient." From this external perspective, human growth appears to inhibit the efficient expansion of the farm as an economic enterprise.[8] This difference between two metrics, "*their*" slow-moving, growth-oriented values, and "*our*" short-term view of profits, is at the heart of "the problem of the peasantry" as we see it – their reputation for "laziness," inertia, and inefficiency. Because their behavior so often seems to defy the logic of the marketplace, they have not been credited with modern economic minds. But while modern economists take such little account of the logic of growth, most peasants are well enough aware of the advantages of engagement with markets when it suits them. They have also become aware of the disadvantages, the appropriations, swindling, and other abuses to which "market penetration" from the outside exposes them.

Early in the twentieth century the Russian economist A. V. Chayanov proposed an explanation of the apparent underproductivity of the peasant farm which linked these two metrics.[9] Patient examination of the deluge of statistics collected through the *zemstvo* local government system indicated a high degree of variation in the management and yields of peasant farms. Chayanov argued that this was because the relatively self-sufficient peasant family farm "exploited" its variable capacity, using its own labor and pulling in extra land to supply its own variable needs. In the early stages of its establishment, the household had to work very hard to make ends meet, but as the children grew and the ratio of hands to mouths improved, life eased considerably. The family could now enjoy *leisure*, a commodity which capitalist economists – and those who live off peasants – tend to regard as an ill-deserved luxury.[10] Chayanov pointed out that whether or not peasants want and can get more depends on wider political integration, especially the efficiency of markets. Given the right sort of "vent" for surplus production, peasants are ready enough to step up their efforts. But by the same token, peasants whose "surplus" capacity is being squeezed out of them by landlords, tax collectors, or zealous Soviets will have no enthusiasm for substituting drudgery for leisure.

Hunger, envy, and inertia

It has always been comforting to those who live off peasants to imagine them as shackled by their own feeble ideas. A particular object of scorn has been the peasants' dedication to their families – an immersion in biological processes which gives them a pathetic inability to think rationally. In his classic account of *The moral basis of a backward society* in southern Italy, Banfield attributed poverty and lack of communal initiative (the *"miseria"* of which the people often complained) to an ethos of *"amoral familism."* The people of Montegrano, he reckoned, *behaved as if* they were following this rule: "maximize the material, short-run advantage of the nuclear family; assume that all others will do likewise." Although the Montegranesi themselves might not recognize it in this form, *familism* was a "predictive hypothesis" in understanding their behavior and suggesting remedies. Banfield concluded that being "prisoners of their family-centered ethos – that because of it they cannot act concertedly or in the common good – is a fundamental impediment to their economic or other progress."[11]

Banfield's critics were quick to point out that "familism" in Montegrano was more obviously a historical and material consequence than a psychic cause, and that an aggressive concern for family welfare was a reasonable response to centuries of economic repression.[12] Similar criticisms were levelled at Oscar Lewis who, in a series of finely observed empirical studies in Mexico and Puerto Rico, attributed the persistence of poverty to defeatist, fatalistic ideas passed from one generation to the next.[13] This "Culture of Poverty" had a sameness around the world, because the material and political conditions of the poor were so similar. However, Lewis's argument had much the same awkward circularity as Banfield's: ideas cause poverty and poverty generates debilitating ideas. Lewis implied that remedies should be pursued at both the material and the ideal levels – investing and educating. But tinkering with how poor people think has to reckon with the protective value of their ideas, especially their justifiable suspicion of outsiders. Latterly, peasants in many parts of the world have become case-hardened by official development projects which promised the earth, gobbled up energy and resources, and achieved little.

Invidiousness is a central motif of these cultural explanations of peasant inertia, the notion that poor people are set against one another in an ethos of dearth and neighborly fears of unfair advantage. George Foster's model of the peasant "image of limited good" explains how simple, child-like people lack the notion of expandable wealth which has been so vital to the development of capitalism, and operate instead with a conviction that one person's winnings in the game of life must equal other persons' losses.[14] Peasants are caught in a low-level equilibrium of expectations, in which accumulators (proto-capitalists) are snuffed out by the policing action (isolation, innuendo, "accidental" damage to crops) of their neighbors. Notions of life as a "zero-sum" game – your getting more implies less for someone else – do seem to lurk in our suspicions of greed. But as a general characterization of peasant life, the "notion of limited good" makes less sense if we remember that growth persistently *obliges* people to expand and contract wealth. With every household in a community at different stages of growth and decline, "richer" and "poorer" in varying degrees, there is no stable collective "good" to be perceived, no loading-line stretched through the community, no fixed quanta (babies, hands, mouths, fields, bags of corn) against which gains and losses can be measured. There is only the mainly visceral understanding that growth generates and justifies variation in these things, that there is a need, not simply a right, for more or for less. Outsiders are generally impatient about this visceral tempo of the economy, but peasants themselves, inured to poverty, have a particular suspicion of *fast* wealth, accumulation which outpaces what is expected to support growth.[15] As Chayanov pointed out, the economic assessment is rooted in bodies rather than minds, by sensations of hunger and satisfaction, drudgery and leisure. This is the chemistry of envy and sloth, the source of accusations of witchcraft or greed, to which we are as susceptible as any peasant.

In my experience, restrictive images of "familism," or of stable norms of production and consumption, or of a generalized "limited good," can never be elicited from peasants themselves in any form resembling an explicit moral code. This is probably because such ideas are a product of modern reasoning about the failure of rural people to meet *our* expectations (progress, the accumulation of wealth), rather than the authentic sentiments of rural people themselves about the meaning of growth and what inhibits it. No amount of clever economic, psychological, or sociological reasoning can get closer to the agony of peasant life than the sensible human body. The notion that always being a little hungry is a sign of decent restraint is widely reported.[16] However, moderation is the key, for being skinny can suggest that accumulation is taking place elsewhere, out of sight. In rural Jamaica, if families share what they have, no one gets rich and no one gets thin: "Cultural logic has it that people tied firmly into a network of kin are always plump and never wealthy." Rich, fatty foods are most suspect: they clog the gut and must be dislodged with vigorous enemas and purgatives – "The most important cure-all" in Jamaica.[17]

Hunger and growth

Our modern interpretations and explanations never seem to do justice to the persistent agony of peasant life. All is hazard, from the uncertainties of weather and other variable aspects of the environment, to unstable markets and governments. In the thick of it is the unfolding drama of human reproduction, the creative disruption of family growth and decline. To suggest that peasants are "mindless" in their efforts to come to terms with growth is of course prejudicial nonsense. They are as anxious as the rest of us about the exercise and outcomes of skill, judgment, and material investment. The air of resigned fatalism which they often present to outsiders is not the principle by which they actually work the land. You do not need a degree in agricultural economics to be aware of inter-seasonal shifts in surplus and deficit, and their bearing on consumption, saving, investment, and external appropriations. But the long-term complexities of bearing and raising children, of marrying and endowing, are of overarching practical importance, even if they are not explicable in formal economic terms. Survival is not simply a string of short-term decisions, it depends on the elaboration of human relations through successive generations, which makes the durable fabric of local communities. Anxiety and mistrust are endemic in all the peasant communities in which I have lived and worked, but these sensations are counteracted by rigorous rituals of politeness and toleration (which urban life now so painfully lacks). On the dark side, these tensions include accusations of envy, malice, or greed, mostly by innuendo. These are most likely to surface in oppressive or recessionary times, but when the cake is expanding, larger slices attract less critical attention.

In the ordinary course of our lives we do not discriminate between growth in its biological and its political-economic senses – that is something scholars do. *All* growth disequilibrates, and making sense of change and responding to it is a perpetual human challenge. For peasants who, perhaps for centuries, have lived at the mercy of outsiders, factoring external pressures into the management of family and farm is no novelty. Changes in their wider world – colonization by foreigners, industrial expansion, pestilence, war, are not dealt with as a separate category of experience or the disruption of some timeless "traditional" calm, but as an extension of the dynamism of ordinary life. Exotic forces, from hurricanes to irrigation projects, must be accommodated along with the turbulence of birth, maturation, and death. No intrusive force has attracted more attention than *money*, with its insidious capacity to put simple, externally defined values on objects and relationships which have hitherto had much more complicated, locally established meanings. Everybody – ourselves included – puts up barriers to distinguish where and when money cannot be used (selling a child, buying votes), and crossing these lines can arouse feelings of disgust, anger, or fear. Shifting its use to something like buying labor from a neighbor involves complicated adjustments. To people who are unfamiliar with it, money in the form of wages or profits from commercial farming often has evil or foul associations, and may have to be processed to make it morally "clean" in family and community contexts.[18] Malay peasants symbolically "cook" their wages or market profits when they take the cash home and turn it into food for the family hearth.[19] Home cooking makes rural Jamaicans plump and happy, but bought food is thin, mean fare; money is *shit*.[20] The disruptive effects of money are often expressed in "witchcraft" accusations, especially where younger people with the advantages of education have become more prosperous than their elders.[21]

It should not be surprising that where external intrusions have been most drastic, their accommodation within the processes of human growth has been *felt* most painfully. Few regions of the world have had to sustain the pressures of global marginality for so long, or so painfully, as Melanesia. Throughout a century of forced labor, world war in the Pacific, imperialism and neocolonialism, some of these "peripheral" peoples have been tortured by anxieties of greed for so long that the trauma has become endemic, normal, "cultural." The people of Wamira in southeastern New Guinea inflicted their pre-occupation with greed on their ethnographer Miriam Kahn, divert-ing her from her own research agenda (the construction of gender relations). For them, greed was an all-pervasive, inescapable force. "Wamirans fear not only the greed that lurks within themselves, but also that which exists within their fellow human beings, even, as can be seen from the examples of the myths and stories, one's closest kin." Their understanding of the vice is stripped down to the core: "Need, in Wamira is perceived as greed."[22] The Wamirans are locked into a Hobbesian war against themselves, in which the very act of eating is full of menace.

Kahn could find no biological or ecological justification for the Wamirans' passionate insistence that they were, and should be, "*Always Hungry.*" The Wamirans, she concluded, are not (like Turn-bull's Ik) demoralized by the actuality of having too little food, they are moralized by the dreadful possibility of having too much. The well-adjusted Wamiran is "hungry but controlled."[23] Unlike other people, the Wamirans seem to get little joy from sharing a slap-up meal. Such excess would amount to a collective admission of guilt. Eating is secretive, and inviting someone to dinner runs the risk of unleashing an "avalanche of uncontrollable lusts and desires." Gen-erosity is highly valued but tightly contained. Hunger is the best demonstration that one is worthy of affection: it is the knife-edge between love and hate and, as such, means much more than an empty belly. "Hunger, which is perceived more as an emotion than a physi-cal state, indicates need, neglect, and antagonism. 'Enough food' sug-gests cooperation, sharing, and amity."[24]

Kahn traces the Wamirans' fixation on hunger into underlying con-cerns with growth and reproduction. Graphic myths and stories weave together eating and copulating, snakes and the oral-vaginal "tube," desire and fear, the ambivalence of hunger and lust, fertile youth and barren age, temptation and restraint, abandonment and control, raw and cooked meat, feeding and killing, production and consumption, affinity and kinship, life and death. In the symbolic mélange, pigs are women, and marriage – the regulation of sexual desire – is a quest for "meat" outside kin relations. For women, powers of production are all about children: blood, breast milk, and the growth of the matrilineage. For men, the focus is on the subsistence crop taro, whose tubers are "people" who are gendered, have blood, and must be "brought up." The symbolically distinct foods of pork and taro are brought together in feasts, a collective ordeal which Kahn dissects skillfully. Leaders express their (superhuman?) elevation above "the needy, greedy masses" by neither eating nor excreting at feasts.[25] The conflation of people and food raises the topic of cannibalism, a deeply ingrained motif in the agony of Melanesian relations with the wider world, which has teased anthropologists from the earliest days. "According to Wamirans, 'before the missionaries arrived, the only meat eaten was human flesh; the missionaries taught villagers not to eat people and to eat pigs instead.'"[26]

Wamirans, according to Kahn, "see human beings as innately selfish and greedy. They integrate this understanding of their biological needs and desires with their social values, which are those of sharing with and caring for one another."[27] Wamirans work hard to maintain something which Kahn herself values very highly: their *culture*. The obsession with greed which "suffuses their total cultural orientation" is "their psychological technique to keep their passions and desires in check."[28] It is clear from Kahn's account that the Wamirans are aware of their obsession, and know that there are people outside the moral boundaries of their community who are less tormented by hunger and greed. It seems to be this, rather than the agony of inventing culture for its own sake, which prompts their fears. Freedom from hunger and the guilt of greed are possible only in the context of "town," to which Wamirans migrate for work. Greed is a guilty passion you feel *at home*, and satisfy abroad. White people in particular are associated with an inability to share, and thus with uninhibited greed. Wamirans told Kahn: "We are taro people, but where you come from, people are money people."[29] One of them says:

> I wish we could be like white people. I want to be rich and have many possessions. I want to dress up in fancy clothes and go out. I want to eat lots of food in restaurants. But I never will. We have too many laws governing our taro garden. That is why we shall always be hungry![30]

It is their recognition of a common humanity which gives the Wamirans some perspective on their own moral clutter. Human beings everywhere, they say, "have a mouth" or "a mouth and an anus" and do much the same sorts of thing with them. What might seem to us a pathologically narrow interpretation of their plight is actually part of a remarkably broad view of the cosmos and its dynamism: "Both food and human beings are integral parts of a total system of energy exchange" which requires persistent monitoring.[31] People in this region react to change as they do because they are cosmic "lumpers" – they do not see their being, and the being of other people, as divided up into discrete intellectual packages. The long history of millenarian movements ("cargo cults") in Melanesia reveals a startlingly total, revolutionary approach to change. They are passionate, thoroughly physical responses to world disorder, ranging from abject, masochistic rejection of defunct morals to the rigorous construction of entirely new systems.[32] All are moved bodily by outrage at the separations which the modern world has thrust upon them, especially the inequitable partitioning of wealth. All are premised on the moral obligations of a common humanity, and all make sensual appeals to the common human condition in rituals of stripping, scourging, starving.

History and the mobile peasant

For modern theorists, the challenge is to decide which sort of "growth" peasants in a particular place and time are involved in: the "merely cyclical" and temporary, or the "definitively historic" and permanent. Even the most detailed census of a peasant community will not provide an answer. How can we tell whether this big, prosperous household is about to fall into a routine "substantive" process of decline, or will "go historical" by consolidating its capital, buying out its neighbors, and escaping the confines of peasant life? For Marx, the evidence was irrelevant because the making of history was in the hands of a particular modern class, the industrial proletariat. Peasants were like potatoes in a sack – some big, some small, but always the same boring carbohydrate.[33] For others like Lenin, peasants were more interesting because in countries like Russia capitalism was largely rooted in the countryside. The advance guard of this movement were the *kulaks*, literally the "tight fists" among the peasants who took advantage of economic links with the metropolis to "bourgeoisify" themselves. The key question was whether *kulak* enterprises would simply dissolve back into the peasant mass after a generation or so. While Lenin saw variation among family farms in the Russian statistics as proof of a definitive historical transformation of the peasantry, Chayanov saw the same data as evidence of the cyclical *persistence* of the peasantry.[34] This collision of the "historical" and the "substantive" meanings of time was resolved, at least for a while, by the victory of Lenin's bolsheviks, the forced communalization of the Russian peasantry, and the "disappearance" of Chayanov.

These arguments are as much about the theories we have invented to measure historical "progress" as about peasants themselves. Peasants slither around the categories we have set up to place them in the modern world. They have both "persisted" and "changed," depending largely on how we apply our ambiguous indexes of growth. Being a peasant is not, as town dwellers so often imagine, a static condition. During their lives a great many peasants dodge back and forth across the historic lines *we* have drawn. The dilemma for all peasants is that to secure a living you have to be flexible: you have to play it safe *and* you have to take risks. Farmers have to juggle so many variables – fields, seeds, labor, skills, yields, patronage, cooperation, prices, taxes. They have to seize any opportunity which comes their way, whether it is a good harvest, healthy children, or favorable government. In peasant lives, these many processes do not resolve into two opposed types, the "substantive" and the "historical." They merge in the single process whose meaning *we* have divided: growth.

This is evident in the arrangements generally known as "sharecropping," a feature of farming systems all over the world, from ancient times to the present.[35] The basic principle of sharecropping is deceptively simple: two or more parties agree to combine their resources of land, labor, and capital in a productive enterprise, and to share the output in proportions they agree beforehand. For example, you contribute two fields and some harvesting labor, I do everything else, and we split the crop fifty-fifty. It all looks very fair, the perfect antidote to envy and greed. However, the political and economic complexities have teased social theorists for more than two centuries. If land is scarce, or you are powerful, I may have to make do with a third share, or less. Such exploitative systems of sharecropping in France and Italy dismayed economists like Adam Smith, who argued in favor of the more advanced "English system" of fixed rents and wage labor – that is, capitalism.

By the mid-twentieth century, the negative view of sharecropping was firmly established, but for reasons which diverged according to the ideological preferences of the theorist. Those on the left saw it as straightforward exploitation of laborers by the landowner, an excellent device for squeezing peasants to the point "just consistent with the reproduction of the peasant household."[36] A shift to "more progressive" capitalist relations was historically inevitable. On the right, liberal "neoclassical" economists reckoned that sharecropping would disappear because it was inefficient: if he was rational, a tenant receiving only half of the crop would work half as hard, and the landlord would be half as likely to invest in capital improvements. Agriculture in these circumstances would stagnate because neither party would want to innovate. Progress, in the liberal view, depends on whether one of them feels the urge to "improve" the contract in his own interests, by assuming full control of the farm's resources, taking all the profits along with all the risks.

Having rung the death knell on sharecropping, economic theorists have been embarrassed by its persistence. Regarding sharecropping as historically a "transitional" form of rent or labor hire, or as "intermediate" between feudalism and capitalism, now seems unhelpful. The thresholds are in our minds rather than in the contracts themselves – hence our schizophrenic hyphenations such as "semi-feudal" or "quasi-capitalist." However, sharecropping has persisted alongside the "more progressive" fixed rents and wages for long periods, and has violated historical expectations often enough by appearing *after* "more capitalist" arrangements. Italian peasants in the past, for example, moved in and out of the *mezzadria* sharecropping system, shifting to wage labor or working their own smallholdings when conditions were suitable; and many Malay peasants have had all three sorts of relationship simultaneously.[37] More recent inquiries have made it clear that *either* party, not just the one who supplies capital, can have the upper hand in the contract. In Europe and Asia, land has usually been the scarce resource, but in Africa it is commonly the supplier of labor who is better off. Even more surprisingly, share contracts have resurfaced around the world as part of the apparatus of advanced, transnational capitalist enterprise. Recent studies in Asia, Latin America, and Africa indicate that sharecropping need not be as repressive or underproductive as has been supposed. It has not only survived major economic changes like the "green revolution" or land tenure reform, it has even facilitated them.[38] Sharecropping can be a "rational" arrangement where farming is very risky, for ecological or for economic reasons. Farm produce is shared whatever the outcome, whereas "modern" farmers take the burden of risk on themselves while paying fixed wages to laborers and/or a fixed rent to the landowner.

Close examination of contracts within a locality often reveals little evidence of "feudalism" or low yields. Instead of one distinct historic type of contract we find a highly fluid and versatile range of collaborations, some apparently distributing costs and benefits equitably, others coming very close to Adam Smith's "more progressive" – and thus more inequitable – modes of wage labor and fixed rents. Indeed, the efficiency of the contract for either or both parties turns largely on this flexibility. By corollary, trying to "freeze" share arrangements in written contracts reduces this utility – a negative consequence in efforts to reform and codify land tenure. The complexity of contracts, extending from season to season, depends largely on *not* spelling out the details, but depending on the unspoken qualities of long-term relationships to make pragmatic adjustments on the basis of mutual dependence and trust.

Abstract categories of "landlord" and "tenant" make little sense of contracts (often very rigid and demanding) between father and son, or neighbors who have lived and worked together since childhood. Accounts of sharecropping often allude to arrangements which meet the capital deficits of young people on the one hand, and labor shortages of old people on the other.[39] Commonly these are close kin, and the flexibility of arrangements allow the *gradual* transfer of resources as part of the process of inheritance. In the American Midwest, for example, sharecropping was "part of a two-stage system for gradually passing on control and ownership of the family property from one generation to another."[40] In a similar process in Malaysia, a son after he marries may continue to work on his father's farm, on rigorously formal terms which give him an agreed proportion of yields. The son thus acquires a significant measure of independence, while the father retains access to resources (including his son's labor) to keep his own household going. But over a number of years the terms of the contract improve in the son's favor until eventually the father's "rental" share reduces to zero and the son becomes in effect the owner of the farm.[41] The investigator bent on discovering all the "clauses" of such a contract is likely to be frustrated by its stealthy growth, and by the bland assurance that it always "just feels right." Adding to the complexity, each party to a contract may explain it quite differently, each claiming that the other is the strategic beneficiary, or the more exploited. Describing yourself as a "tenant" rather than a "laborer" in such arrangements is largely a matter of self-esteem. Similarly, where share contracts have been prohibited by reformist governments on grounds of inefficiency or inequity, they can be relabelled to look legally more acceptable ("tenancy" or "smallholding").[42]

The virtue of sharecropping, and a good reason for its historical persistence, is that it absorbs much of the instability and uncertainty of the world in which farmers live, and at the same time provides a medium for people to change productive relationships in both the short and the long term. Share contracts played a central role in what was known in the US as "the agricultural ladder," an upward progression of the young, capital-deficient wage laborer towards a fixed rent tenancy and thence, savings permitting, to ownership of a farm of his own.[43] Where it has such mediating functions in the process of growth, it makes little sense to describe sharecropping as a relationship between fixed agrarian classes – a division into "capitalists" and "proletarians."

Again, because they are so fluid, the general appearance of share contracts in a particular region can change, looking "more capitalist" (fixed rents and wages) or "more feudal" (sharecropping) as local people respond to changing political and economic conditions. Thus a contractual pattern which looks exploitative in one period may appear more egalitarian later. This sort of movement has been very apparent in Lesotho (southern Africa) during the course of the twentieth century. It is reflected in two terms for sharecropping: *seahlolo*, regarded as more traditional and equitable; and the more businesslike *lihalifote*. Farmers I talked to found the words difficult to distinguish categorically, because a contract which lasted several years could look more *lihalifote* to one party at one stage, and more *seahlolo* to the other party at another stage. In repressive and recessionary times (notably the heyday of South African apartheid during the 1960s and 1970s), when Sotho farmers were forced into closer cooperative dependence on one another, the poverty-sharing *seahlolo* was the characteristic mode. But in more prosperous times it was *lihalefote* – when, for example, Sotho farmers worked the land of capital-deficient white immigrant farmers in the latter part of the nineteenth century (the word incorporates the Afrikaans word for "half"). Meanwhile, the various gradations and ingredients of share contracts in Lesotho also formed an "agricultural ladder," as in the US Midwest: as it "grew" the contract included a typical stage when a younger farmer establishing his own family and, with some savings from migrant mine labor, took the field of an impoverished widow on shares which were *lihalefote* for him, and decidedly *seahlolo* for her.

Seahlolo and *lihalefote* have simultaneously substantive *and* historical meaning – they refer to changes in the lives of individual farmers, and changes in the agrarian system of this region of southern Africa. A one-sided "substantive" or "historical" interpretation of contracts will not reveal the dynamism and versatility of sharecropping in Lesotho. From this point of view, "capitalism" is not the monolithic, relentless force we have generally supposed. Its components (wages, rents) come and go, not simply by the force of major historical movements or macroeconomic cycles, but according to the life processes of the farmers themselves. *Seahlolo* and *lihalefote* are aspects of a repertoire of working arrangements which have grown over more than a century, but not in the historical direction – *towards lihalifote* – which Adam Smith would have predicted.

The persistence of the peasantry into the capitalist epoch has been a topic of endless theoretical debate. A good deal of energy has been expended on trying to figure out if "peasants" even exist as a single, homogeneous category. It is the historical destiny of the peasantry to *become* rather than to *be*. "Peasants" have responded often enough to the caprices of the twentieth century (imperialism, depression, war-fueled boom, planned development) by moving back and forth across the threshold of modernity as *we* have defined it. But if they do this with any sort of ease it is because in the processes of their own lives they have been making similar "historic" moves, routinely, over very long periods.

It seems we need peasants as much as ever – both as psychic reference points and as part of the apparatus of modern economies. As Karl Kautsky and Rosa Luxemburg prophesied, peasants did not "disappear" during the twentieth century, but have adapted as a mass of small-scale producers within the processes of global capitalism. The external restrictions on peasant growth are as strong as ever, and are now reinforced by late-modern intellectual neuroses. Disgust with our own experience of "development" and fears of environmental degradation have made peasant "apathy" or "conservatism" look sensible and politically attractive. If peasants now *seem* to want less, that is a good example to the rest of us. Their economic "irrationality" (preferring a traditional, lower-yielding crop variety) may make good ecological sense. After all, experienced farmers surely know more about local conditions than a kid fresh out of agricultural college.

Our admiration of peasants is almost as perverse as our contempt. The redemptive images we seek in their ways of life is more fundamentally an expression of the dissatisfaction *we* feel about the meanings of modernity – meanings which we ourselves have devised. But whatever it is, modernity is the product of the vitality of the very same people – our own forebears – whom we now marginalize as "peasants." Their world is bonded to ours not just by the chaotic processes of "global development," but by the historical dynamism of bodily growth.

9

The Avaricious Pensioner

The grievance against old people is ancient and visceral. The idea that they fortify their waning powers by sapping the energy and resources of the young underlies beliefs in vampires and witches in Europe and in many other parts of the world. Aging can evoke the nastiest mixture of feelings – love and rage, guilt and grief, envy and despair – probably because aging moves us all so inexorably towards dependency and death.

Aging becomes the axis along which the accusations of greed ebb and flow. We owe it to our parents to take care of them, but as they decline they should be letting go of what they have, not wanting more. Retentive avarice confronts cupidity as elders cling to their resources and adults with growing children of their own resent their seniors' leisure, luxury spending, or sterile stockpiling of wealth. The self-recrimination of the elderly, wishing not to be a burden and dreading the lapse into second childhood, only adds to the anguish.[1]

If this drama has been embedded in family life throughout human history, it is little wonder that people everywhere have sought ways of dispersing the responsibilities and agonies of aging out into the wider community. In the nineteenth and twentieth centuries, industrializing populations seized on the opportunities of expanding political-economic scale to break the family bounds and make new sorts of pensioning deal with worker associations, corporations, and gov-

> ## Carking for wealth
>
> Four centuries ago, Montaigne lamented: "mee thinks our soules in age are subject unto more importunate diseases and imperfections then they are in youth . . . In truth wee abandon not vices, so much as we change them; and in mine opinion for the worse. Besides a sillie and ruinous pride, combersome tattle, wayward and unsotiable humours, superstition and a ridiculous carking for wealth, when the use of it is well-nigh lost, I find the more envie, injustice and leaudness in it. It sets more wrinckles in our mindes, then on our foreheads."
>
> Montaigne, *Essays* vol. 3 ch. 2, [1603]; translated by John Florio. David Nutt, London (1892), p. 35.

ernments. For a while the modern welfare state seemed the perfect solution, but as a new "Old Age Crisis" threatens to engulf the industrialized world, the moral tide has turned. Accusations of senile greed are once again in the air.[2] However, even politicians and officials seem to understand that blaming an entire generation of old people for fiscal failures doesn't make much sense. Instead, they fall back on a very old intuition that the ultimate remedy for the pensioning crisis must be found where it supposedly originated: not "out there" in national political domains, but within the personal web of family relations.

Too late – the genie of growth is out of the bottle. If the family of modern nostalgia ever actually existed, it has yielded too many of its welfare capacities to new public institutions. But the assumption that the welfare state has wiped out caring relations in household and community is as false as the expectation that these relations can simply "resume" their old responsibilities. Our understanding of pensioning has dissolved into a confusion about the rights and duties of citizenship on the one hand, and of parent–child relations on the other. These misunderstandings are strung out between the two sundered meanings of growth, the biological and the political-economic. Unless we can grasp more clearly how these meanings mesh, the misunderstandings will only multiply.

Plate 5 Avarice: detail from Quinten Massys (c.1466–c.1530), *Caricature of four usurers* (Galleria Doria Pamphilj, Rome)

The golden age

If public pensioning is a popular conspiracy it is a very old one. In England, the principle of getting public authorities to support the indigent aged goes back far beyond the Poor Laws of the seventeenth century. Thomson challenges the "simple minded premise that families cared for their disadvantaged members" in the "traditional" societies of the European past. Care of the sick and the elderly has been passed back and forth like a hot potato between households and public bodies of various sorts – guilds, parishes, municipalities, and now states.[3] Private mutual assurance funds, to which individuals contribute while they are able-bodied and from which they draw benefits later, are at least as old as the medieval guilds, and are the forerunners of employer-sponsored ("occupational") and public systems.

It is important to understand that in modern times the pressure for public pensions did not come from old people themselves, but from the able-bodied laboring poor. It was not, as is often supposed, the political action of a *generation*, but of an emergent *class* in industrial capitalist societies. The working poor, removed from what little security the rural life could offer and lacking disposable income to invest in future protection, looked first to their own peers and then increasingly to employers and governments to underwrite the costs of sickness and old age. The political struggles of the nineteenth and twentieth centuries turned on the claims of workers for more secure lives, in the face of the capitalists' assumption that labor was an impersonal commodity to be purchased by the day, the task or the piece, without long-term commitment. Throughout the nineteenth century wage earners worked until they dropped or were made redundant, many of them beginning their downward drift through the job hierarchy in early middle age.[4] Since very few employers felt any obligation, workers themselves struggled to secure their own welfare. The need, in order of urgency, was assurance for injury, sickness, decent burial, and then provision for old age – which was regarded as a dire but less immediate form of incapacity. These working-class initiatives, the penny credit clubs and friendly societies, became the basis of modern welfare institutions.

Proletarian pressure, first in Europe and later in North America, changed the notion of old age as a disability and a personal liability to a risk which should be socially insured through the state.[5] Private organizations lacked the political capacity and institutional stability to accumulate, protect, and transfer funds on such a large scale through time from one generation to the next.[6] In the 1935 Social Security Act, Roosevelt very explicitly constructed a long-term commitment for government and the electorate in the US: payroll contributions were to remind everyone of future rights and continuing obligations – "With those taxes in there, no damn politician can ever scrap my social security program."[7] However, governments might never have been moved to control these large-scale transactions if the popular friendly societies and mutual funds had not already accumulated large sums of money. Towards the end of the nineteenth century the sheer bulk of these savings invited professional management and official regulation.[8]

Employers in the nineteenth century were quick to see the advantages of pensioning, especially where workers themselves were contributing to the cost, or where states helped to foot the bill.[9] Encouraged by tax-breaks after World War II, US firms provided an increasing proportion of workers with contributory pension schemes, and by 1981 50 percent of men and 37 percent of women were covered. These are best thought of as a deferred wage or salary, useful to the firm in retaining services up to, but not beyond, a specified age. They were negotiated by more privileged workers, an upper tier who stood in contrast to the poorer un- and under-employed recipients of flat-rate pay. Now, virtually every privately pensioned employee in the US is also covered by state benefits – the dependable long-stop in welfare support. Today's contributory schemes have important advantages for employers in shifting "dead wood" out of the workforce: "The typical firm plan provides a very large reward for remaining with the firm until some age, often the early retirement age, and then a substantial inducement to leave the firm, often as early as age 55."[10]

Similar motives influenced governments. The application of Keynesian macroeconomics to the crises of the early twentieth century made the fiscal manipulation of the elderly a vital part of the larger employment, prices, incomes, and savings calculus. The means-tested pension, introduced in Britain in 1908 and progressively extended over the next forty years, served to move low-paid and casual employment down the age scale to un- and under-employed youth.[11] Likewise, the pensioning provisions of the 1935 Social Security Act in the US were more immediately concerned with releasing employment to younger people in the post-Depression years than with rewarding the elderly.[12] These political manipulations have always generated fierce argument, liberals complaining that public pensioning undermines labor markets, socialists that it bolsters the bourgeois state.

The successes of public pensioning after World War II are remarkable: between 1960 and 1980 poverty among the over-65s in the US was reduced by half.[13] Pensioners were no longer just lucky survivors, they were normalized as a statutorily entitled, statistically defined segment of the population. State regulation played a key role in defining old age as a modern social and political category. In Britain, the threshold was set at 50 years by the Friendly Societies Act of 1875, and later raised to 65.[14] A new profession of actuaries measured lives and predicted the costs of liability. Old age was no longer seen just as an insurable risk, but as a life-stage with civil entitlements, underwritten by the state. Early public pensions were flat-rate, means-tested poverty alleviation programs, but increasingly the idea gained ground that pensions should be a form of *income maintenance*, paid not according to dire need but as deferred earnings. The political implications were enormous: unlike private schemes where the insurer simply pays out to those who pay in, public pensioning redistributes incomes fiscally, collecting from the haves and giving to the have-nots. Little wonder that the welfare state has met with so much resistance from the rich, and that public pensions should be seen by some as pandering to the greed of the senile masses.[15]

As Myles points out, public pensioning has become a politically and economically hazardous business for governments. On the one hand, redistributing national wealth to the elderly poor just looks like liberal democracy at work. But it also subverts liberal democratic principles because the "citizen's wage" paid to old people is not reckoned by the value of *their* labor on a free market, but by taking the current wage-rates of *non*-pensioners as an index. Using labor markets to define the social liabilities of one category of citizen and the entitlements of another soon rebounds on the markets themselves, thus undermining the index. The resulting "mixed economy" is "a system of tolerated contradictions" which, exacerbated by the relentless expansion of the cohort of pensioners, seems set on "a collision course."[16]

The old-age crisis

From 1940 to the mid-1960s there was a steady and relatively uncontentious growth in public pension coverage and levels of benefit in the US, fueled by expectations of surging economic growth. The number of recipients rose from 222,000 in 1940 to 14,800,000 by the end of 1960, and by 1983 in US, 82 percent of population was covered by Old Age, Survivors, and Disability Insurance (OASDI).[17] Thereafter, the stagflation of the 1970s and 1980s raised "future shock" fears about the national economic capacity to pay inflated benefits, and the threat which this "burden" imposed on capital growth.[18] Established welfare states like Denmark and Germany reduced the indexes for pensions and raised the retirement age.[19] In Japan the postwar "old people boom" lasted barely twenty years. Japanese pensions are still well below American levels and pension shortfalls mean that "many Japanese 'retire' twice – first from their career jobs and finally from jobs which pay much less." About 70 percent of Japanese elderly live with children, five times the American rate, but this is not necessarily indicative of harmony.[20] "The family" in East Asia is widely reputed to be "stronger" than anywhere else on earth, a convenient alibi for governments which are now seeking to dump the unfulfilled promises of public pensioning.

Blame for the "crisis" falls on surging growth of the wrong sort: a rapid expansion of the proportion of old people in the industrial populations. Over two centuries, the technologies of modernity have halved the birthrate and doubled the human lifespan, changing demographic structure from the squat pyramid of agrarian societies to the elongated barrel of the late industrial world. Japan has the fastest-growing proportion of over-65s, rising from 7 percent of the population in 1970 to 12 percent in 1990, and projected to increase to 23.6 percent by the year 2020. Over the thirty years following World War II, life expectancy for Japanese women has risen from 54 to 80.5 years, and from 50 to nearly 75 for men.[21] Between 1900 and 1980 the proportion of over-65s in the US population tripled to 12 percent. The likelihood that the demographic pyramid will continue to "spindle" in the twenty-first century has raised fears that there will not be enough physical growth – the production of children – to sustain the expanding geriatric mass. In West Germany the ratio of pension contributors to pension beneficiaries had dropped below 2 : 1, a critical threshold which may be reached in the US around 2030.[22] In the industrial democracies a fiscal crisis is anticipated around that date, when the 1950s-1960s cohort of "Baby Boomers" retire.

Inevitably, fears have focused blame on the aged themselves as "perpetrators" of the crisis. "I suggest that generational tensions will increase in all societies," says Thomson. "Among the immediate indicators are the affluence of large fractions of the middle-aged and elderly, the rapid removal of the aged from poverty, the growing proportions of the young sinking into poverty, mounting youth homelessness, and stalled and declining health and education levels of children and young adults." We must now scrutinize the entitlements of old age: "is 'right' at century's end more than 'want' in fancy garb?" Thomson concludes that "To those born after World War II the message throughout will be 'Few of these rights are for you.'"[23]

Other social scientists reject these premonitions that a geriatric urge to monopolize public welfare will erupt into "intergenerational 'class struggle.'"[24] By the 1980s 18 percent of West German tax revenue was devoted to supporting old-age security, 20 percent in Sweden, and 25 percent in the Netherlands, but "despite *official* concern over rising costs, *public support* of old age security systems remains high in these countries."[25] Talk of crisis, says Walker, is not just ill-founded, it is "a dangerous diversion of policymakers' and the public's attention from the major sources of inequity and dependent economic and social status."[26]

One aspect of the growth of public services for the aged is the expansion of the professions caring for them. As advocates of the elderly they have entered the intergenerational fray, and have acquired more voice in policy-making than the aged themselves.[27] Their discipline is gerontology, more specifically the new sub-discipline of "social gerontology" which has moved beyond clinical concerns with the aging individual to the social implications of longevity. The literature is already massive, and bears the imprint of the full range of modern social theory. Concern has become international: a "United Nations Year of the Aged" (1982) was followed by a major World Bank publication, *Averting the old age crisis: Policies to protect the old and promote growth* (1994). The role of these professionals in propagating the crisis has attracted some criticism.[28] Lawrence Cohen declares that the prime purpose of gerontology in India has been "not to study aging but to create it." An alliance of elite, neocolonial, and academic influences has convinced itself that "*India needs aging.*" Indian scholars and policy makers have embraced a "universal gerontology of the pensioner," an international "science of aging," and have whipped up fears that old people who were once absorbed convivially in "multigenerational 'joint' households" will become a massive public burden. If it happened in the West, it has to happen in India too.[29]

Critics point out that the crisis is anticipated rather than current, more actuarial than actual, more metropolitan than global. The proportion of over-60s in the rich countries will exceed 30 percent in 2030; in Africa and the Middle East it will be barely 7 percent.[30] Alarm has ebbed and flowed throughout the twentieth century as demographers have reinterpreted the statistics.[31] The tendency to confuse numbers of old people with proportions is of particular relevance in populations which, as in India, are actually expanding. As with the threat of eco-doom (decimated rainforests, ozone depletion), people in poor countries are becoming resistant to invitations to share our guilt and fears.

The World Bank's recipe in *Averting the old age crisis* worldwide "is to assist in the selection and design of policies that facilitate growth and enable the old to secure an equitable share of that growth."[32] However, it was the failure of such policies in the liberal democracies which has made pensioning a crisis: the incapacity of markets to fulfill official promises that the expansion of national wealth would cover the needs of aging citizens. Underlying this is a misunderstanding about the two meanings of growth – the economic and the physical. In the face of insolvency, governments have two solutions to offer: citizens should buy their own pensions and gamble on the market on their own account, as the provident middle classes have always done. Or, if they have nothing to invest, they should reckon that *people* ultimately afford better assurance than money or markets, especially people to whom one is bound by long-term reproductive ties – "the family."

Generation war?

As the belt tightens, media references to greed and the elderly have multiplied. But the accusations still run in both directions: against the asset-hogging of the elderly themselves, and against the asset-stripping by those paid to take care of them. Wicked people (kin and strangers) take advantage of the physically and mentally frail to extract their savings on the pretence of guarding their interests. On the other hand old people tend to sit on badly needed housing equity, partly as assurance against the soaring costs of geriatric care.[33] In Britain young adults, especially those plunged into negative equity by the collapse in house prices in the early 1990s, "reckon, with some cause, that the economy is being run for the wrinklies."[34]

The rhetoric has settled on one of the most subjective of social categories, the *generation*. In the context of an individual's network of reproductive relations, "generation" is immediately meaningful, and designated clearly enough by such terms of address and reference as "grandfather" or "niece." But the extension of this metaphor from the relations of reproduction out to whole segments of the population is a source of much confusion. Our assumption that our own or an adjacent generation can *act concertedly* is an illusion which has for long fascinated sociologists.[35] Whatever affinity we may feel for age-mates who enjoyed the 1960s or experienced Vietnam, we should not assume that we think or act alike. Nor should we ascribe collective ideas or actions to the demographic phenomenon of the age cohort ("the 40–49-year-olds"), even when it acquires special historical significance by sheer weight of numbers ("the Baby Boomers"). To imagine that "generations" think and act concertedly inspires us to make policies for largely illusory categories of people – possibly to their disadvantage. It also obscures the importance of *other* social categories (women, the poor, ethnic minorities) whose interests and identity have different and more compelling sorts of reality.[36]

As an age cohort, the elderly in the liberal democracies would seem to have formidable powers of self-expression through the ballot box. Does the privacy of the voting booth simply cater to the greatest greed of the greatest number? The electoral disadvantage of children must surely have some impact on the fact that public expenditure in a country like Canada is 3:1 in favor of old people.[37] It seems that children are generally accepted as a private responsibility, perhaps because the neediness of infants, though absolute, decreases mercifully fast, while the neediness of elders runs the other way, increasing slowly and chronically. Everyone knows we must have children, but our need for the very old is much less obvious. Old people have always struggled to maintain their share of resources, but it seems that in the Western democracies they have used their preponderance inertially, rather than actively and concertedly. There are numerous "political" organizations for the elderly, the largest being the American Association of Retired People (AARP).[38] But Achenbaum insists that "Despite its wealth and savvy leadership, AARP can rarely mobilize its membership around any specific policy issue. The assets, interests and needs of the elderly population are simply too diverse to rally them as a monolithic, single minded political force."[39] According to Pratt, older people share the frustrations of inflation, increasing medical costs and property taxes, but their political cohesion is inhibited by "sectional, partisan, class, and racial" divisions, by physical isolation from one another, as well as by disability, poverty, and political inexperience.[40]

There are better grounds for thinking that younger people are more inclined to, and have more opportunity for, generational solidarity. They assemble in schools and colleges, and extend their contacts through leisure (music and sport) and media skills. An obvious source of unrest are the meager prospects for growth which confront youth:

the lack of employment, and thus the inability to leave the parental home, raise families, and solve the economic problems on which welfare provision for everyone must depend. If this is expressed in a low-level guerrilla war on adults, it is nothing new.

A few in the middle generation have responded to the perceived threat of "the gray lobby" with organizations like Americans for Generational Equity (AGE) and the American Association of Boomers (AAB). But for all the media hype, these groups are more concerned with advocating the young than assaulting the old. "There is, in fact, no evidence that those who advocate the rights of the elderly take a position on social insurance at odds with the views expressed by groups advancing the interests of children or young people. All age groups say they are willing to support the old."[41] Political activism for the young and the old, like most "grassroots" campaigns in the liberal democracies, is more an expression of people's adversarial view of "the state" and its agents than intergenerational war. It is significant that AGE, AAB, and similar organizations were products of the Reagan era of spending cuts and regressive taxation.

Misunderstanding growth

Modern private pensioning institutions foster magical beliefs: advertisements tell us we simply put money in the bank today, listen to it grow, and go cruising when we are 65. That dream of course depends on there being not just money but a viable economy when we retire, for the goods we enjoy are not produced by the bank but by the willing labors of the young and the active. Our belief that this will happen is a measure of our faith in efficient markets or strong states, but it depends more radically on an unspoken assumption that life, in a more complex sense, will go on.

From an accountant's point of view, a pension is a tricky sort of time transaction, a sort of wager involving faith, hope, and charity. It is an obligation which I try to place on other persons in the future to commit resources (food, shelter, cash) to meet my persisting needs in the face of my dwindling capacities. Trust is inherent in this relationship, whether I am depending on my children, my employer, my assurance company, or my government. Those who can afford to, spread their bets as widely as they can.

From the perspective of the national economic planner, public pensioning presents a microeconomic puzzle: why should young people allow themselves to be taxed, and forgo current income, to pay the pensions of an expanding mass of old people who are very evidently *not* their own parents or grandparents? Would it not be more rational for young people to advocate a drastic pruning of the older population? The most plausible utilitarian explanation is that self-interested youngsters are prepared to pay for public pensioning because the system relieves them of a direct responsibility for their own parents. They play along in "a politics of consensus" because they realize that they themselves will, in the fullness of time, benefit.[42] But in these uncertain times, it is surprising that anyone should have so much faith in a return on investment thirty or forty years hence.

Liberal economists, whose tools are best adapted to short-term transactions, are hard put to explain how people "make decisions" which stretch so far into the future.[43] Trying to reduce what goes on within the reproductive organism of "the family" to the familiar

---

Snuff 'em!

In *Soylent Green*, a front-runner for the title of most fascinatingly awful movie, oldies in post-Armageddon America are politely snuffed and turned into cookies (Soylent green, Soylent red) by the all-powerful Corporation that feeds the masses. This wickedness is revealed by Charlton Heston in a melodramatic dying gasp: *"Soylent Green is people!"*

Richard Lamm, former governor of Colorado and board member of Americans for Generational Equity (AGE) "sees merit in late-life euthanasia to counterbalance the excesses of the 'prodigal father' " (Achenbaum 1989: 113). The idea also apparently occurred to that great euthanasia enthusiast Adolf Hitler (von Balluseck 1983: 233). Generalized senilicide, it is comforting to hear, is not substantiated ethnographically, despite tales of hard times in adverse arctic or desert environments (Simmons 1945). Braybrooke (1987: 50) briefly raises the interesting question about whether we can be greedy for *life*. In what ways does the protraction of life constitute a *need* rather than a desire? An ironic counterweight to the desire for protracted life is the fear of protracting death. "This is why Japan has *pokkuri jinja* and *pokkuri otera*, 'popping-off' shrines and temples, visited by a steady stream of old people who have come to pray for a speedy death" (Kiefer 1990: 191–2).

microeconomic logic of a business firm reveals a little but obscures much. How ordinary citizens save and invest has massive implications for national economies, but how they actually make these "lifetime choices" remains largely mysterious.[44] Milton Friedman argued that many of our decisions on these matters may look unreasonable because we are less interested in quick profits than in keeping our consumption levels steady over the long term. This "permanent income hypothesis" explained why we might prefer to forgo an obvious benefit today if it served to pension us in the future. Since it seemed unlikely that people carry around in their heads for years a fixed idea of what they want while other aspects of their lives change, various "life-cycle" refinements of Friedman's model followed.[45] But because these "life interests" are usually very tacit (the desire to be a parent, or not to die in penury), and are being revised continually as life progresses, their presence in the economic calculus is enigmatic. Life is uncertain, markets are imperfect, governments are unstable, and people are irritatingly "myopic."[46] Gary Becker asserts that "each family maximizes a utility function spanning two generations," but he has no means of spelling out what this "function" actually consists of, and how it is transacted. The uncertainties which such a timespan entails oblige him to factor in a very old-fashioned ingredient – *luck*.[47]

However, the burden of such theorizing is that in bringing *lifetime* interests to bear in today's markets, young people will allow more benefits to their seniors today because they are in the process of constructing *better retirement prospects for themselves than explicit market rationales might currently indicate*, and certainly better than any government policy could presume to fix.[48] The cheering news from the economists, therefore, is that the apparent inequities of pensioning are only a fleeting image of an enduring social contract which is continually being "perfected" by the invisible hand of the market. But this is not a "contract" in the rational and legal sense elaborated by the Enlightenment philosophers. It is a vague assumption about growth, the "natural" reproductive processes which hold families together through time.[49] The prevalent fear is that this ancient pact between the generations is collapsing under the weight of disputes about taxation and welfare spending: promises will not be fulfilled, public welfare will not be able to bear the burden of support, children will suffer. The decrepit elderly will eventually overwhelm us, resorting to the brute force of numbers to pursue their own short-term gains.

There is no evidence that family relations have ever consisted of a stable and harmonious "intergenerational contract." The most obvious reason for this is that growth perpetually undermines any temporary balance we may achieve. "Retirement," implying pensioning in some form, is a political issue in every family system and not, as is often supposed, simply a modern invention.[50] These transactions, so important in European social history, give the lie to romantic images of the family as the heartland where selfish material calculation yields to perfect altruism.[51] The older generation is formally obliged to abdicate control of scarce resources in exchange for often elaborate guarantees for their welfare. In the sheaves of documents which transfer rights and obligations between parents, children, and siblings, "one is astonished to see the way that filial piety has to stand up and be counted, spelt out in exact quantities and decked out in lawyer's jargon."[52] Reading these wills and marriage depositions dispels the notion that intergenerational transfers in households are unthinking, or that competitive self-interest is a modern novelty. Little wonder that such complex transactions often ended up in the courts, and that the legal profession has thrived on the efforts of each generation to manipulate property and wealth in its own interests.

Economic analysis has notoriously little patience with our idiotic explanation that what we do "just feels right." In the slow-moving somatic economy of the family and the household, "generation" is a grammatically broader term: it is not just a passive category ("that which is generated"); it is an active experience ("the act of generating").[53] Our interests in generation are not narrowly associated with an age cohort, they entail lifetimes of transactions linked by sentiments which develop slowly within the context of personal relations. These include the "irrational love" which, says Rossi, will always frustrate economic reckoning of rational choice.[54] But it also includes many other less attractive sentiments (grief, hate) which move us through life. All of these can be manipulated, and as elders lose the moral justifications of physical growth and relinquish material control, they can turn their life experience to psychic advantage in their struggle against the fear of dearth and destitution. This may be particularly important in societies where there is *no* property to manipulate. In the Kalahari desert, older !Kung grind away on the theme that "nobody" looks after them. Their elaborate, melodramatic narratives are full of dark threats of supernatural retribution for negligence which, according to Rosenberg, is belied by family attentiveness. This persistent "squeaky wheel" behavior is considered normal – even a sign of mental acuity: "It is hardly surprising that the elders are good at it, as they have been practicing their whole lives."[55]

In our societies accusations of greed track the fears and anxieties of aging out from the family domain into the public welfare systems on which we now depend. But "the old-age crisis" is now less a matter of filial impiety and senile avarice than of declining public confidence in the capacity of national welfare systems to meet the demands of human growth.[56] The idea that we can look to the "the family" for support when public pensions fail, is a *non*-policy which preys above all on the " 'natural' reciprocity and altruism of female kin" and serves "to perpetuate the myth of the family as a private domain" distinct from the state.[57] There is no shortage of economistic rationales for this maneuver. "The family is the cheapest institution for the care of the aged" – but only if we strip our accounting of its functions down until it crudely resembles the business firm of classic microeconomic analysis.[58]

With the erosion of public welfare, people with lower incomes are indeed forced into dependence on ties of family and friendship, but these relations are now far removed from the fanciful memories of "life on Grandma's farm" which linger in the conservative mind. The incapacity of households to absorb welfare burdens is regarded as delinquency: moral collapse has reduced "the family" to sub-nuclear "matrifocal" units of welfare mothers and their illegitimate offspring. In a classic trick, women who are not at home to pick up the burden, but are "out to work" picking up wages, are accused of *greed*.[59] One part of the web of official confusion which enshrouds these issues is that the *household*, which statisticians and demographers still identify as the base unit of modern society, is not necessarily the *family* as ordinary people think of it. Like "generations", "families" defy formal institutional definition for the simple reason that they are not mutually exclusive groups, they are subjectively based ("ego-centered") networks. In this contingent sense, "the family" may be as large and as vital as it ever was. However, governments can neither "see" nor make reliable judgments about such networks and their welfare capacities, not least because increased longevity – the perceived source of the pensioning problem – has been complicating family forms. To have four living generations has become common, five less of a rarity. Parenthood now extends through as many as fifty years, and grandparenthood through twenty.[60] The focus on "parents" in the pensioning crisis tends to obscure the advancing age of "children", who may be old enough to be co-residents of the same retirement home.[61] On the other hand, the "principal care-giver" for young children may now be a grandparent, even a great-grandparent.[62]

The statistics also suggest that if there is indeed an "aging crisis", it is emphatically a crisis for women *of all ages*. We can certainly make no general assumptions about "the family" as it affects the demands placed on women. The number of years in which a woman has both parents alive has quadrupled since 1800, which indicates that the daughters available to care for increasingly aged parents are getting fewer, older, and poorer.[63] Anderson reckons that a woman born in Britain in 1951 could expect fifty-two years of life ahead of her after bearing her last child, and that the "empty nest" phase after the departure of her last child could extend for several decades.[64] Women aged 70–74 are four times more likely to be widowed than they were in 1800, and in that age group there are now five times as many widows as widowers. Over the age of 65, women are twice as likely as men to be living alone and in poverty.[65] In such circum-stances, the assumption that there is some ready-made family cap-sule which can, at short notice, close protectively around a woman, or within which she can apply her caring energies, is dangerous nonsense.

Accusations of greed are eloquent about the intergenerational transfers and tensions endemic in all forms of pensioning. "Greed" marks the hot spots where growing (and declining) bodies merge with economic processes. This is as true today as it was when welfare was organized in the microscopic domains of "family" and commu-nity. But now the ancient struggle between the generations has been translated into a contest between people and state. What the linger-ing accusations of greed tell us is that old people themselves are not unilaterally responsible for either the problems or the solutions of pensioning. Everyone from the smallest infant to the most decrepit elder is a moving force in the welfare calculus. The great irony – possibly the great tragedy – of modern times is that the processes of government are now so profoundly out of phase with the processes of human life. While the focus of national economic attention closes in on the fleeting minutes of stock market fluctuations, the motion of human growth extends into ever-widening reaches of world history. In these circumstances, the notion that the problems of mass aging will respond to short-term fiscal manipulations is very improbable.

10

The Venal Professional

There is nothing very mysterious about the greed of the great modern capitalists. The robber barons are known in caricature to all of us, and the monuments to their excesses are everywhere. Our images of these great accumulators are drawn in sharp contrast to the lives of their asset-stripped victims, the workers.

We, the professionals, live somewhere in the moral twilight between these two classes. We are laborers of a sort, but our business is the manipulation of ideas, mostly for capital, sometimes for labor, but always for ourselves.[1] We have cashed in on the Cartesian trick of putting a higher value on the mind than the body. We like to think of ourselves as even-handed servants of the public – discreet, trustworthy, knowledgeable, and thoroughly adult. Our rights to larger rewards rest on the comfortable assurance that we have a "legal monopoly" on the services we provide.[2]

Our nineteenth-century champions (Tawney, Ruskin, Tocqueville) saw us as a vital mediating and moderating force in the turbulent expansion of capitalism, the enlightened and self-disciplined managers of public affairs. In our time we have enjoyed great power and privilege, but we have not fulfilled these earlier moral hopes. Inflated in numbers and in self-esteem, our ranks are now fragmenting and collapsing, and we are losing the public credibility on which everything we are depends: "the most common accusation leveled at professions is (1) that they are greedy ... And if their pursuit of the dollar is cause for suspicion, their (2) pursuit of the aesthetic delights of expertise in their own professional art is simply infuriating."[3]

The rise of the salariat

In bourgeois folklore there are four classic professions: the church, the army, law, and medicine. To the church, we may owe the vocational element in "profession": an avowal, a commitment of one's life, a dedication of learning in the service of others. To the army we may trace some crude elements of professional *trust*, with all the anxiety which that notion entails: we commit the defence of the realm and the safety of our women and children to the soldiers. On the lawyers we pin our hopes for justice; and on a more private level we commit the care of our souls to the clerics, our bodies to the doctors and, more recently, our money to the managers. We trust them to make judgments on the basis of reliable knowledge, which is why the scholars who organize and certify that knowledge were admitted (usually as clerics) to the professional circle from the beginning.

The fortunes of the four "classic" professions have been far from stable: in the eighteenth century, before the expansion of industrial capitalism brought a slew of new opportunities, the reputation and earnings of law and medicine were at a particularly low ebb.[4] "Professing" has always been an assertive act, claiming the moral high ground and closing ranks without attracting too much hostile attention. Although professionals like to see their functions and privileges as "natural," even divinely inspired, maintaining credibility and building an intimidating relationship with clients has involved centuries of hard political-economic work. "Amateur" is a significant counterpoint to "professional," a distinction between love and money, with the implication that others may do our work for pleasure but we do it full-time, and we do it better because our livelihood depends upon it. Subtle ideas and exclusive rituals are vital in keeping idiots out of the game, but discipline, in all its senses, is at the core of every profession: lose it, and the game is up. In Platonic terms we are the "Guardians" over whom hangs the perennial question of who monitors *us*. To be above suspicion, professionals must make a business of suspecting themselves.[5] The bigger the responsibilities, the grander the opportunities for corruption, which is why the most senior guardians must not only police their lower ranks, but must make regular displays of their own probity – with the aid of large quantities of ermine, silk, gold braid, marble, and other impressive materials.

As the professions have expanded and mutated in modern times, sustaining credibility has become increasingly complicated and costly. The boom years of professional growth were around the turn of the twentieth century. Between 1900 and 1930, when the US population increased 162 percent (to 123 millions) the ranks of accountants and auditors grew by 835 percent, college faculty by 342 percent, and government officials by 191 percent. On one estimate, the ranks of those calling themselves professionals rose from less than 1 percent of the population at the end of World War I, to something approaching a quarter by 1980. The biggest boost was the transfer of control of the industrial and commercial corporations to the rapidly expanding core of " 'scientific managers,' lawyers, financial experts, engineers, personnel experts, etc."[6] They used their ascendant powers to secure some old professional privileges, and to invent a few new ones.

In the core principle of the *salary* the professionals tied their rewards to the moral logic of growth in both its somatic and its political-economic senses, defying the short-term material logic of the marketplace by arranging for their income to be distributed in an incremental pattern over the lifetime of each individual. Many a capitalist might envy the long-term material security of this clever invention. Unlike the history of industrial wages, the development of the salary is not easy to trace because its principles were constructed within the networks of the elite itself, beyond the scrutiny of open labor markets, and therefore on terms which have eluded formal economic analysis. It thus provided a sublime rationale for expanding gains, and a near-perfect alibi for greed.

Salary *versus* wage

Salary: the term exudes worthiness and trust, something natural and necessary, aloof from the taint of lucre. The word derives from the allowance paid to Roman soldiers to buy salt, the classic symbol of dignity and the sustainer of life in the heat of military campaigns. As a middle-class institution, the salary can be traced to the development of professions and new forms of work contract in the medieval guilds. Apprentices lived with their masters and were contractually bound to learn and be taught, often over many years (eleven for a harness-maker in Paris in the thirteenth century, four for a baker). They were rewarded on an age-related scale which included benefits like food and accommodation, but when they graduated as journeymen they were paid daily fees.[7] The notion of making a *career* in a guild-protected occupation has been carried over into the "salary" of modern times, distinguishing the privileged rewards of the professionals from the proletarian *wage*.[8] The term asserts differences of social status as well as types of employment, as expressed in speech and dress, diet and residence. In the workplace, the privilege of a salary is reflected in apportionments of space (a private office or desk, separate washrooms) and time (meetings, appointments, flexible hours). "Salary" asserts the superiority of thinking over doing, and is part of a vocabulary of privilege which includes words like "office" and "staff."[9]

The most straightforward material expectation of a salary is that it pays more. However, this disguises a more important principle, the temporal flow of rewards. The salary is a special sort of *time payment*, a transaction removed from the immediate give-and-take of the marketplace, and delayed or spread out over longer periods. In technical jargon, "A salary field is characterized by pay progressions (published or undisclosed) related to increasing experience, quality of performance, and career expectations, through the use of such procedures as incremental scales, pay ranges, merit additions, or promotions."[10] While neither the middle-class bureaucrat nor the proletarian owns the productive resources on which his income depends, the professional sells his labor by the *lifetime*, the proletarian by the hour, day, or week. A salary connotes permanent rather than temporary or casual employment. The salary is closely linked to the notion of a "career," and usually rises incrementally over many years to several times the entry level. It also incorporates long-term perquisites such as pensioning, life insurance, mortgage assistance, and health and education programs.[11]

Wages, in contrast, are characteristically "flat," measured by much shorter units of labor time, or by the piece produced. Although some wage earners may take home more at the end of the week than some salaried employees, it is usually more advantageous *in the long term* to have a salary than a wage. While salary increments are, as the Japanese put it, "person-related," wages are impersonal and work-related.[12] Pay is raised by working overtime or by moving between differently rated jobs, and rates are "improved" by collective bargaining and across-the-board hikes rather than by personally adjusted increments. Wages offer much less job security: notice of termination

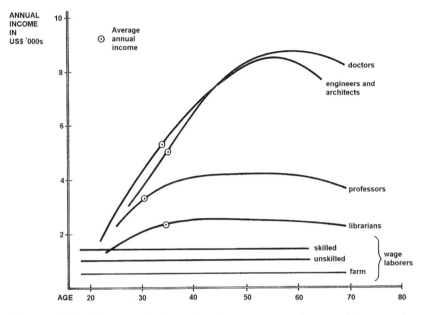

Figure 10.1 Wage and salary structures compared: annual income by selected occupations in the US, 1920–9 (after Clark 1937)

is typically much shorter than for salaried staff. Wage structures can be "improved" by adopting some of the appearances, though rarely the basic principles, of the salary, such as extending the term of contracts, or paying monthly by check rather than by weekly pay-packet.[13]

Figure 10.1 is an early illustration of these distinctions, drawn from Harold F. Clark's survey *Life earnings*, among various occupations in the US during the 1920s. Over the course of their careers, the average income of professionals, notably doctors, engineers and architects, rose steeply to about ten times the annual earnings of an unskilled laborer. Young professionals might initially be paid less than wage earners in their age cohort (an awful temptation for middle-class youth) but income soon rose in a pattern of increments accelerated by promotions, leveling off somewhat in middle age, but sustained at a high level beyond retirement by pensioning arrangements and accumulated savings. For more humble professionals like college professors, the curve flattened out quite soon, even more so for semi-clerical occupations like librarianship. At the level of the unskilled laborer, much closer to the threshold of poverty, the pattern of life earnings was virtually flat: "in unskilled and semi-skilled labor the pay is determined by the kind of work done and not by the length of service."[14] Figure 10.2, drawing on Lydall's 1953 survey of life earnings in Britain, likewise reveals the steep upward curve of the professional's salary and the much flatter, declining earnings pattern of the "unskilled" worker. Not much has changed: in the early 1970s Dore noted that "manual workers reach their peak earnings in their twenties. Thereafter there is little change in their earnings level until (for those who are not made foremen) they decline somewhat in their fifties and rather more in their sixties."[15]

"Traditionally, a salary was regarded as a close secret between an employer and the salary earner."[16] The professional is nothing if not discreet. Efficient markets, on the other hand, are grossly indiscreet, which is probably why professionals avoid them when transacting their services. Nevertheless, liberal economists would regard the basic differences between wage and salary as the result of "free" bargaining in the market for labor: those with greater skills and capacities command a higher price, have more opportunities to set contractual terms, and thus enjoy greater prestige. However, the logic of the marketplace does not in itself explain the disproportionately high rewards for professional "mind-work," the inflated cost of access to professional employment (diplomas, certificates, etc.) nor, especially, the age-related incremental structure of salaries. Efforts have been made to justify these in terms of *human capital*, the notion that people build up investments in their own skills and capacities, which can also depreciate or become obsolete as they age. The Nobel laureate Gary Becker was struck by the "impressive piece of evidence . . . that more highly educated and skilled persons almost always tend to earn more than others." This, Becker argued, was "as true of developed countries as different as the United States and the Soviet Union, of under-developed countries as different as India and Cuba, and of the United States one hundred years ago as well as today."[17] The income of skilled people rose more steeply and peaked later in life because this was when returns to investment in human capital, mainly the cost of an education, were reaped. It was young rather than older people who invested in human capital "because they can collect the return over more years." Becker was so convinced that the accumulation of human capital explained the pattern of life earnings that he regarded the proposition as reversible: "if two [earnings] profiles differed in steepness, the steeper could be said to indicate the presence of greater

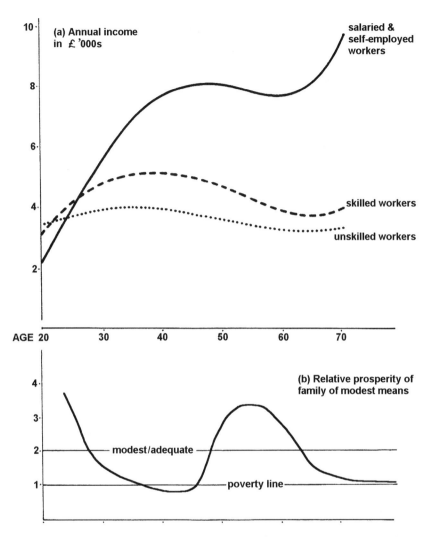

Figure 10.2 Wage and salary structures (after Lydall 1955: 141–2) in relation to the "family life-cycle squeeze" (after Wynn 1970: 168)

human capital." You don't have to look at what a person actually does, the salary itself tells you the worker is worth more.[18]

Becker's ideological commitment is clear: free and expanding markets stimulate investment in human capital through diversifying opportunities for specialized skills, allowing individuals "to *become more efficient*" and thus earn more.[19] But for all its flashes of insight, the notion of a market for human capital has raised more questions than it has answered.[20] How should an economist set about measuring the costs and returns to investment in human capital, or its depreciation with age? Why should cash earnings be regarded as a reliable indicator of holdings of human capital? Why should an unskilled lawyer get ten times what we pay a skilled stonemason? If senior doctors are paid five times the salary of junior doctors, does this mean that we are five times more likely to seek the services of an older doctor when we are sick? Might we not feel more confident about one who was trained more recently? On the other hand, do we care so little about whether our plumber is 18 or 50 that we reckon his work is worth the same flat *wage*?

Something more complicated than the market is securing a salary and defining professional worth. Most of us don't know enough to assess the "real" skills of a professional, nor do we weigh up his years of patient self-improvement. We hire a "certified" or "reputable" doctor or lawyer.[21] Becker's assurances that "some persons earn more than others simply because they invest more in themselves" and because they are "abler" than others does not take account of the way professional organizations have worked to *exclude* the majority of workers – especially women – from the privileges of a salary. Becker concludes that women don't "want" to invest in human capital because as wives and mothers they don't hold a job long enough to make it worthwhile.[22] And since married women's wages do not change much over their lives, "human capital production by married women can safely be ignored."[23] *Why* women are employed sporadically and earn less is a question which has little to do with markets and much more to do with social rules about being a wife and mother. If these activities are not accountable as "human capital" the failing is in economics.

Modern economics was designed to explain – and to regulate – wages rather than salaries. Pay is immediate rather than deferred, rates respond quickly to short-term economic shifts, and because there are so many more wage earners in the workforce, pay is negotiated more publicly, either within enterprises or across whole industries. One reason why salaried employees resist unionization is because collective bargaining has the tendency to expose their rewards to the same disadvantageous short-term scrutiny as wage earning.[24] Salaries, related in a much more complex way to individual *lives*, do not depend on what employers are prepared to pay for particular services on any particular day. *Who* you are, in some durable and socially complicated sense, matters a great deal in determining a salary, and even within families how much a professional earns can be a status-laden secret. Complicated personal screening (manners, appearance, associates) plays an important part in recruitment to professional employment, especially in the higher echelons. By contrast, there is no suggestion that the wage earner "might be paid for what he 'is' rather than what he 'does'": he lacks the *curriculum vitae* of the professional. One effect of this is that salary scales are notoriously difficult to concoct and justify, in the absence of clear market cues. The essence of such a privileged system of rewards is its dependence on implicit social rules about growth, such as "the young ought to defer to the old" or "the young ought to be asked to contribute their energies and skills that their youth endows them with."[25]

The salary is not just a more elaborate sort of wage, it is a distinct social institution. At best, it represents what economists quaintly call an "imperfection" in labor markets. Quite simply, the terms of trade are such that laborers cannot and do not bargain for salaries. They bargain for wages. Recruitment to salaried positions is not from the lower ranks of wage earners but from separate social groups, filtered through special organizations like colleges. Who gets a salary is not determined by today's markets, but by "traditions" which have been centuries in the making.[26] Notice the different power implications in talking about *"drawing"* a salary, and *"getting paid"* a wage. Through their guild organizations, the professions have protected the privileges of their own people – especially their children – by restricting admission to their ranks. This "requires persistent, inventive action," a monopolistic and nepotistic urge which, for those who in other contexts believe devoutly in free markets, is a perpetual source of embarrassment.[27]

Durable, dependable institutions are absolutely essential to the salary principle. They have to be sufficiently large and well protected (big firms, or public institutions like hospitals and universities) to ride out economic fluctuations in the short and medium term, and to absorb the costs of time payments, especially long-term pensioning commitments. Small unstable businesses cannot support careers or offer deferred rewards, although there are some advantages (loyalty, specific knowhow) in trying to do so.[28] Without such support the earnings of self-employed professionals characteristically peak earlier and tail off more steeply.[29] The salariat thrives in large bureaucracies which provide the vertical structures for career advancement, and through the centuries professionals have devoted much time and attention to building and maintaining these organizations. The mother of all reliable institutions has been the modern state, which is why civil servants have always been prepared to trade added security for lower rates of pay.[30]

Institutions like the salary are not simply the cumulative logic of millions of individual exchanges, they are expressions of the power which one smaller and more cohesive class of employees has established in relation to others. Thus political-economic explanations from the left, dwelling on the history of social power, seem more likely to come to terms with such questions as why, in bargaining for a wage rather than a salary, workers seem to accept a system of rewards which keeps them – and their dependents – in their economic and political place. If a salary is such a good deal, why do the wage-earning masses not rise up and claim it?

From a socialist perspective, wage labor is an essential symptom of the rise of capitalism and the making of an industrial working class. When the workers wake up to the conditions which the bosses (including their clever professional agents) have foisted on them, the *wage* will be seen for the miserable, repressive device it is. The value of the time which the worker sells by the hour or day bears no direct relation to the value of the products which the owner of the enterprise sells. The difference is profit, which feeds the growth of capital not the worker, and pays for the managerial and other services on which the owners of capital depend. The connection between work and profits has little to do with markets, and everything to do with history. The Marxist economic historian Michel Aglietta ridicules the "human capital" notion that salaries are simply the fair and free market price of the high cost of producing a professional. He insists that "the wage relation is not an exchange relation, even at the point of the wage contract." It is defined by processes much more complicated than what individual people want to buy and sell on a particular day. "The two 'players' are not playing the same game, they do not have the same goals, and they are not subject to the same rules."[31] Their interests in the job, the enterprise, and in society generally are entirely different.

It is not the players who determine the wage, it is the wage which determines who the players are. So – what sort of player is determined by a *salary*, and what is his role in Marx's historic scheme? Finding a place for the professionals in the Marxist logic of conflicting classes has always been a problem. For Aglietta, the salary is part of the "notoriously ambiguous" position of managerial staff, who appear as an "intermediate category" between the capitalist and the proletariat.[32] The professional does not very obviously squeeze surplus value from others, nor does he have it squeezed from him. In many respects he is just a souped-up proletarian, dependent like all the others on the largesse of capital. Downwardly mobile professionals (e.g. clerical or para-legal staff) subside into the ranks of the wage earners, while the upwardly mobile (the managers of giant corporations) have been nudging the old robber barons aside. All of this amounts to an admission that Marxist analysis works no better than liberal economic analysis when it comes to explaining professionals and their rewards. Nor does class analysis say much about why *women* generally get lower wages, or why *juniors* get lower salaries. It is the theories, rather than the people and their activities, which don't fit; which is interesting, because it is we – the professional mind-workers who teach and certify other professionals – who invent the theories. Would it be too cynical to suggest that there is some advantage in keeping the rationales and tactics of our own mode of livelihood in the dark?

Growth and increments

The most mystifying aspect of salaries has been the timing of payments. The salary operates in a theoretically inaccessible timespan between the instant of liberal economic analysis and the epoch of Marxist economics; between the short-term transactions of individuals competing in free markets on the one hand, and the long-term political conflict between opposed classes on the other.

The missing logic is human growth, in which the salary offers some remarkable advantages. It adjusts the flow of income to a family's changing needs over several decades. Salary structures guarantee that families will get what they need, independently of their capacity, *at the right time.* Salaries rise most steeply during the period in family growth of most acute demand, when children are young and adolescent. The curve levels and drops somewhat in the "empty nest" stage, but may rise again as the parents age, and savings and pensions mature. The correspondence between the periods of deepest family need and the steepest upward trajectories of the salary is illustrated in figure 10.2, which compares Wynn's reckoning of the changing levels of prosperity in a "family of modest means" with Lydall's account of lifetime earnings patterns in approximately the same geographical and historical context.[33]

Given these advantages, it is little wonder that the idea of a "family wage" for all workers was widely mooted from the start of the industrial era. Since starving workers were useful to nobody, the idea that employers should pay workers what they *needed* rather than what the market would bear made good sense. However, in discussing the "family wage" the early economists were interested in *how little* workers should be paid, not how much. Thus David Ricardo declared that "the natural price of labor is that price which is necessary to enable the laborers, one with another, to subsist and perpetuate their race, without either increase or diminution."[34] Anything beyond this low-level equilibrium was a superfluous "want," which the shrewd employer could resist. However, the calculation failed because the wage rate was rarely adjusted to *changing* needs. On the relatively few occasions on which it was paid, the "family wage" was usually reduced to averages, such as a "normal family of five," not to a flow of timely increments in the manner of a salary.

Discussing wages in terms of wants and needs always puts workers at a disadvantage. With somebody else (employers, legislators) deciding their needs, workers have to put their claims for fair recompense in the morally suspect language of short-term *wants*. In the noisy clamor for hikes in piece-, job-, and hourly rates, workers' demands can easily be represented as a massive, greedy threat to social stability. The salariat, on the other hand, is funded for a lifetime of expanding *needs* which avoids undignified public quibbling about their personal desires. The marvel of the system is that its rewards bear no direct relationship to effort or skill or hours of labor. Moreover, while "family supplements" for wage workers (welfare checks, child allowances) are paid as public charity after the need has arisen, a privilege of the salary is that it *anticipates* rising expenses. And yet, getting the money does not even depend on actually delivering the babies – which is a great deal for double-salaried childless couples.

For a while it seemed that Japan might have found the means of "salarizing" the whole workforce.[35] In many enterprises Japanese workers received specific allowances for each family member, and special funds contributed not only to education but to the cost of weddings and other rites of passage. It is often supposed that this was an old Japanese tradition, part of the secret of the postwar "economic miracle." In fact, salarization arose from the need for family-based rationing strategies in the face of widespread poverty after World War II. It depended on the creation of long-term paternalistic bonds between worker and organization, allowing the latter to buy "not a skill but a lifetime's work."[36] The system offered a loyal workforce secure employment in exchange for deferred earnings and benefits, but while this version of the "family wage" undoubtedly strengthened and stabilized the larger Japanese industrial enterprises in a period of intense international competition, it also undermined the bargaining power of labor. The steady drift towards conventional wages in Japan confirms the view that it was neither inherently efficient nor a solid national tradition. The typical "salaryman" in Japan today is now much more like his European counterpart than the family-waged factory employee of the 1950s.[37]

Salaries, as we knew them in the twentieth century, could only be the privilege of a minority. No social or economic system is robust enough, or affluent enough, to allow every worker to be rewarded in this way. The benefits of long-term security are too costly to share with the masses – especially if all the pensioning, mortgaging, health and child allowances that are wrapped up in the salary package are taken into account. In contrast to the generous convexity of the salary curve, soaring to anticipate needs, we can picture the growth of working-class families compressed against the unyielding ceiling of the wage rate. The childrearing squeeze "is more intense for blue-collar and lower-white-collar men, whose earnings flatten around the point when their children become teenagers, than it is for professional groups," whose income curves enjoy a steady upward swing until the mid-50s.[38] It is a cruel irony that while bodily growth does not define the wage, bodily *decline* does: physical incapacity reduces earnings very quickly, and soon leads to redundancy.[39] As figure 10.1 indicates, the working life of wage laborers (with the exception of the poorest, the farm workers) ended earlier than that of professionals. At retirement the salariat can look forward to pensions and other deferred benefits, while wage earners are confronted with another trough of material need.

Compared with the privileges of a salary, the wage is a useful political device for keeping workers in their economic place, by capitalizing on the life-cycle squeeze. While this makes workers more dependent on public welfare institutions (run, of course, by the professionals), it is the families themselves that have to cope directly with the stress of growth. This exposes the inequities of gender and generation at the reproductive core: it is women who cover most of the costs of family welfare by their unpaid and undervalued labor. As employers know to their benefit, family responsibilities stabilize a workforce, since workers "prefer" the security of long-term employment to the hazards of job-shopping. The cyclical squeeze means tightening belts, begging and borrowing, and strategies of "self-exploitation" reminiscent of Chayanov's Russian peasants. In the industrial world, formal piecework or overtime systems, or moonlighting and other illegal earnings, allow some scope for this "intensification" of labor, but the main effect is to force women (and often children) out into the lower reaches of the labor market. This has always been resented as a deflationary assault on men's earnings, and part of the argument for the "family wage" was to stem the hemorrhaging of women's work out of the home.[40] Although a man's salary has also "freed" his wife to attend to her domestic duties, the higher levels of compensation seem to have dampened the same criticisms. Indeed, the recent rise of the salaried wife is viewed with some unease (one male informant called it "double-dipping"), especially if there are no children.[41]

Growth – the keyword of modernity – is deeply embedded in professional ideals.[42] It applies interdependently to the career advancement of the healthy young professional and to the maturation of industrial society. In its heyday, the salary tied the professional body to the national economy, with the welfare of the bourgeois family as its justification. A salary structure "programs" reproduction, allowing professionals to plan ahead, and to move wealth and class status from one generation to the next in ways which are denied the proletariat. A reliable flow of wealth which expands over the long term makes family projects possible, while wages reduce economic perspectives to daily or weekly reckonings. Dependence on "family ties" is a *physical* survival strategy for the working class, and a *political* tactic ("good breeding") for those who dominate them. This sheds further light on the sanctimonious "family values" which the middle classes have always tried to foist on the wage-earning masses.

The decline of the salariat

Up to the middle of the twentieth century, salary-earners were the fastest-growing component of the professions.[43] Salaried lawyers, and most other professionals working for institutions, earned more than their private-practice, fee-earning counterparts until after World War II, when the position reversed.[44] The salariat has been weakened by the inflation of its own ranks, by the restructuring of the industrial economies which has polarized wealth and squeezed the middle classes, by the diminished capacity of organizations to fund careers, by the rise of market individualism over ideals of social equity, and by a decline in the value of formal learning on which the claims of professional authority have hitherto depended.

Up to the 1960s, any occupation offering services to the public, from shop assistants to masseuses, sought admission to the professions. They formed associations, certified and disciplined members, and hoped to offer recruits the dignity of a career. Lacking solid institutional support, increasing numbers of professionals have been obliged to work for fees – the elite term for piecework or time-work. Superficially, this has been no great hardship: by the 1960s self-employed professionals in the US outnumbered the salariat but earned on average almost twice as much ($12,048 a year).[45] By 1981 recruits to private law firms earned 50 percent more than those entering public service, and nearly three time more when they reached the top ranks.[46] As professionals were pitted against each other in short-term competition the old guild structures began to crumble, along with the promise of lifetime increments in earnings. Fewer than half of doctors and lawyers are members of the American Medical and Bar Associations, even though the lawyers doubled their numbers in the US to 732,000 between 1960 and 1985.[47] "Professionalism is the law's apple pie and motherhood," but while publicity seeks to pump up self-esteem, critics speak "with some emotion about a decline in values, the triumph of greed, the transformation of law from a public good to a marketplace commodity and a 'profession' degenerating into a mere 'business.'"[48] Broader solidarities among the professions were also eroding: "When physicians threatened to exchange information about prospective patients who had previously sued for medical malpractice, lawyers responded with a threat to provide patients with a list of doctors who had been sued."[49]

These movements reflect major changes in the industrial economies. The liberal dream of a "post-industrial" society in which we could all be middle-class has been shattered by the relentless polarization of wealth and power. "Corporate restructuring" since the 1970s has shifted industrial production to peripheral countries and transformed the structures of employment. The new vocabulary of "downsizing," "outsourcing," "flexibility," etc, disguises what Harrison and Bluestone have called a "one-sided class war" on labor, involving shrinking earnings, increasing workloads, and cuts to part-time employment. Operating in rapidly changing global markets, firms have lost both the need for and the ability to sustain long-term employment patterns of the sort associated with salary structures. The "vertical disintegration" of big corporations means that they can no longer provide their own employees with opportunities for upward mobility.[50] Managers, acutely aware of the surge in the number of workers in the US below the poverty line from around 23 million in 1973 to 32 million in 1986, have been especially beset with a "fear of falling." With fractured careers becoming the norm rather than the exception, the maxim is "take what you can get – today." For the younger generation especially, respect for professional privileges is fading along with prospects of long-term security. Their seniors have always promised them that if they wait they will be rewarded, but now they find their upward mobility blocked by elders who won't get off the gravy train. Rather than making personal sacrifices, senior professionals have usually responded to economic downturns by shrinking their junior ranks.[51]

The pervasive effects of "deskilling" in the restructured industrial economies have extended to the professional managerial class. Today's financial or computer moguls have little need for college degrees, and managers of today's fast-moving enterprises prefer to train their own staff on the job. In the heyday of the professions, academics played a central role in turning knowledge into salaries and building the paper barriers (the highest of which must, of course, be reserved for the professors themselves). Historically, medicine and law set the standards, and thereafter people were made to plod through examinations before they could sell houses or insurance – usually on the pretext of protecting the public from unscrupulous agents. Thus "it is virtually impossible to work as a clown in a major American circus today without a diploma from Clown College in Venice, Florida, which admitted only 60 out of the 3,000 applicants in 1985."[52] Until the middle of the twentieth century a certifiably "good education" subsumed a broad range of other social aptitudes and graces, ranging from probity and prudence to talk and table manners. These took a generation or two to consolidate, and maintaining them was hard social work. They were necessary to resist the intrusion of outsiders into the established professional ranks. The declining value of certificates in buying secure employment has contributed to the much-lamented "dumbing-down" of academic studies, and the loss of both tenure privileges and self-respect among faculty. The gap between the academic and practising wings of each profession has widened dramatically. In 1954 Harvard President Derek Bok's options for a career in law (city or town, public or private, teaching or practicing) entailed just a few hundred dollars difference in annual starting salary, but by 1987 the choice was between teaching for $16,000 a year, or working on Wall Street for $65,000–70,000.[53] Scholars have become increasingly interested in their own survival, and have been moved, perhaps by jealousy, to make potentially suicidal assaults on the wickedness of their more successful professional colleagues.[54]

"Executive overcompensation"

Although the pay differentials are not in themselves new, their extremities and some of the devices used to secure these are. The contrasts are stark and much cited. While the real value of the wages of the 80 percent of Americans who are "production and non-supervisory workers" fell 18 percent between 1979 and 1989 to $258 per week, "the real annual pay of corporate chief executives increased by 19 percent, and by 66 percent after taxes."[55] By the end of the 1980s "the total compensation of CEOs in the largest two hundred companies *averaged* almost $3 million per year."[56] The number of persons declaring annual *incomes* in excess of $1 million rose sixfold in a decade to 52,019 in 1991. Fifty companies examined by *Fortune* magazine each paid its leading executive in excess of $5 million, rising to $11 million at Philip Morris and $15 million at General Electric.[57]

Plato thought that no one in a community should earn more than five times the pay of the lowest-paid worker. At the end of the nineteenth century the financier J. P. Morgan thought it should not be more than twenty times. Subsequently national leaders have dickered about the proportion and its effects on inflation, but today the sky is evidently the limit for executive pay. Differentials in big corporations in excess of a hundred to one are quite normal. "There's no question that in the mind of the general public top executive pay constitutes a national scandal."[58] "The corporate boss is now Hollywood's favorite villain," John Stossel reports.[59] But the cries of "shameless-

"I'm overcompensated, but I'm not overcompensated enough."

Plate 6   Overcompensation; cartoon by Weber in the *New Yorker* (1998)

ness" seem to have done little to stem the "gluttony" and "bloat." Surveying these complaints, Callinicos notes that the new corporate elite seem infatuated with their own individuality and oblivious to public perception of themselves as a new rapacious class which "overconsumes," spends rather than saves, displays rather than listens, prospers pathologically, instigates the polarization of rich and poor, and wallows in the sensuousness of wealth.[60] An earlier generation of reformers who pinned their hopes on sane "Scientific Management" by a professional elite would have been aghast. Walter Lippmann once hoped that the graduates of the new business schools would lift American business out of the "cesspool of commercialism."[61] Instead they, especially the overpaid lawyers and doctors, stand accused of dragging the whole professional cadre down into the mire.[62]

In 1963 Burgess noted that "the largest and most significant part of the top executive pay package" was still the salary. He reckoned

Lecherous pirates go gluttonous

In February 1997 shareholders raged over the Walt Disney Company's cash-and-stock payoff of its departing President, Michael Ovitz ($96 million for less than a year's work, with estimates still rising). Then in December of the same year, in what the *Los Angeles Times* called "a watershed event for American business compensation," Walt Disney chairman Michael Eisner exercised accumulated stock options to the tune of about $565 million. The 7.3 million shares Eisner sold were from a deal to retain his services struck in January 1989. In 1992 he cashed in $202 million worth of options, and after the record breaking payout in 1997 he still had options on an estimated 8.7 million shares. Graef Crystal, who designed Eisner's contract, estimated that his total take from Disney was close to a billion dollars. "In a statement, Eisner acknowledged that his action 'will undoubtedly provoke much discussion.'" He donated 300,000 of his shares to his family charitable foundation.

Meantime, public attention was focused on the company's efforts to make "Pirates of the Caribbean," the highly popular ride set up by Walt Disney himself thirty years ago, more morally respectable. Ironically, the motif has been shifted from lechery to gluttony: "Critics howled at the park's decision to tinker with the famous chase scene to depict pirates in hot pursuit of a good meal rather than terrified village maidens . . . A hungry buccaneer who used to chase a young maiden now swipes at fleeing chickens with a net. A drunken brigand still stalks the cantina waitress – but only for the wine she now carries on her tray. A big-bellied pirate now holds a turkey leg aloft in triumph, rather than the woman's shoe and negligee from past years."

Disrespect for women is out, leaving the bad name of piracy to ride on greed, alcoholism, domestic violence, cruelty to animals, theft, and a few other vices. Disney executives acknowledged with some pleasure that the controversy had revitalized public interest in the ride.

Los Angeles Times, February 26, 1997, March 8, 1997,
December 5, 1997.

that salaries accounted for 74.1 percent of the total earnings of top executives in 1937, 60.9 percent in 1948, and 55.5 percent in 1958. The "career salary curves" of CEOs were extraordinarily steep – rising by a multiple of as much as 160.[63] At this level rewards were already parting company with the notion of professional career-linked increments. Although technically the salary remains the basis of executive payments, the word rarely appears in Graef Crystal's

---

Graef Crystal

"To justify my existence as a compensation consultant," says Graef Crystal, "I always liked to think that I was ultimately working for the shareholders, using that second-most ancient motive, greed . . . to help make society more productive and hence improve the lives of everyone, not merely CEOs." He declares, "I don't think I was ever for sale" but he now takes moral comfort in writing "critical articles for publications like *Financial World, Fortune*, and the *New York Times*." As an adjunct professor at Berkeley, Crystal teaches a course on "Management Reward Systems" which "is known more informally among the Berkeley Business School students as 'Greed 259A.' "

Executive pay in the US is "out of control," says Crystal. "It is not the core which is rotten, it's also the system." But for all his piety ("at least I've never been rewarded for being a gobbler"), Crystal has had something less than a Pauline conversion from his service to mammon. His faith in "the market" remains unshaken – as does his belief in some very old passions: "we have a decent chance to put greed to work in the service of the U.S. economy and to begin to regain the economic glory that once was ours. If we do nothing, our dwindling competitiveness will dwindle even more. And, irony of ironies, the widening gap between CEO pay and worker pay may even inspire a new Marx and a new Lenin, but with American names, and all at a time when the original Marx and the original Lenin have been so discredited." Crystal wants to see executive excesses taxed out of existence, greater accountability to shareholders, and "proper" behavior in the marketplace – which he quaintly defines as "arm's length negotiation involving an informed buyer and an informed seller."

Crystal 1991: *passim.*

1991 critique of "executive compensation," *In search of excess.* Base salaries are still staggeringly large, but executive earnings have been inflated by other sorts of payment, the most infamous of which is the *stock option* (in UK "share option"). This gives the executive the right to claim company shares at prices current when the deal was struck some months or years earlier (the "strike price"), and to sell them at today's market value. Stocks held this way doubled during the 1990s to 6.6 percent of all outstanding shares in the US.[64] The idea is to induce executives to do things which will boost the value of company shares, but criticism of such deals centers on the short-term rather than growth-promoting tactics they encourage. Cashed-in stock options do not come from company "earnings" but from stock market value, which can be pumped up by a couple of words to the media, a change of faces at the top, the mere hint of a new project, an advertising blowout, or (a ruse favored by shareholders) some brisk pruning of the labor force. The very notion that a new CEO is likely to take such action is often enough to push up share values, and the CEO does not have to be very smart to anticipate when to cash his options. Crystal, architect of many such deals, points out that stock options are virtually risk-free, since the executive has no obligation to buy. They are monuments to risk-aversion rather than speculative imagination, part of an elaborate set of safety nets which CEOs have constructed for themselves – at the corporation's expense. And "since key executives receive not one but many stock option grants during their careers, the chances to become seriously rich are multiplied."[65] Ironically, some of the largest gains are made when mergers, which cost the CEO his own job, drive up stock values. Despite the conflict of interest which stock options imply, they are legal and even enjoy fiscal protection.[66]

Stock options have mutated into a wide array of executive pay tricks, such as the "Bonus Units" in which the "strike price" is raised *above* that day's market price, conveying an immediate profit plus the dividends which would routinely accrue to the shares over time. If it seems that share options may attract too much hostile attention, they can be cosmetically repackaged as "Performance Units," one unit often comprehending thousands of shares. According to Crystal, the "Golden Parachute" is "one of the most egregious perks of all." This is an agreed sum payable to an executive "in the event his company is taken over and he is turned out." Since it is usually underperforming companies which get taken over "the CEO ends up getting paid lots of money for abysmal performance."[67] Public reaction being intense, stiffer tax was slapped on these parachutes – but companies responded with supplementary "Tax Benefit" agreements to cover losses the executive might suffer. Nothing, it seems, will thwart executive overcompensation. Another ruse is the "Supplemental Executive Retirement Plan," which is a means of evading the 1974 Employee Retirement Income Security Act cap on pensions. Special "non-qualified" pensions give the executive extra, much bigger benefits on top of the "ordinary" pension associated with his salary, the costs and the risks being borne out of the company's running costs. And so the list of perks continues, through inflated health plans, to the payment of elaborate housing, travel, entertainment, and other "allowances." Finally, if all these were not enough, there is the

"Golden Coffin," a contract paid to an executive for a period extending beyond his death, for the benefit of his family.[68]

Any moral cover which the metaphor of growth may have provided has been blown away by the breathtaking scale of these gains. The link between inequity and illegitimacy is captured in the characteristically British epithet "*greedy bastard*," much used in press assaults on the new executives of recently privatized public utilities.[69] In their rare attempts at apology, CEOs declare that life at the top is short, brutish, and ugly, and that as doyens of the free market they are bound to take whatever they can get, as fast as they can. In all the arguments about just and unjust deserts one thing is certain: they have little to do with the modern logic of the marketplace, over which the CEOs themselves are supposed to have some special mastery. All the talk of head-hunting and blood-letting, of life in a corporate jungle where survival depends on "rugged individualism," must be taken with more than a grain of salt.[70] The existence of a "market for executives" has long been in doubt. Very few top executives change jobs often, and the most conspicuous scandals have been about contract *re*-negotiation. CEOs like to compare their rewards with those of stars in sports or entertainment – who are also frequently accused of greed, but whose rewards are more easily justified by box office receipts or goals scored. It is virtually impossible to gauge what a CEO is worth: "In the perfectly competitive world so dear to classical economists, all chief executives would receive amounts approximating what they added to the net profits of their company," says Bok. But "While everyone can point to serious flaws in the market for executive services, no one knows exactly what a truly competitive paycheck would be."[71] Warren Buffett, doyen of the super-rich, thinks the very idea is absurd: "You'll never pay a really top-notch executive . . . as much as they are worth. A million, $3 million, or $10 million, it's still peanuts."[72]

"Reputation" is usually offered in a last-ditch defence of executive worth, but the reckoning is still strictly cash. Publications like *Forbes Magazine*, responding to prurient interest, keep the tally. "You're on this list, you see, and you want to move up the list. You want to be number one," says media mogul Ted Turner. "America is about competition and rising above that competition. That's the basis of what makes our economy and our society tick . . . Why sure it's greedy."[73] In this sense, securing a "reputable" CEO is an end in itself: a record of overpayment is now valued above any other socially vested skill or formal qualification. The idea of an *under*-compensated CEO

Private greed in the public corporation

In mid-1997, the British Broadcasting Corporation's 22,000 employees accepted a 2.8 percent wage increase. Justifying his own 18 percent pay hike (to £354,000 [$566,000]) the BBC's Director General, Mr John Birt, blamed the market: "We've no choice but to be in the market if we want this institution to remain strong . . . The market moves and we have to move with it." The raise was to bring Mr Birt's pay more into line with other (commercial) broadcasting chiefs. But journalist Rob Brown complains that Mr Birt is not a media mogul, he is a privileged public servant. The BBC does not have to compete in the media marketplace, because 95 percent of its programming budget comes from the licence fees all British viewers are obliged to pay.

The Independent [London] July 9, 1997; *The Times* [London], July 10, 1997.

How rich?

To be *rich* these days you need a lot of income and the leisure to enjoy it, which means living on invested assets. According to *Barron's Magazine*, to have about $100k to spend each year ("Beer and Pretzel rich" – in the top 5 percent of individual taxpayers) you'll need $2.2 million in assets. To be "filet mignon rich" on about a quarter of a million dollars a year (the top 1 percent of taxpayers) you'll need an investment portfolio of $4.55 million. And to be "yacht and limo" rich, with something approaching $2 million a year, you should reckon on investment wealth of about $38 million. But for today's super-rich this is still peanuts.

Barron's Online, October 20, 1999.

violates both how the executive niche is defined and conceptions of corporate fitness. Thus CEOs have acquired the extraordinary entitlement to pay themselves more or less what they want, without any recognizable "market" constraints, but at the expense of the corporations they are supposed to serve.[74] If shareholders ask questions, escalating rewards are justified by what CEOs in rival corporations are paid. Early critics like Schumpeter and Veblen pointed out that professional roles could be better grasped through their parasitic organization of *consumption* rather than conventional liberal economic categories of exchange or Marxian categories of production.[75]

Professionals measure their worth by visible affluence: the right address, the right car, the right clothes. But not even Veblen could have imagined that *professional* worth (as opposed to capitalist or proletarian worth) could be reduced to such a crude, absolute, and apparently limitless index as gross income.

In many ways the portfolio of plutocratic tricks is just a more flagrant version of the old game from which the construction of the modern salary emerged more than a century ago: manipulating ideas and organizations to secure privileged rewards. But although stock options and golden parachutes are "time payments" of a sort, they are not geared to a career or a life. They are related in no positive way to growth, either in the metaphoric sense of corporate progress or, as any idiot can see, in terms of physical needs and capacities. The salary, for all its vices, was based on patience, discreetness, durable service to a single enterprise, and the deferral of rewards in status as well as cash. Without this sort of life-bound discipline, the greed of people masquerading as professionals is starkly exposed.

11

Corporate Greed

> **Corporation:** a succession or collection of people author-
> ized by law to act as one individual and regarded as
> having a separate existence from the people who are its
> members . . .
> a belly, *esp* a pot belly (*colloq*).
>
> *Chambers dictionary*

The big difference between greed now and in the past is that
today we can do it on a larger scale than ever before. There is much
more to want and it can be pursued with fewer inhibitions within the
protective cover of much bigger groups of people. But none of this
means that greed has become superhuman, or more justifiable.

One of our most important inventions to absolve us from the guilt
of greed has been the *corporation*. Dating back to the early mercantile communities, it teased individuals out of the community networks
in which their lives and activities were embedded, and regrouped
them according to more narrowly defined interests and purposes.
Repackaged into new corporate bodies, people could do business
with one another more concertedly and at less personal risk, in ever-
expanding arenas. Once the principle that many people could be entitled to act as one was established, it could be extended indefinitely
to embrace the city, the nation state, even the international confed-
eration. This powerful idea has been indispensable in the making
of the modern world, and we have many pressing needs to believe

in it. But the fiction that corporations *are* bodies can be lethally confusing.

In legal terms, the corporation is a super-person with a single identity, name, and official seal, whose purpose is to transcend the rights, obligations, and *lives* of its individual members, for their joint and long-term benefit. As elaborated in English law, the corporation can contract debts without obligating its members personally, and hold property beyond their individual claims. Like any body, it is reckoned to have a mind of its own and a need to grow, but in other respects it is very different from the real bodies on behalf of whom it does business. For example, it defies death: through the right of *succession*, the corporation is entitled to move the property and interests of its members through time indefinitely, regardless of their individual comings and goings. Only the law can declare the corporation dead. And yet, in an ultimate reckoning with physical decay, the law is also obliged to do so when the last member dies. The corporation's claims to immortality can make the bodily metaphor look morally grotesque. "Did you ever expect a corporation to have a conscience," asked an eighteenth-century Lord Chancellor, "when it has no soul to be damned, and no body to be kicked?"[1]

This is probably why corporate bodies tend to avoid anatomical images of feeding, sex, and death in their official publicity, trademarks, etc., favoring the botanical symbolism of flowering, fruiting, and sturdy arboreal growth. Real bodies have a furtive existence within the modern corporation, apparent in the jokes which pile up around toilets and cafeterias, the mock privacy of work cubicles, or the legendary subversive lust at office parties. Being drawn into a bigger and better sort of body can never fully release the corporate member from the real agonies of physical growth and decay. Nor has life within the new metaphorical body freed the merchant from old-fashioned accusations of greed. Since the days of the medieval guild, each corporation has had to justify its selfish interests in progressively larger arenas and, more starkly, against that vague super-corporation, "The Public." The biggest firms now spend vast sums of money on spectacular effusions about their value to such transcendent entities as "The American People," "The Environment," "The Planet", or even "The Future."

To the extent that their lives have depended on it, the middle classes have struggled long and hard to put the best appearance on their corporations, but they have always been regarded as "conspiracies to defraud the public."² The dilemma at the heart of every corporation is that it is an alliance of selfish individuals, united mainly in their opposition to other corporations (including the city, the state). Its purpose is to cut through some of the social complexities in which real bodies have to develop, and to reassemble *aspects* of those personalities as *members* of a new, synthetic body. The burning question is whether this new body, defined by law rather than by nature, has the obligations, as well as the rights, of the old. If a basic purpose has been to escape the moral density of real life and allow freer trade, is the morally thin atmosphere of company law enough to sustain the corporation?³ Some businessmen fear that markets will not "work" if they are fettered by motives like public-spiritedness. Some believe that such motives are an essential part of efficient business practice anyway. And others argue that social obligations are a cost all reputable businesses *ought* to bear, for without moral discipline the fabric of democratic society on which free markets themselves depend will collapse. And when a big corporation falls apart, the people who comprise it stand starkly revealed in the media spotlight in all their human frailty.⁴

However, the real moral hazard is that most of the "members" of big modern corporations have little to do with its activities. Today's capitalists are not robber barons but the mass of small investors who put their money in trust funds and bonds which are managed by the executive officers of big financial corporations. The corporate executive would say with little hesitation that his primary obligation is to the corporate "shareholders" or "stockholders," large and small. Their gain is his sacred trust; but as a professional his own gains are none of their business. The executive does not rub shoulders with small investors and, as the stage-managed annual meetings make clear, has little accountability to them. The "shareholders" who matter are mostly other corporations (pension and mutual funds, money-management firms) whose interests are transacted in huge block "votes" by the professional managers. Since the executive often owns or has options on blocks of these shares himself, there is an obvious conflict of interest. Whatever his legal obligations, an economic agent cannot rationally pursue his own interests *and* the diverse interests of many others simultaneously. Liberal economics has no theory of, and no prescriptions for, corporate morality or the social responsibility of businessmen. But the basic assumption that self-interest is socially beneficial, and will deliver the best possible moral outcome, simply acknowledges that efficient executives will always put their personal interests first. A social conscience, says Milton Friedman, is socialist claptrap which is directly at odds with free market principles. But by the same token the idea that an executive officer "represents" his stockholders even-handedly is capitalist claptrap.[5]

So long as we, the private investors, can satisfy our greed under the cover of corporate transactions, we have no need to complain. When markets are bullish, who cares about executive overcompensation? If everyone's shares are appreciating, there's no cause for recrimination or guilt. By the same misplaced logic we sat back and watched the US government bail out the delinquent savings and loan funds in the 1990s, under the delusion that it was not "our money" which was paying the villains. The Robin Hood morality that "it is not greedy to take something from someone who can afford it" has rebounded on corporations that are being bilked by alienated employees. The new cosmetic term for these people who actually produce the goods and services is "stakeholder." As unions and the apparatus of collective bargaining have collapsed, efforts have been made to draw these "stakeholders" into the corporate ethos, but many of them see themselves as victims, and the corporate body as fair game. "Long Hours, Low Pay and Plain Old Greed Motivate Thieves" declares a *Los Angeles Times* headline. "Workplace fraud" in the US amounts to an estimated $400 billion a year – equivalent to 6 percent of the total US gross domestic product. The Association of Certified Fraud Examiners in Austin, Texas, computes the loss as $9 per employee per day for the average company. Urged by relative deprivation and "disgust with corporate greed or dishonest executives," employees feel entitled to adjust their own wages by theft.[6] The more the corporate body distances itself from the lives of its personnel, the more it sheds both the costs and the benefits of moral restraint. If everyone knows the corporation cannot really "get hurt," it is more exposed to internal predation.

With its claims to immortality the corporation has become the vehicle for "millennial capitalism," the intoxicating, pot-of-gold dream that riches come from nowhere, instantaneously. The old, magical notion of money with a reproductive life of its own has resurfaced in a new generation of capitalist miracles. More than seventy high-tech companies in California's Silicon Valley went public during 1996, creating an average of sixty-two millionaires every day.[7] These tales wreak havoc in countries which have recently turned to capitalism for redemption. A booming firm in Changsha, China, which produces foot massage machines, distributes its product through a teetering pyramid sales scheme from which only a tiny number of people near the apex can possibly profit.[8] Little wonder that at the turn of the millennium political commentary is in the grip of pessimism, dominated by the idea that we are about to be overwhelmed and repossessed by our own destructive nature.[9] Kim Polese, the 38-year-old co-founder of Marimba Inc., a software firm whose share values soared to $1.4 billion at its public offering in 1999, fears that "there will be a backlash against all the greed." Her new-rich friends are depressed. "I feel more and more the greed factor, and these absurd expectations that you should be worth $50 million by the time you are 30, or you have failed in some way."[10]

The fears are of social as well psychic damage. Luttwak links the wealth-polarizing effects of "today's technology-powered, deregulated, globalizing 'turbo-charged' capitalism" to the expansion of a criminalized underclass. The "United States is on its way to acquiring the income-distribution characteristics of a Third World country, with a truly very rich top 1 percent and a substantial minority (about 12 percent) which remains in poverty even though fully employed". In December 1994, one in 189 Americans was incarcerated, an increase from one in 480 in 1980. While truly hi-tech global firms like Boeing trim costs and expand profits as never before, their staffs declare – with good reason – that they do not feel "secure." The political response, evocative of inter-war Europe, is the expansion of repressive, punitive law. "It is no coincidence that prohibitions multiply when the middle class is especially insecure."[11]

People around the world now look to the corporation not for a long-term commitment to the fulfilment of needs, but for the instant satisfaction of consumer desires. The metaphor of organic growth is drained of meaning, and the corporations themselves expand by conspicuous cannibalistic consumption, the larger monopolies gobbling up the smaller. The tiny chance of getting rich has all but demolished the ancient quest of the middle classes for *security*, and with it the ambition of a *career* which will support the raising of the next generation. Now that the carefully forged institutional links between human growth and wealth are crumbling, the professional can only hope to seize the moment and pursue rapid, short-term gains. But to be wealthy is to be insecure, turning the provision of physical security itself (alarm systems, armed rapid-response agencies) into one of the fastest-expanding industries.

The question is not, as it once seemed, whether the modern jug-gernaut of growth is unstoppable, but whether growth in its most meaningful bodily sense still has any place in our corporate interests and activities. Back in the 1950s and 1960s, every state in the world, with the exception of the USA and a handful of trade enclaves like Hong Kong and Liechtenstein, tried to make integrated, long-term development plans. Now these five-, ten-, or twenty-year national projects have succumbed to annual unbalanceable budgets and blind faith in the Invisible Hand. However much we may sympathize with the utopian plea that "Small is Beautiful", all we have left as a measure of progress is *scale*: bigger and badder executives, corporations, states, confederations.

As the grand dreams of steady progress towards worldwide moder-nity fade and disillusionment with global capitalism takes over, our time horizons have shrunk to the fleeting instants of market transac-tions. Banks are shedding their old pretence of permanence: marble pillars have yielded to plasterboard and "virtual" electronic pres-ences. Everyone waits for the software giants to vaporize in a few minutes of hectic stock-trading. The imagery draws in towards the gut, with talk of feeding and glut. The dynastic pretensions of some of the old robber barons at least expressed a longer-term interest in growth, images of lust and avarice rather than gluttony, albeit dogged by fears that the house would collapse within the proverbial three generations. Today's enterprises are caught in a vicious circle: where capital lacks a close connection with real lives, enterprises can be very short-lived. In the past, when productive enterprises were *necessarily* locked into human life processes (the family farm or firm), these pro-vided a fabric of continuity, a program of obligations which tran-scended the fast talk of the marketplace and the short cycles of production. While we are warned that America will degenerate like Nigeria into "A Nation Ravaged by Greed,"[12] it is just possible that on the periphery of the world system, in Trinidad or Kenya, new "organic" forms of capitalism are emerging which are more tightly linked to the lives of local people.[13] But there is another, ugly side to the coin: seeking a measure of stability, big business has once again been taking a predatory interest in that old, life-defined corporation "the family." As manufacturing collapses in rich countries like the US, exploitative tactics of "putting out" minor industrial processes to underpaid "homeworkers" – mostly women, and mostly in regions of poverty – have been revived.[14] Pushing what is euphemistically called "flexible accumulation" far beyond the cover of the law rebounds in bizarre ways on legislation itself: in April 1999, European countries struggling to meet the terms of admission to economic union were formally allowed to take account of prostitution, drug dealing, tax evasion, and other vices when describing the size of their economies. "We are actively working on how to pick up any illegal activity which isn't already showing up," an official of the UK Office for National Statistics promised.[15]

As complaints of greed have become more strident, moral apologies for it have become increasingly brazen. In his Cato Institute web page on "How to fight the greed-and-envy lobby," Stephen Moore complains that "Class envy is not just wrongheaded but dangerously subversive to the uniquely American idea that success and reward in this country are interlinked." He urges that "Republicans should – no, they must – launch a vigorous counterassault."[16] According to Tad Tuleja,

> public opinion is not the last word on ethics, and in spite of what the Bible says about avarice, greed is not itself unethical. Using a "checked utilitarian" standard, we can say that the gobbling CEO becomes unethical when, in the act of gobbling, he takes food out of somebody else's mouth. To determine the rightness or wrongness of the bonuses we need to know who was harmed.[17]

This statement is heavily loaded: something or someone knows better than the "public" – and God – what is right and wrong; science (that "checked utilitarian" standard) tells us when greed can be OK; executive greed is OK so long as it harms the right people. The only glimmer of redemption in this dismal logic is its gravitation to the belly: greed is still, basically, about *gobbling*.

Panic lurks beneath the surface of modern life: *"Wacky Week Mixed Greed and Fear"* declared a *New York Times* headline, as stock prices collapsed in the Fall 1997. "The marketplace is made of human beings," wailed Alfred Goldman of A. G. Edwards & Sons. There was "real depression among supposedly professional money managers who panicked." The Psychology Correspondent told *Times* readers that "Some See 'Herd Behavior' Behind the Market Swings . . . emotions, not rational analysis, may be driving fund managers and others, social scientists say."[18] When the corporation falls apart, the little people within it stand revealed. "The institutional infrastructure may do the dirty work," says Berke, "but behind faceless mandarins and impenetrable group processes there lies personal praxis – that is, the specific actions of strong-willed, aggrandizing, hate-filled personalities."[19]

Today we need social theory as never before, but we need it to reunite us with our estranged bodies, and to rediscover the sense of humility which a view of the world at this scale entails. The idea that desires are infinitely expandable without moral cost is historically recent, and we will have to use our wits and our guts to resist this self-destructive urge. Any tendency for meanings to get separated from our frail bodies is neither in our personal nor in our collective interest. It seems the idiots, a step or two ahead of the scholars as usual, have already taken note of this. In the cinematographic images of the 1980s, heyday of corporate scandals, vomit was a recurrent motif: hardly a movie appeared without its puking scene – startling, repulsive, darkly satirical. "In its purest form, as defined by Veblen, conspicuous consumption is consumption of the totally useless."[20] Corpses and feces are the epitome of disutility, and their consumption – a society engorged on decay – has been a recurrent, savage image of younger artists.

The specter of greed takes its seat at the corporate banquet, cutting the diners down to size, questioning their individual motives in the collective pursuit of more. Greed will not be duped by the idea that it is institutions which are "greedy" – it's *us*. Corporations provide the scale economies which help us grow, but when the real link with our bodies is ignored they provide opportunities for excesses far beyond our needs. This is where that old, critical instrument greed jabs its accusing finger. Greed drags the behavior of the elegantly tailored business executive down to those root feelings of hunger, glut, and disgust. Elaborate pretenses to the contrary, everyone is reducible to the functions of their own bodies. The community, the corporation, the class can offer no lasting protection from this scathing critique. Nor should our scholarly apologies remain exempt from the indictment.

Notes

1 Introduction

1 On poetry see for example Wakoski 1969. The song "More" by Stephen Sondheim is rendered with exquisite passion by Madonna on her album *I'm Breathless* (Sire/Warner Brothers, 1990).
2 Ryvita advertisement, *Radio Times* (UK) July 1–7, 1995.
3 Hendra 1994: 57.
4 *Los Angeles Times*, November 11, 1997.
5 *Los Angeles Times*, March 16, 1985.
6 Michael Douglas as Gordon Gekko in *Wall Street*. Twentieth Century Fox 1987, directed by Oliver Stone, screenplay by Stanley Weiser and Oliver Stone.
7 *The Economist*, November 1, 1997: 27.
8 www.softdisk.com/sd/greed/cdrom.html (January 1997).
9 www.weeworld.com/greed.
10 "I can grow" says an investment banker in a mug-shot advertisement. "I work for J. P. Morgan" (*New Yorker*, July 19, 1999).
11 MGM, *c*.1921. See Weinberg 1972; Rosenbaum 1993. The movie *Greedy* (Universal Studios 1994) starring Michael J. Fox is a playful update on the McTeagues.
12 Hendra 1994: 57–8.

2 What do We Mean by Greed?

1 See Bynum on the conflation of gluttony and lust in medieval Europe. In this period of resurgent famine, "gorging and vomiting, luxuriating in food until food and body were almost synonymous, became in folk literature an image of unbridled sensual pleasure" (1997: 139).

2 "Lechery" derives from the old French *lechier*, to lick.

3 As far afield as China, dictionaries of the communist era recognize a distinction between greed for *food* and greed for *profit*. The Chinese character in question alludes loosely to *wealth*. Classical Chinese dictionaries evoke avarice, covetousness, and grasping corruptness, as in the behavior of *officials*.

4 *Reader's Digest encyclopedic dictionary*; also issued as *Funk & Wagnalls standard college dictionary* (New York 1966). Note the reversed order given in the 1902 edition of *Webster's dictionary*: "Having a keen appetite for food and drink; ravenous; voracious; very hungry . . . (2) Having a keen desire for anything; vehemently desirous; eager to obtain; avaricious; as, *greedy* of gain." See also *Webster's new international dictionary* (2nd edn, 1955): "1. Having a keen appetite for food and drink; ravenous; very hungry . . . 2. Having, or characterized by, eager or keen, and often selfish desire; specif. eager for wealth; avaricious . . . GREEDY implies keen and excessive appetite or craving for food or (figuratively) gain."

5 In similar vein, the fifth-century monk John Cassian viewed sin as a causal progression from gluttony to lust to greed, and thence to anger, sadness and sloth, vainglory and pride (Falk 1994: 47).

6 Common responses to my request for a definition of greed are "Just wanting more;" "more than you've got already, always more;" "*sheer* more."

7 Harris 1971: 1372.

8 See Willard 1983: 96–7.

9 Mintz 1996: 6.

10 Mennell 1997: 316.

11 Berke 1988: 14, 26.

12 This was the visceral, pragmatic definition of greed proposed to me by one informant. Chocolate often figures in allusions to greed, presumably for a very wide range of historic, economic, metabolic, and other reasons.

13 B. Williams 1993: 219, 222. Neu (1980) has made a somewhat similar transactional exploration of jealousy, with its implications of love, fear, and a rival, real or imagined.

14 *Chambers dictionary* points out that this "Inner Man" facetiously mistakes the soul for the belly. In family lore, my cousin was inhabited during his adolescence by "Timothy Tapeworm." I simply had "hollow

legs." In ch. 4 of her book *Always hungry, never greedy* (1986: 60–73) Kahn gives a vivid account of the myth of the ravenous Tamoduko-rokoro – "the monster within" – which plagues the people of Wamira, Papua New Guinea (see chapter 8).

15 Interview by Kitty Felde, *Los Angeles Times*, January 23, 2000.
16 Hendra 1994: 57, 123–4.
17 William Shakespeare, *Henry V*, act IV, scene 3.
18 *The Times* [London], March 7, 1998.
19 Berry 1994: 46. In Plato's "model of the first city based on need satis-faction . . . we have perhaps the first enunciation of the crucial principle that need should be the measure or guideline of desire" (Berry 1994: 61).
20 Drug addiction is commonly assumed to proceed from an excess of desire, or the foolish exercise of a preference (see Braybrooke 1987: 265–8). In "an emotional statement" at the court hearing, Downey explained that he had been addicted since 8 years of age (*Los Angeles Times*, December 9, 1997).
21 See Berry 1994: 51, 49.
22 Berry 1986: 82.
23 Braybrooke 1987: 36.
24 See especially Sen 1981, 1994.
25 Mennell 1997: 316.
26 Many readers want to "correct" this to "desserts."
27 Rousseau 1911: 57.
28 The word "kleptocracy" was used to describe the regime of Mobutu Sese Seko, President of Zaire, until shortly before his death in Septem-ber 1997. At around $8 billion, his personal fortune was as large as his country's national debt (obituary and editorial, *The Times* [London] September 9, 1997).
29 See Frankfurt 1984: 12.
30 See for example Streeten 1981 and Stewart 1985. The notion of "basic needs" has acquired great currency, if only as a disembodied abstrac-tion. Consider, for example the first item on the International Organi-zation of Consumer Unions (now "Consumers International") basic charter: *"The right to basic needs"* (Tansey & Worsley 1995: 247–8). Can a need be right?
31 Tansey and Worsley 1995: 49, 55–6.
32 Advertisement, *Los Angeles Times*, January 4, 1998.
33 William Godwin 1793, *An enquiry concerning political justice*, 12.18.

3 Beastly Passions and Legitimate Desires

1 See especially Onians 1951.
2 Well into the nineteenth century, physician-philosophers like Cabanis and Moleschott reckoned that the brain secretes thoughts just as the

liver secretes bile, or the kidneys urine. If such ideas seem idiotic, we should ask ourselves how current scholarly assertions that the brain "*is*" a computer, and the mind merely "software," will look a few decades hence.

3   Nutton 1993: 288.
4   See Bunge 1980: 26.
5   Genesis, ch. 3. These biblical themes are explored by Sekora (1977: 23–29) in relation to the idea of *luxury*.
6   Aquinas, *On evil*, question XIV, article 1 (1995: 411, 418).
7   On Thomists, see especially Skinner 1978, vol. 1.
8   Skinner 1978: 2.358.
9   See Spicker 1970: 8–10.
10 Paradox 6: That the gifts of the body are better than those of the mind, or of fortune. From John Donne, *Prose and poems*, Everyman edition, Knopf, New York 1995, pp. 190–1.
11 Husserl 1960: 2.
12 Descartes, *The discourse on method* [1637] (1968: 54).
13 See Astington 1993.
14 See Dennett 1996: 2.
15 Russell 1961: 543. Descartes eventually died of cold in 1650, trying to teach philosophy at five in the morning, in Stockholm, to the young Queen Christina of Sweden.
16 This problem of "theory-theory" or "thought-thoughts" is nicely captured by H. A. Prichard [1940] (1968).
17 Descartes, *The meditations* [1641] (1968: 159, 167–8).
18 Russell 1961: 550.
19 See Matson 1966: 98.
20 See Leder 1990: 139; Wagner 1984.
21 Bunge 1980: 83.
22 Lockwood 1989: 310.
23 See especially J. Foster's defense of Cartesian dualism (1991).
24 Descartes, *Les passions de l'âme* [1649] art. 31 (1996: 119).
25 Ibid., art. 50 (1996: 132).
26 Ibid., art. 211 (1996: 228).
27 Spicker 1970: 11.
28 Arendt 1958: 287; and see Prigogine 1994: 95–6. One of the most passionate defences of dualism as the basic premise of liberal science was mounted by the historian of ideas Arthur Lovejoy [1930] (1996).
29 See Warner 1994: 13–14; Searle 1997: 198.
30 Descartes *The meditations* [1641] (1968: 164).
31 Searle 1997: 6.
32 J. Foster 1991.
33 See Searle's critique (1997).
34 Mandeville, *Fable of the bees; or, Private vices, publick benefits* (1714); and see Dumont 1977.

35 Hobbes, *The elements of law natural and politic* 1640: part one, *Human nature*, XIV (1994: 4, 11–14).
36 "Solitary, poore, nasty, brutish, and short" (Hobbes, *Leviathan* 1651: XIII).
37 See for example Gaskin (1994); Tuck (1996: 189–93).
38 Hobbes, *The elements of law natural and politic* 1640: part one, *Human nature*, IX (1994: 15).
39 See Gert 1996: 169.
40 Hume, *A treatise of human nature* [1739–40] (1972: 223).
41 Ibid., [1739], book II part 1 (1972: 37).
42 Hume, *Enquiries concerning human understanding* [1777], book III, part 2, section 2 (1975: 216–30).
43 Ibid., appendix II (1975: paragraphs 247–54).
44 Hume *A treatise of human nature* [1740], book III, section 2 (1972: 222–3).
45 Hirschman 1977: 42.
46 Hume *A treatise of human nature* [1739], book II, section 3 (1972: 98–102).
47 Hume *Enquiries concering the principles of morals*, para. 139, p. 176; *A treatise of human nature* [1740], book III, section 2 (1972: 229).
48 Dumont 1977: 79.
49 A. Smith *Theory of moral sentiments* I.ii.1.1 (1976: 27–8).
50 A. Smith, *An enquiry into the nature and causes of the wealth of nations* [1776], book 1, chapter 2 (1976: 26–7).
51 Ibid., book IV.i.10. (1970: 184–5).
52 Hirschman 1977: 107–8, 109.
53 Sen 1977: 343, 336.
54 Midgley 1995: 120. Anticipating a visit to the shopping mall, a friend of mine likes to exclaim "I feel a purchase coming on." Shopping to excess is now recognized as a treatable (i.e. embodied) disorder which Graham (1968: 43) calls "*oniomania.*"
55 For a critical view, see Gray 1987. A prime example is Nobel prize-winner Gary Becker's conviction "that the economic approach is applicable to all human behavior" and "to the biological world as well" (Becker 1981: x).
56 Frank 1988: ix, 254–5.
57 Alexander Pope, *An essay on man* 1732–4; 1: 207–32.
58 Mueller 1984: 159.
59 Kant [1796] 1978: 173, 174, 157.
60 Rousseau 1911: 56, 117.
61 *Forbes Magazine*, March 9, 1998.

4 Disciplining Greed

1   Searle 1994: 288.
2   See Tansey & Worsley 1995: 250.
3   Searle 1994: 288, 291.
4   See Masters & Carlson 1984: 438–9.
5   Campos & Barrett 1984: 229. See also Foster's explanation (1991) of the various "Identity theses," and Lockwood's characterization of cognitive scientists as "unregenerate Cartesians" (1989: 303).
6   See Davidson 1984; Kagan 1984.
7   The classic account of this mind-body integration is Onians, *The origins of European thought about the body* (1951).
8   Freud [1930] 1962.
9   Sarbin 1986: 84; and see for example the collection edited by Harré (1986). Prime influences have been the psychology of William James (see Kagan 1984: 38), and G. H. Mead's *Mind, self and society* (1934).
10   Geertz 1973: 81.
11   Armon-Jones 1986: 57.
12   White 1949: 141.
13   Durkheim [1914] 1960: 337, 326, 329; and see Durkheim [1895] 1938.
14   Friedman 1994: 74; and see Stocking 1982: 232.
15   See Barth's discussion (1975) of the Baktaman of New Guinea.
16   See Friedman 1994: 69.
17   Malinowski [1941] 1960.
18   See Lockwood 1989: 310.
19   Sahlins 1999: 407.
20   Lévi-Strauss 1964.
21   Chomsky 1968.
22   See Hammel 1972; MacCormack 1980: 3–4.
23   See for example the piling-up of symbolic oppositions by "Irresistible analogy" in Bourdieu's account of Kabyle culture (1990: 200–70).
24   Leach 1991: 108.
25   Boyer 1994: 296.
26   E. O. Wilson & Lumsden 1991: 403.
27   "The dirty secret of contemporary neuroscience," says Searle, is "the lack of a theory of how the brain works" (1997: 198).
28   Geertz 1973: 62.
29   Ingold 1990: 210.
30   Sahlins 1976: 66.
31   Geertz 1973: 82, 36.
32   See Kuper 1994. An example of the disjunction: "My theses are (1) that the capacity for ethics is a necessary attribute of human nature; and (2)

that moral norms are products of cultural evolution, not of biological evolution" (Ayala 1987: 235).

33 For approaches to bio-cultural "coevolution" see Durham 1978, Chagnon & Irons 1979, Boyd & Richerson 1986, Lumsden & Gushurst 1991, and Lopreato 1984; and see critical comments by Ingold (1990: 219–20; 1991: 241) and Robertson 1996. The coevolutionary hypothesis was earlier floated by Geertz (1973: 43–51). See also the bio-cultural "interactionism" sketched by Lewontin, Rose & Kamin (1984: 266, 282).

34 Daly & Wilson 1988: 5.

35 Ibid.: 6.

36 Goodwin 1985: 54.

37 Ingold 1990: 210.

38 Goodwin 1985: 46, 47, 49.

39 Rose 1998: 98.

40 See Ingold 1991: 368; and Midgley 1995: 161.

41 The new disciplinary framework of evolutionary psychology has been bold enough to seek a realist link – an "artificer" as Symons (1989, 1992) puts it – between genes and culture in the material structure of the adapted human mind. It is not yet clear what contribution this approach may make to closing the material–mental gap. For a discussion see Sinha 1985, Barkow 1984.

42 E. O. Wilson & Lumsden 1991: 410; and see the critical comments of Rose (1998: 296).

43 See B. Williams 1995: 97, 87.

44 Dawkins 1976.

45 As Hermann-Pillath points out " 'fitness' . . . cannot be the goal of individual behavior" (1991: 134) – there is no planning in the Darwinian adaptationist scheme (ibid.). See the attempts by Daly & Wilson (1988) to apply the tautologous notion of "expected fitness" to the analysis of homicide – in which it is apparently the genes, not the man with the pistol, which are doing the "expecting." For a radical attempt to justify evolutionary "intentionality" see Dennett 1996.

46 Rose 1998: 246; Kuper 1994: 153.

47 See Dawkins 1986; and Blackmore's *The meme machine* (1999).

48 Alexander 1987: 33, 139, 37.

49 Ibid.: 6, 31.

50 Oyama 1985: 153, 37, 44.

51 Rose 1998: ix, 18. Ingold insists that "organic form is a property not of genes but of developmental systems" (1998: 30).

52 Stoller 1997: xii.

53 Jackson 1983: 327–8 and 341 n. 1.

54 Shilling 1993: 39.

55 Husserl 1960: 157, 155.

56   Merleau-Ponty 1964: 3, 5.
57   Merleau-Ponty 1962: xiii.
58   On this predicament of dualism, see Foster 1991: 203.
59   Johnson 1987: xxxvi.
60   Csordas 1994: 12.
61   Comaroff & Comaroff 1992: 90.
62   A. Strathern 1996: 202–3.
63   Ibid.: 181.
64   Merleau-Ponty 1964: 10.
65   Lakoff & Johnson 1980: 10.
66   Ibid.: 146.
67   Ibid.: 76, 46.
68   Geertz 1973: 44.
69   Shilling 1993: 39.
70   Falk 1994: 10–44.
71   Stoller 1997: 47.
72   Bourdieu 1984: 190.
73   Bourdieu 1977, 1990.
74   See especially Connerton's account in *How societies remember* (1989), much influenced by Bourdieu.
75   Ingold 1998: 27.
76   Bordo 1993: 17.
77   Foucault 1970: 387, xx.
78   Turner 1994: 36, 44.
79   Foucault 1979: 298, 304; and see the critique by Shilling (1993: 75–80).
80   Falk 1994: 1.
81   Damasio 1994: 249–50, 252.
82   "Hypodermic Philosophy – the doctrine, resulting from the application to a cognitive animal of the biological concepts found sufficient in the study of animals assumed to be non-cognitive, that the organic phenomenon of knowing may be exhaustively described in terms of molecular displacements taking place under the skin" (Lovejoy 1996: 15–16).
83   Damasio 1994: 139, 124.
84   Ibid.: flyleaf.
85   Blacking 1977: 2, 18.
86   Stoller 1997: xi–xiii; and see Turner 1994: 29.
87   See Shilling 1993: 48–55; Tooby & Cosmides 1992.
88   Harré 1991: 257.
89   Two examples: "It is indeed a humbling experience to recognize, like wise Songhay sorcerers and griots, that we do not consume sorcery, history, or knowledge; rather, it is history, sorcery, and knowledge that consume us" (Stoller 1997: xvii). Emily Martin, writing on the effects of immunology on American perceptions of the body, declares that "The self has retreated inside the body, is a witness to itself, a tiny figure in

a cosmic landscape, which is the body. The scene is one that is both greatly exciting and greatly bewildering" (1992: 125).
90 Turner 1994: 44; see also Emily Martin's *The woman in the body* (1987: xiii); and A. Strathern's critical commentary (1996: 139–44).
91 Ingold 1998: 26.
92 See de Zengotita (1984) on Locke; and Booth (1993) on Aristotle.
93 See Silver 1985.
94 See especially Zelizer's *Pricing the priceless child* (1985).
95 Bicchieri 1988: 104.

5 Scholars and Idiots

1 *Los Angeles Times*, March 20, 1998 – entries to nymills@uslink.net. My emphasis.
2 See Berry 1986.
3 Quoted in Classen 1993: 63.
4 See especially the philosophy of G. E. Moore, notably his essay "A defense of common sense" (1959 [1925]). The anti-dualist tradition sympathetic to "Common Sense philosophy" now includes Blakemore and John Z. Young among neuroscientists; Craik through Piaget to Zangwill among the psychologists; and Ryle, Quine, Rorty, Smart, and Searle among the philosophers (see Bunge 1980: 28–31).
5 Rousseau [1762] 1911: 122.
6 Kant [1796] 1978: 23–4.
7 Gellner 1964: 72.
8 Huxley 1881: 128–48 ("On the method of Zadig").
9 Atran 1990: 269.
10 See Warner 1994.
11 Husserl 1960: 152–3.
12 See for example Bogdan 1991.
13 Stich 1983: 1.
14 Astington 1993: 27.
15 Stich 1983: 5–6, 8.
16 Dennett 1996; and see Stich 1983: 10, 242.
17 Like many anthropologists I keep finding myself appealing to my early fieldwork in Uganda and Ghana for norms of childrearing, or neighborliness, in my complaints about my own society.
18 A. Strathern 1996: 62; and see for example Heelas 1986: 244; Matson 1966: 93; Skultans 1977: 148.
19 Lambek 1998: 107.
20 Matson 1966: 94, 93, 101.
21 Lienhardt 1961: 149, 151; see also Hallpike 1976.
22 "Ethnographers studying societies which do not employ the category

'emotion' clearly have not found it easy to identify what counts as emotion talk" (Heelas 1986: 237). See for example Lutz's efforts (1986) to study Ifaluk "emotion words" from the cultural inside – in the absence of any Ifaluk category translatable as "emotion."

23   Leavitt 1996: 518.
24   Turnbull 1972: 295,
25   Turnbull 1961.
26   Kenny 1981: 490–1.
27   Clastres 1977: 179–80, 181.
28   Ibid.: 165, 37.
29   Errington 1974: 19, 252, 21, 58.
30   These are terms in, respectively, the Zande (Sudan), Ganda (Uganda), Safwa (Tanzania), and Nyakyusa (Tanzania) languages.
31   The ethnographic collage is justifiable to the extent that the basic traits to which I shall refer have been so extensively reported – indeed much of the description would be recognizable in other regions of the world. I have drawn mainly on these texts: Abrahams 1994, Evans-Pritchard 1937, Foner 1984, Green 1994 and 1996, Harwood 1970, Krige & Krige 1943, Lienhardt 1961, Marwick 1970, Mayer 1970, Middleton 1960 and 1967, Middleton & Winter 1963, M. Wilson 1951, and Winter 1956.
32   M. Wilson 1951: 215.
33   See especially Green's graphic account (1996) of the Pogoro of Tanzania. Andrew Strathern notes the "classic complex of symbolic associations between witchcraft, greed, incest and cannibalism" around the world. Among the Melpa of Highland New Guinea, *Kum* is "inordinately strong desire" which Strathern translates as witchcraft. When *Kum* gets into people they can turn into birds and fly out and attack their victims, "entering them by the anus, eating their insides and emerging via the mouth." After driving the witch to these "immoderate acts of consumption," the *kum* finally turns on its host and eats him or her too (1982: 111–12, 122, 117).
34   M. Wilson 1951: 214–15.
35   Rothman 1998: 14.
36   Marwick calls this aspect of witchcraft "constitutional" (1970: 13).
37   Krige & Krige 1943: 263.
38   See especially Foner 1984: 161–5.
39   Evans-Pritchard 1937: 338.
40   Middleton 1960: 239.
41   Ibid.: 242. Images of witchcraft in Europe are replete with such reversals, from flying to saying the mass backwards.
42   See especially Middleton & Winter 1963; Harwood 1970.
43   If the functional difference between a psychologist and a psychiatrist is that the latter can prescribe medicines – he can invade your body,

whereas the psychologist can only tinker with your mind – then East African witch-doctors more closely resemble our psychiatrists.

44 See for example Abrahams 1994.
45 See for example Winter's account of the Bwamba (1956).
46 Harwood 1970: 133.
47 Fulani (West Africa) witchcraft, says Riesman, "is part of the protective force that maintains order in the community" (1986: 81).
48 Middleton 1960: 240.
49 Robertson 1978: 168–70.
50 See for example MacCormack & Strathern 1980; Ortner 1974; Riesman 1986: 81; A. Strathern 1982.
51 *Chambers dictionary.*
52 Compare Scott's use of the term *metis*, which "denotes the knowledge that can only come from practical experience," to be contrasted with "more formal, deductive, epistemic knowledge" (1998: 6).
53 See for example Eichner's critique of professional economics as a social system (1983: 225–35).
54 See Williams 1995: 91; and see Gould (1990: 4–5, 14–15) on "common misunderstandings" of Darwinian theory.
55 A recent example is E. O. Wilson's plea for *Consilience* (1998).
56 B. Williams 1973: 149.

6 Feeling and Meaning

1 For accounts of gender modification with the lifespan, see Carucci 1985: 108–20; Counts & Counts 1985: 135, 149; Flinn 1985: 77; Foner 1984; Noddings 1989: 120; Rossi 1987 and 1993: 193.
2 Farb & Armelagos 1980: 17.
3 See Hammond & Marshall 1952: 829–38; Bogin 1988: 38–41.
4 G. Lewis 1980: 137–8; and see Green (1996: 491) for an East African example.
5 See M. Strathern 1988: 13, 131–2.
6 Lafleur 1992: 33–5.
7 See for example Jorgenson (1985: 210) on the Telefol of Sepik, Papua New Guinea; Astuti (1998: 35) on the Vezo of Madagascar.
8 Counts & Counts 1985: 151, 145, on the Lusi of New Britain.
9 Rabain 1979; and see Riesman 1986: 112.
10 Von Kondratowitz 1984: 31, 37.
11 Woodward 1995: 85–6.
12 See especially G. C. Williams 1966, Comfort 1979, and Stini 1991.
13 See Anderson 1985: 70–5; Kruse 1984.
14 Ingold 1990: 221.

15   See for example Rose 1998.
16   See Gould 1990; Lewontin 2000.
17   Alexander Pope *An essay on man* (1733), Epistle 2, 1.3.
18   Lucretius *De natura rerum* iii. 450.
19   Polanyi 1969: 212.
20   Searle 1997: xiii.
21   See Bateson 1972: 471.
22   See Searle 1997: 204–5.
23   Leder's example (1990: 52–3).
24   Leder 1990: 51, 52.
25   See Izard 1984.
26   See Campos & Barrett 1984: 229.
27   Kagan 1984: 70.
28   Hendra 1994: 123.
29   E. O. Wilson 1978: 54.
30   Hallowell 1955: 75.
31   See Farb & Armelagos 1980: 80; and also Rabain's perceptive account
      (1979) of weaning among the Wolof of West Africa.
32   Kagan 1984: 62; and see Hoffman 1984: 125.
33   Jackson 1983: 336.
34   Jackson 1983: 337; and see Polanyi 1969: 152.
35   See Loudon 1977: 165; and Classen's cross-cultural study of the senses
      (1993). Classen notes that *sagacious* derives from the Latin *sagire*,
      meaning to smell, to perceive acutely.
36   See Hampshire 1989: 123. Bloch (1998) gives vivid illustrations of the
      often wordless communication of meaning from one generation to the
      next.
37   See Bloch 1991: 185; Rabain 1979: 76; and on houses-as-bodies see A.
      Strathern 1982: 124; Gell 1992: 15; and Carsten & Hugh-Jones 1995.
38   Blacking 1977: 5.
39   "The organism is both the weaver and the pattern it weaves, the chore-
      ographer and the dance that is danced" (Rose 1998: 171). See also
      Toren 1993: 474, Riesman 1986: 112.
40   Geertz 1973: 81.
41   G. Lewis 1986: 414, 423.
42   See Toren 1993: 469; Morgan 1995.
43   See Margaret Mead's account (1967) of the conversion of Manus chil-
      dren from little realists to mature, mystified animists; and see Benedict
      1938: 377; Matthews 1994.
44   Lerner & Hultsch 1983: 485; Erikson 1985: 26–8.
45   See Spear & Campbell 1979; Boyer 1994: x.
46   See Lerner & Hultsch 1983: 443–85.
47   See Mines 1981, 1994.
48   See for example Holy 1990: 180–1; Woodward 1995: 87–91.
49   See Rodeheaver & Datan 1981: 186; Erikson 1985: 8–9.

50 Haddon 1890: 297.
51 See Lerner & Hultsch 1983: 443–85. Erikson notes that "we must acknowledge in old age a retrospective mythologizing that can amount to a pseudointegration as a defence against lurking despair" (1985: 65). See also Labouvie-Vief 1984 on the skepticism of the aged, a parallel for the ingenuous realism of children noted by Mead.
52 See for example Foner 1984: 162–3; MacCormack 1980: 117.
53 Thomas Hobbes 1914 [1651] *Leviathan*, chapter VI: "Of the Interiour Beginnings of Voluntary Motions: commonly called the PASSIONS," p. 24.
54 With such diverse luminaries as Cicero, St Augustine, and Jack Goody warning us of the enmity in family life, the socio-biological view that "Kinship" . . . should be seen to mitigate conflict, all else being equal, and to do so in proportion to its closeness" (Daly & Wilson 1988: 10) seems wildly optimistic.
55 See Izard 1984: 26–7; Farb & Armelegos 1980: 25.
56 MacCormack 1980: 117.
57 I am grateful to Tetsuro Nakaoka for this example.
58 Worthman 1993: 341.
59 Gow 1989: 567, 578–9.
60 Berry 1994: 74.
61 Tansey & Worsley 1995: 75.
62 G. Lewis 1980: 140, 163.
63 Farb & Armelagos 1980: 90.
64 Green 1996: 488–90, 494, 496.
65 *Chesapeake Family*:
    www.family.go.com./Features/family_1998_12/cspk/cspk128gimme
66 Brain 1970: 176
67 Ibid.: 173.
68 The American National Center for Health Statistics announced that 59% of men and 49% women surveyed between 1991 and 1994 were officially "overweight," compared with 51% and 41% 10 years earlier. People in their 50s are fattest: 73% of men, 64% of women. (Reported in the *Los Angeles Times*, October 9, 1996). Farb & Armelegos (1980: 18–19) reckon that the energy equivalent of the excess fat would be enough to run 900,000 automobiles for 12,000 miles a year.
69 On anorexia nervosa and bulimia see Bordo 1993: 139–64, who notes that these disorders were "barely known a century ago."
70 See Robertson 1991.
71 See for example Gove et al. 1973; and Oppenheimer 1974.
72 Ehrenreich 1989.
73 Coser and Coser 1974: 98.
74 See Demos 1970; Errington 1974: 58–60; Garrett 1977; Noddings 1989.

75   Counts & Counts 1985: 138. Fearing that the comforts of home are unexpandable, little children may also challenge the *need* for a baby brother on the same zero-sum terms.
76   Kant [1796] 1978: 182.
77   See especially Meillassoux 1981.

7 Growth and History

1   Robeco Bank (Suisse) advertisement, *Guardian Weekly*, April 4, 1999.
2   "[M]en do not make history," says Braudel chillingly, "rather it is history above all that makes men and thereby absolves them from blame" (1991: 679). Compare Marx's famous declaration that "Men make their own history, but not of their own free will; not under circumstances they themselves have chosen but under given and inherited circumstances with which they are directly confronted" (1973b: 146).
3   Berry 1994: 23, 5, 9, 34.
4   Ibid.: 41–2, 38.
5   Ibid.: 203.
6   Ibid.: 177.
7   See Collingwood 1945; Ryan 1973: 15.
8   See Berry 1994: 182.
9   Baudrillard 1981: 71, 80; and see Berry 1994: 35.
10   Booth 1993: 248.
11   See Acton 1971.
12   See Elster 1983.
13   Engels 1958: 325.
14   For example Marx 1973a: 471–2 [*Grundrisse*]; and see Soper 1981: 111.
15   Soper 1981: 109.
16   See Eagleton 1997.
17   Marxist understandings of 'reproduction' are well expounded by Noble (1979: 130–40).
18   Soper 1981: 35; and see Heller (1976) for a valiant effort to wring consistency out of Marx's various usages of 'need.'
19   Braudel 1980.
20   Rhoads 1985: 116.
21   A classic account of this is Elder's diachronic study *Children of the Great Depression* (1974).
22   See especially Hareven's exploration of *Family time and industrial time* (1982).
23   Cain 1985: 145.
24   See T. W. Schultz 1973, 1974; J. P. Smith 1977; Montgomery & Trussell 1986.

25 See C. Harris 1983: 181. On how Marxists have failed to take direct account of reproduction – despite Engels's early insistence on its historical importance – see Hartmann 1981: 370–1.
26 Aglietta 1976: 12.
27 See Meillassoux 1972, 1981, 1983.
28 See for example Wolpe 1980.
29 Giddens 1984; Bourdieu 1990.
30 Giddens 1984: 374.
31 *Los Angeles Times*, March 28, 1997.
32 Callinicos 1990: 168.
33 For a classic illustration, see Berkner's study of the Austrian 'stem' family (1972).
34 See Robertson 1991: 106–28.
35 See especially Laslett 1969; Wall 1983; Herlihy 1985.
36 See Mendels 1972: 252, Medick 1976: 301–2; Levine 1977: 147; R. M. Smith 1981.
37 Furstenberg 1966: 327.
38 Le Play 1895; Rowntree 1922.

8 The Gluttonous Peasant

1 Kroeber 1948: 284.
2 See Wolf 1982.
3 See Scott 1976.
4 See Wolf 1969; B. Moore 1967.
5 Malthus 1970 [1798].
6 See Boserup 1965, 1981; Bray 1986.
7 See for example Robertson & Hughes 1978; Durrenberger 1984.
8 This is the basis of the anthropologist Marshall Sahlins's definition of an inherently underproductive "Domestic Mode of Production" (1972).
9 Chayanov 1966.
10 On the modern interpretation of leisure as "waste" or "extravagance" see Veblen: 1934: 85, 97–101.
11 Banfield 1958: 87, 163.
12 See R. A. Miller 1974; Silverman 1975.
13 O. Lewis 1964, 1965.
14 G. Foster 1965.
15 "*'Ntere nfune': alyazaamaanya munywanyi we*," runs a Ganda proverb. "(One who acts on the principle) 'Let me get rich quickly' cheats his own bloodbrother. His greed kills the better feelings" (Walser 1982: 303).
16 This is familiar to me from my own upbringing: as a devout trencherman, I was told that it was polite to leave the table a little hungry. My reply was that I always did.

17 Sobo 1997: 256, 261.
18 Taussig 1980.
19 Carsten 1989.
20 Sobo 1997: 261–2.
21 See for example Ardener 1970: 146.
22 Kahn 1986: 41, 39.
23 Ibid.: 10.
24 Ibid.: 39.
25 Ibid.: 151.
26 Ibid.: 86.
27 Ibid.: 1–2.
28 Ibid.: 59, 58.
29 Ibid.: 26, 41–2, 154.
30 Ibid.: 121.
31 Ibid.: 151, 111. "Wamiran ideas about food and sex constitute part of a larger belief that the universe has a fixed and finite amount of life-creating energies and resources. In simple productive idiom, people expend energy to grow food, and consume food to acquire energy (p. 113). Such images are strongly evocative of the physical biology of Alfred Lotka (1956).
32 See for example Worsley 1968.
33 Marx 1973: 239.
34 Lenin 1964 [1899].
35 This section draws on my book on share contracts, *The dynamics of productive relationships* (Robertson 1987).
36 Byres 1983: 16.
37 Silverman 1975: 45; Fujimoto 1983: 29.
38 See especially Cheung 1969; Hsiao 1975; Newberry 1975.
39 See for example Finkler 1980: 271.
40 Winters 1978: 108.
41 See Horii 1972: 67; Robertson & Bray 1980: 227–30.
42 See Martinez-Alier 1971: 257, 267.
43 See Winters 1978: 78.

9 The Avaricious Pensioner

1 The gerontologist Raphael Ginzberg in an early exploration of "The negative attitude toward the elderly" observed that old people tend to become their own worst enemies: their sense of uselessness disposes them to be "asocial, depressed, desperate, stubborn," a pattern of subversive "protest" which further exasperates those on whom they depend (1952: 298).

2 See Binstock 1983.
3 Thomson 1986: 359–60. See also E. Clark (1982: 307) on welfare tactics in medieval England; and von Balluseck (1983) on Germany.
4 See Anderson 1985: 85–6.
5 See Orloff 1993; Quadagno 1986; Gratton 1986: 18. Ewald (1983) and Trempe (1983) describe this process in France. Myles (1989: 16) traces the growth of modern state pensioning from Bismarck's welfare policies in Germany during the 1880s in Germany. "Some form of national pension legislation has been in effect in Denmark since 1891, in Austria since 1906, in Britain since 1908, in France since 1910, in the Netherlands since 1913, in Italy since 1919, in Belgium since 1924, in Canada since 1927, in the United States since 1935, and in Switzerland since 1946." Initially these provided low levels of support; the main provision of *income security* in old age came after World War II.
6 See Verbon 1988: 5.
7 Achenbaum 1986: 163.
8 See Trempe (1983) on the miners' unions in France.
9 See Wise 1990: 8; Mitterauer & Sieder 1982: 171.
10 Wise 1990: 8.
11 Anderson 1985: 86. Increased pensioning has also reduced the proportion of older workers in the US: 74.1% of men aged 60–64 were working in 1971, 54.9% in 1986 (Wise 1990: 8).
12 Myles 1989: 12–13; and see Quadagno 1986.
13 Hess 1985: 324.
14 Anderson 1985: 70. The 1935 Social Security Act fixed the retirement age in the US at 65 (Achenbaum 1986: 171).
15 See Quadagno 1986: 150; Hess 1985: 325. It is also noted that since rich people tend to live longer than poor people, they stand to gain more from the redistributive effects of public pensions (World Bank 1994: 2).
16 Myles 1989: 57–60, 114.
17 World Bank 1994: 105; Achenbaum 1986: 168–73; Quadagno 1986: 147.
18 Achenbaum 1986: 180; Walker 1993: 150–3; J. H. Schultz 1992.
19 Walker 1993: 145–6.
20 Campbell 1992: 210; Kiefer 1990: 190, 188.
21 Kinoshita & Kiefer 1992: 38.
22 Myles 1989: 106.
23 D. W. Thomson 1993: 217, 234–6.
24 Myles 1989: 104–5.
25 Ibid.: 107.
26 Walker 1993: 141; see also Hess 1985: 324.
27 Jacobs 1990: 354.
28 See Marshall et al. 1993.
29 Cohen 1992: 123, 154, 124.
30 World Bank 1994: 26.

31   On one estimate in 1935, the British population would dwindle to about 5 million in 2035, with nearly half over the age of 64 (Enid Charles, cited in Borrie 1978: C137).
32   World Bank 1994: 3.
33   See especially Wise 1990; Venti & Wise 1990; D. Thomson 1993: 234.
34   Richard Thomas in the *Guardian* [London], October 28, 1995.
35   See Mannheim 1952, 1956; Riley 1978; Riley and Riley 1993. For a history of the idea of "generation" see Kriegel 1978.
36   See for example Walker 1990: 378, 388–9, and 1993: 144; Quadagno et al. 1993: 270.
37   Myles 1989: 107.
38   See Bengtson 1993: 12–13; Pratt 1976; Quadagno et al. 1993: 269; Jacobs 1990: 353. Blaikie (1990) ascribes a more active political role to "grey" pressure groups in Britain during the first half of the twentieth century.
39   Achenbaum 1989: 130.
40   Pratt 1976: 170, 41.
41   Achenbaum 1989: 113, 130.
42   Achenbaum 1986: 171; and see Myles 1989: 107. A curious version of this reasoning sees the pensioner in a sort of contract with *himself*: from an institutional perspective, says Daniels, "transfers *between* age groups are really transfers *within* lives" (1988: 63).
43   See for example Verbon's attempt to model pensioning as an intergenerational "prisoner's dilemma" (1988: 10–11).
44   See for example Lydall 1955; Ando & Modigliani 1963; Meade 1966.
45   See Atkinson 1971; Modigliani 1986; Kotlikoff 1989.
46   Modigliani 1986: 304–5; and see Kessler 1989: 80–2. The World Bank report *Averting the old age crisis* makes the point that it is often governments rather than individuals which are "myopic": constitutional powers do not guarantee farsightedness (1994: 11).
47   Becker 1964: 136–7, 164. "Luck," says Berke, "is a superbly efficient social-sanctioned device to rationalize inadequacy, incompetence, poor judgement, and, in general, dissimilar skills, traits, or resources" (1988: 274).
48   See Kingson et al. 1986; Easterlin et al. 1993: 70, 81–2.
49   See for example Johnson et al. 1989: 5; Bengtson & Achenbaum 1993.
50   See for example Phillipson 1982: 16–38.
51   Gaunt illustrates how a retired couple abstracting food contractually from a child with children to support, could ruin that family (1983: 269–70).
52   Goody 1986: 146.
53   *Oxford English dictionary.*
54   Rossi 1993: 194.
55   Rosenberg 1990: 23–37.
56   Hess 1985: 324.

57   D. Thomson 1993: 143, 155.
58   Von Balluseck 1983: 243.
59   Since the murder of her baby by an au pair nanny, Deborah Eappen has seen herself "transformed by personal tragedy into a public symbol of maternal neglect and yuppie greed," according to Eileen McNamara of the *Boston Globe*. One hate letter accused Eappen of "greed and bad judgment" for leaving her baby with an au pair for the sake of her "lifestyle" (*Guardian Weekly*, October 26, 1997).
60   Bengtson et al. 1990: 263. Anderson (1985: 69–73) reckons that in 1750 the average woman would die *12 years before* the birth of her last grandchild, whereas in 1970 she would live *25 years after* the birth of her last grandchild. With life-expectancy extending into the 90s in the twenty-first century, great-grandparenthood will become a normal experience for most women.
61   See Hagestad 1987: 425.
62   Bengtson et al. 1990: 264, 280; and see Anderson (1985: 75) on increasing "generational overlap" in postwar Britain.
63   Bengtson et al. 1990: 265–70. T. Paul Schulz notes that "families" bear the largest burden – about 70% – of the care of the "chronically ill elderly" (1992: 196, 217).
64   Anderson 1985: 73.
65   See Hess 1985. "Since 1940, the proportion of unmarried noninstitutionalized older people living alone has risen from less than 25 percent to over 60 percent. For people over age 85, the proportion has increased from 13 to 57 percent" (Wise 1990: 5).

10 The Venal Professional

1   "We define the Professional-Managerial Class as consisting of salaried mental workers who do not own the means of production and whose major function in the social division of labor may be described as the reproduction of capitalist culture and capitalist class relations" (Ehrenreich & Ehrenreich 1979: 12).
2   Abel 1989: 32.
3   Newton 1983: 27.
4   See Bok 1993: 25–41.
5   See Shapiro 1987: 645–8.
6   Ehrenreich & Ehrenreich 1979: 18, 20.
7   See Epstein 1991.
8   With interesting semantic variations, the distinction seems to translate into most modern languages: for example, *Lohn* and *Gehalt* in German; *salaire* and *traitement* in French; *gongzi* and *xinfeng* in Chinese; *chingin* and *kyuryo* in Japanese.

9   See Lupton & Bowey 1983: 98. The semantic connotations of worthiness translate into many modern languages. The German *Gehalt* (salary) is an example: *gehalten* is to be obliged, bound, self-controlled, sober, steady; while *gehaltslos* is worthless, shallow, superficial. The Spanish professional receives *honorarios*. Etymologically, we may hypothesize that words for wage are likely to be older, more various, and more earthy than those for salary. While the English middle classes, following their tendency to dignify by shifting from Germanic to Romance roots, recruited the French word for *wage* (*salaire*), the French bourgeoisie constructed new terms (*appointement, traitement*) for what we now call salary.
10 Ibid.: 102.
11 See Rex 1961: 142; Bowey 1982.
12 Dore 1973: 99; Ballon 1982: 2.
13 See Garbarino 1962; Schaeffer & Weinstein 1979: 151.
14 H. Clark 1937: 138.
15 Dore 1973: 110.
16 Genders & Irwin 1962: 51.
17 Becker 1964: 2.
18 Ibid.: 153, 50, 143.
19 Ibid.: 52.
20 See for example the critical commentaries by Ben-Porath (1967), Heckman (1976b), Rosen (1976), and T. P. Schultz (1976).
21 Bok 1993: 224–5.
22 Becker 1964: 153, 51.
23 Heckman 1976a: S30.
24 See Dore 1973: 74; A. Thomson 1975: 38.
25 Lupton & Bowey, 1983: 96, 14.
26 Genders & Irwin 1962: 46–7.
27 Abel 1989: 23–4.
28 Ballon 1982: 5.
29 Lydall 1955: 141.
30 Blau & Duncan 1967: 429n.
31 Aglietta 1976: 186.
32 Ibid.: 174–5.
33 For parallel data on the US, see Oppenheimer 1974.
34 Ricardo 1971 [1821]: 115.
35 For a concise account, see Ballon 1982.
36 Dore 1973: 111.
37 The idea of workforce salarization has resurfaced recently in the campaign for "Stakeholder Capitalism," a liberal "communitarian" commitment to long-term security in the face of "casino capitalism" and "corporate greed."
38 Newman 1988: 39.
39 Oppenheimer 1974: 240.

40   See especially the discussion by Carlson (1986), and Barrett & McIntosh (1980). The family wage arguments are well summarized by Creighton (1996).
41   These issues have been the subject of extensive debate – see for example the historical survey by Haines 1979; also Treas 1987; Oppenheimer 1974; and J. P. Smith 1977.
42   See for example Kelly (1994: 6) on the legal profession.
43   See Lupton & Bowey 1983: 133–41.
44   Abel 1989: 161.
45   Blau & Duncan 1967: 27.
46   Abel 1989: 168.
47   Newton 1983: 26–7; Kelly 1994: 1.
48   Kelly 1994: 14, 3.
49   Abel 1989: 39.
50   Harrison & Bluestone 1988: 12–13.
51   See Abel (1989: 208) on lawyers, and Hacker (1994: 22) on professors.
52   Abel 1989: 21.
53   Bok 1993: v.
54   For a discussion see Wright 1979.
55   Head 1996: 47.
56   Bok 1993: 2.
57   Hacker 1994: 22, 20.
58   Tuleja 1985: 52.
59   *"Greed with John Stossel"* ABC-TV, Tuesday, February 3, 1998.
60   Callinicos 1990: 162–5.
61   Ehrenreich & Ehrenreich 1979: 21.
62   For details see Crystal 1991: 40–1.
63   Burgess 1963: 9, 13, 17, Diagram 2, 20–Diagram 3.
64   *Los Angeles Times*, October 20, 1999.
65   Crystal 1991: 110–32; 63.
66   Burgess 1963: 74; 2; 88.
67   Crystal 1991: 202.
68   See ibid.: 195–7, 109.
69   "A company director taking a £50,000 raise while other employees get a few hundred is indeed a 'greedy bastard,' but establishing, encouraging, and rewarding greedy bastards is the fundamental purpose of capitalism," *Independent* [London], September 16, 1998.
70   See Engler 1995: 65. In South Africa, "swashbuckling survival specialist" Quinton Coatzee teaches Darwinian logic to businessmen by taking them into the outback to observe the struggles of lions, giraffes, and San bushmen. "He is even known to quench his thirst with the stomach contents of animals . . . Dead quarry. Ripped-out organs. No apologies. Is this business at the turn of the millennium?" (*Los Angeles Times*, November 30, 1998).

71   Bok 1993: 96, 114.
72   *Forbes Magazine*, May 20, 1990.
73   Ted Turner, In *"Greed with John Stossel"* ABC-TV, Tuesday February 3, 1998.
74   See Tuleja 1985: 53; Crystal 1991: 214–40.
75   See Schumpeter 1961; Veblen 1934.

11 Corporate Greed

1   Attributed to Edward, first Baron Thurlow, Lord Chancellor 1778–92.
2   An opinion voiced by Adam Smith and Bernard Shaw, among others (Epstein 1991: 7).
3   See Willard 1983.
4   See for example the collapse of Lehman Brothers, as recounted by Auletta (1986) in his *Greed and glory on Wall Street*.
5   Hannaford 1983: 106, 110.
6   *Los Angeles Times*, October 19, 1997.
7   *The Times* [London], August 18, 1997.
8   *Sunday Times* [London], February 15, 1998.
9   See for example Kaplan (1994): The coming anarchy.
10   *Wall Street Journal*, January 1, 2000.
11   Luttwak 1995: 6, 7.
12   *Los Angeles Times*, July 12, 1995.
13   See D. Miller 1997.
14   See for example Beneria & Roldan 1987; Blim 1990.
15   *Scotsman*, August 27, 1997.
16   Cato Institute, August 12, 1999 [www.cato.org/daily/08-12-99.html].
17   Tuleja 1985: 53.
18   *New York Times*, November 2, 1997.
19   Berke 1988: 205.
20   Berry 1994: 30.

References

Abel, Richard 1989, *American lawyers*. Oxford University Press, New York.

Abrahams, Ray (ed.) 1994, *Witchcraft in contemporary Tanzania*. African Studies Centre, Cambridge.

Achenbaum, W. Andrew 1986, The elderly's social security entitlements as a measure of modern American life. In David Van Tassel and Peter N. Stearns (eds) *Old age in a bureaucratic society*. Greenwood Press, New York, pp. 156–92.

—— 1989, Public pensions as intergenerational transfers in the United States. In P. Johnson, C. Conrad, and D. Thomson (eds) *Workers versus pensioners*. Manchester University Press, Manchester, pp. 113–36.

Acton, H. B. 1971, *The morals of markets*. Longman, London.

Aglietta, Michel 1976, *A theory of capitalist regulation*. New Left Books, London.

Alexander, Richard D. 1987, *The biology of moral systems*. Aldine de Gruyter, New York.

Anderson, Michael 1985, The emergence of the modern life cycle in Britain, *Social History*, 10 (1), 69–87.

Ando, A. and Modigliani, F. 1963, The life cycle hypothesis of saving: Aggregate Implications and tests, *American Economic Review*, 53, 55–84.

Aquinas, St Thomas 1995 [1263–72], *On evil*, tr. Jean Oesterle, University of Notre Dame Press, Notre Dame, Indiana.

Ardener, Edwin 1970, Witchcraft, economics, and the continuity of belief. In Mary Douglas (ed.) *Witchcraft confessions and accusations*. Tavistock, London, pp. 141–60.

Arendt, Hannah 1958, *The human condition*. University of Chicago Press, Chicago.

Armon-Jones, Claire 1986, The social functions of emotion. In Rom Harré (ed.) *The social construction of emotions.* Blackwell, Oxford, pp. 57–82.

Astington, Janet Wilde 1993, *The child's discovery of the mind.* Harvard University Press, Cambridge, Mass.

Astuti, Rita 1998, "It's a boy," "it's a girl!" Reflections on sex and gender in Madagascar and beyond. In Michael Lambek and Andrew Strathern (eds) *Bodies and persons.* Cambridge University Press, Cambridge, pp. 29–52.

Atkinson, A. B. 1971, The distribution of wealth and the individual life-cycle, *Oxford Economic Papers,* ns, 23 (2), 239–54.

Atran, Scott 1990, *Cognitive foundations of natural history.* Cambridge University Press, Cambridge.

Auletta, Ken 1986, *Greed and glory on Wall Street.* Random House, New York.

Ayala, Francisco J. 1987, The biological roots of morality, *Biology and Philosophy,* 2 (3), 235–52.

Ballon, Robert J. 1982, *Salaries in Japan.* Business Series Bulletin 91, Institute of Comparative Culture, Sophia University, Tokyo.

Balot, Ryan forthcoming, *Greed and injustice in classical Athens.* Princeton University Press, Princeton.

Banfield, Edward C. 1958, *The moral basis of a backward society.* Free Press, New York.

Barkow, J. H. 1984, The distance between genes and culture, *Journal of Anthropological Research,* 40 (3), 367–79.

Barrett, Michele and McIntosh, Maureen 1980, The family wage, *Capital and Class,* 11, 52–72.

Barth, Fredrik 1975, *Ritual knowledge among the Baktaman of New Guinea.* Yale University Press, New Haven.

Bateson, Gregory 1972, *Steps to an ecology of mind.* Chandler, San Francisco.

Baudrillard, J. 1981, *For a critique of the political economy of the sign.* Telos Press, St Louis.

Becker, Gary S. 1964, *Human capital.* National Bureau of Economic Research, New York.

——1981, *A treatise on the family* (enlarged edn). Harvard University Press, Cambridge, Mass.

Ben-Porath, Yoram 1967, The production of human capital and the life cycle of earnings, *Journal of Political Economy,* 75 (4/I), 352–65.

Benedict, Ruth 1938, Continuities and discontinuities in cultural conditioning, *Psychiatry,* 1, 161–7.

Beneria, Lourdes and Roldan, Martha 1987, *The crossroads of class and gender.* University of Chicago Press, Chicago.

Bengtson, Vern L. 1993, Is the "contract across generations" changing? Effects of population aging on obligations and expectations across age groups. In Vern L. Bengtson and W. Andrew Achenbaum (eds) *The changing contract across generations.* Aldine de Gruyter, New York, pp. 3–23.

Bengtson, Vern L. and Achenbaum, W. Andrew (eds) 1993, *The changing contract across generations*. Aldine de Gruyter, New York.

Bengtson, Vern, Rosenthal, Carolyn, and Burton, Linda 1990, Families and aging: Diversity and heterogeneity. In Robert H. Binstock and Linda K. George (eds) *Handbook of aging and the social sciences*, 3rd edn. Academic Press, New York, pp. 263–87.

Berke, Joseph H. 1988, *The tyranny of malice*. Summit Books, New York.

Berkner, Lutz K. 1972, The stem family and the developmental cycle of the peasant household: An eighteenth-century Austrian example, *American Historical Review*, 77, 398–418.

Berlin, Isaiah 1948, *Karl Marx: His life and environment*, 2nd edn. Oxford University Press, London.

Berry, Christopher J. 1986, *Human nature*. Macmillan, London.

—— 1994, *The idea of luxury*. Cambridge University Press, Cambridge.

Bicchieri, Cristina 1988, Should a scientist abstain from metaphor? In Arjo Klamer, Donald N. McCloskey, and Robert M. Solow (eds) *The consequences of economic rhetoric*. Cambridge University Press, Cambridge, pp. 100–14.

Binstock, Robert H. 1983, The aged as scapegoat, *Gerontologist*, 23 (2), 136–43.

Blacking, John (ed.) 1977, *The anthropology of the body*. Academic Press, London.

Blackmore, Susan 1999, *The meme machine*. Oxford University Press, Oxford.

Blaikie, Andrew 1990, The emerging political power of the elderly in Britain 1908–1948, *Ageing and Society*, 10 (1), 17–39.

Blau, Peter M. and Duncan, Otis Dudley 1967, *The American occupational structure*. John Wiley & Sons, New York.

Blim, Michael 1990, *Made in Italy*. Praeger, New York.

Bloch, Maurice 1991, Language, anthropology and cognitive science, *Man*, NS 26 (2), 183–98.

—— 1998, *How we think they think*. Westview, Boulder, Colo.

Bogdan, Radu J. (ed.) 1991, *Mind and commonsense*. Cambridge University Press, Cambridge.

Bogin, Barry 1988, *Patterns of human growth*. Cambridge University Press, Cambridge.

Bok, Derek 1993, *The cost of talent*. Free Press, New York.

Booth, William James 1993, *Households*. Cornell University Press, Ithaca, NY.

Bordo, Susan 1993, *Unbearable weight*. University of California Press, Berkeley & Los Angeles.

Borrie, W. D. 1978, Demographic perspectives on aging in an affluent society. In L. Evans (ed.) *Psychogeriatrics*. Geigy Psychiatric Symposium, University of Queensland, pp. 5–17.

Boserup, Ester 1965, *The conditions of agricultural growth*. Allen & Unwin, London.

Bourdieu, Pierre 1977, *Outline of a theory of practice*. Cambridge University Press, Cambridge.
——1984, *Distinction*. Harvard University Press, Cambridge, Mass.
——1990, *The logic of practice*. Stanford University Press, Stanford, Calif.
Bowey, Angela (ed.) 1982, *Handbook of salary and wage systems*, 2nd edn. Gower Press, Aldershot.
Boyd, Robert and Richerson, Peter J. 1986, *Culture and the evolutionary process*. University of Chicago Press, Chicago.
Boyer, Pascal 1994, *The naturalness of religious ideas*. California University Press, Berkeley & Los Angeles.
Brain, Robert 1970, Child-witches. In Mary Douglas (ed.) *Witchcraft confessions and accusations*, Tavistock, London, pp. 161–79.
Braudel, Fernand 1980, *On history*. Chicago University Press, Chicago.
——1991, *The identity of France*. Collins, Glasgow.
Bray, Francesca 1986, *The rice economies: Technology and development in Asian societies*. Basil Blackwell, Oxford.
Braybrooke, David 1987, *Meeting needs*. Princeton University Press, Princeton.
Bunge, Mario Augusto 1980, *The mind–body problem*. Pergamon Press, Oxford.
Burgess, Leonard Randolph 1963, *Top executive pay package*. Free Press, Glencoe, Ill.
Bynum, Caroline Walker 1997, Fast, feast, and flesh: The religious significance of food to medieval women. In Carole Counihan and Penny Van Esterik (eds) *Food and culture*. Routledge, London, pp. 138–58.
Byres, T. J. 1983, Historical perspectives on sharecropping, *Journal of Peasant Studies*, 10 (2/3), 7–41.
Cain, Mead 1985, Fertility as an adjustment to risk. In Alice S. Rossi (ed.) *Gender and the life course*. Aldine, New York, pp. 145–59.
Callinicos, Alex 1990, *Against postmodernism*. St Martin's Press, New York.
Campbell, John C. 1992, *How policies change*. Princeton University Press, Princeton.
Campos, Joseph J. and Barrett, Karen Caplovitz 1984, Toward a new understanding of emotions and their development. In Carroll E. Izard, Jerome Kagan, and Robert B. Zajonc (eds) *Emotions, cognition, and behavior*. Cambridge University Press, Cambridge, pp. 229–63.
Carlson, Allan C. 1986, What happened to the "family wage"?, *The Public Interest*, 83, 3–17.
Carsten, Janet 1989, Cooking money: Gender and the symbolic transformation of means of exchange in a Malay fishing community. In J. Parry and M. Bloch (eds) *Money and the morality of exchange*. Cambridge University Press, Cambridge, pp. 117–41.
Carsten, Janet & Hugh-Jones, Stephen (eds) 1995, *About the house*. Cambridge University Press, Cambridge.
Carucci, Laurence Marshall 1985, Conceptions of maturing and dying in

the "Middle of Heaven." In D. A. Counts and D. R. Counts (eds) *Aging and its transformations*. University Press of America, Lanham, Md., pp. 107–29.

Chagnon, Napoleon and Irons, William (eds) 1979, *Evolutionary biology and human social behavior*. Duxbury Press, North Scituate, Mass.

Chayanov, A. V. 1966, *On the theory of peasant economy*. Richard Irwin, Homewood, Ill.

Cheung, S. N. S. 1969, *The theory of share tenancy*. University of Chicago Press, Chicago.

Chomsky, Noam 1968, *Language and mind*. Harcourt Brace, New York.

Clark, Elaine 1982, Some aspects of social security in medieval England, *Journal of Family History*, 7 (4), 307–20.

Clark, Harold F. 1937, *Life earnings*. Harper & Brothers, New York.

Classen, Constance 1993, *Worlds of sense*. Routledge, London.

Clastres, Pierre 1977, *Society against the state*. Blackwell, Oxford.

Cohen, Lawrence 1992, No aging in India: The uses of gerontology, *Culture, Medicine and Psychiatry*, 16, 123–61.

Collingwood, R. G. 1945, *The idea of nature*. Clarendon Press, Oxford.

Comaroff, John and Comaroff, Jean 1992, *Ethnography and the historical imagination*. Westview Press, Boulder, Colo.

Comfort, Alex 1979, *The biology of senescence*. Elsevier North Holland, New York.

Connerton, Paul 1989, *How societies remember*. Cambridge University Press, Cambridge.

Coser, Lewis A. and Coser, Rose Laub 1974, The housewife and her "greedy family." In Lewis A. Coser (ed.) *Greedy institutions*, Free Press, New York, pp. 89–100.

Counts, Dorothy Ayers and Counts, David R. (eds) 1985, I'm not dead yet! Aging and death: Process and experience in Kaliai. In D. A. Counts and D. R. Counts (eds) *Aging and its transformations*. University Press of America, Lanham, Md., pp. 131–55.

Crane, Tim 1995, *The mechanical mind*. Penguin Books, Harmondsworth.

Creighton, Colin 1996, The "family wage" as a class-rational strategy, *Sociological Review*, 44 (2), 204–24.

Crystal, Graef S. 1991, *In search of excess*. Norton, New York.

Csordas, Thomas J. (ed.) 1994, *Embodiment and experience*. Cambridge University Press, Cambridge.

Daly, M. and Wilson, M. I. 1988, *Homicide*. Aldine de Gruyter, New York.

Damasio, Antonio R. 1994, *Descartes' error*. Grosset/Putnam, New York.

Daniels, Norman 1988, *Am I my parents' keeper? An essay on justice between the young and the old*. Oxford University Press, Oxford.

Davidson, Richard J. 1984, Affect, cognition, and hemispheric specialization. In Carroll E. Izard, Jerome Kagan, and Robert B. Zajonc (eds)

Emotions, cognition, and behavior. Cambridge University Press, Cambridge, pp. 320–65.

Dawkins, Richard 1976, *The selfish gene*. Oxford University Press, London.

——1986, *The blind watchmaker*. Norton, New York.

de Zengotita, Thomas 1984, The functional reduction of kinship in the social thought of John Locke. In G. W. Stocking (ed.) *Functionalism historicized*. University of Wisconsin Press, Madison, pp. 10–30.

Demos, John 1970, Underlying themes in the witchcraft of seventeenth-century New England, *American Historical Review*, 75 (2), 1311–26.

Dennett, Daniel 1996, *Kinds of minds*. Basic Books, New York.

Descartes, René 1968 [1637, 1641], *Discourse on method* and *The meditations*. Penguin Classics, Harmondsworth.

——1996 [1649], *Les passions de l'âme*, ed. Pascal D'Arcy. GF-Flammarion, Paris.

Dore, Ronald 1973, *British factory – Japanese factory*. George Allen & Unwin, London.

Dumont, Louis 1977, *From Mandeville to Marx*. University of Chicago Press, Chicago.

Durham, William H. 1978, Toward a coevolutionary theory of human biology and culture. In Arthur L. Caplan (ed.) *The sociobiology debate*. Harper & Row, New York, pp. 428–48.

Durkheim, Emile 1938 [1895], *The rules of sociological method*. Collier Macmillan, London.

——1960 [1914], The dualism of human nature. In Durkheim et al. *Essays on sociology and philosophy*, Harper & Row, New York, pp. 325–40.

Durrenberger, E. Paul 1984, *Chayanov peasants, and economic anthropology*. Academic Press, New York.

Eagleton, Terry 1997, *Marx and freedom*. Phoenix, Orion Publishing, London.

Easterlin, Richard A., Macunovich, Diane J., and Crimmins, Eileen M. 1993, Economic status of the young and old in the working-age population, 1964 and 1987. In Vern L. Bengtson and W. Andrew Achenbaum (eds) *The changing contract across generations*, Aldine de Gruyter, New York, pp. 67–85.

Ehrenreich, Barbara 1989, *Fear of falling*. Harper Collins, New York.

Ehrenreich, B. and Ehrenreich, J. 1979, The professional-managerial class. In Pat Walker (ed.) *Between labor and capital*. South End Press, Boston, pp. 5–45.

Eichner, Alfred S. 1983, Why economics is not yet a science. In A. S. Eichner (ed.) *Why economics is not yet a science*, M. E. Sharpe, New York, pp. 205–41.

Elder, Glen H. 1974, *Children of the Great Depression*. University of Chicago Press, Chicago.

Elster, Jon 1983, *Sour grapes*. Cambridge University Press, Cambridge.

Engels, Frederick, 1958 [1884], The origin of the family, private property and the state. In Karl Marx and Frederick Engels (eds) *Selected works*, Foreign Languages Publishing House, Moscow, pp. 170–327.

Engler, Allan 1995, *Apostles of greed*. Pluto Press, London.

Epstein, Steven A. 1991, *Wage labor and guilds in medieval Europe*. University of North Carolina Press, Chapel Hill, NC.

Erikson, Erik H. 1985, *The life cycle completed*. Norton, New York.

Errington, Frederick K. 1974, *Karavar*. Cornell University Press, Ithaca, NY.

Evans-Pritchard, E. E. 1937, *Witchcraft, oracles and magic among the Azande*. Clarendon Press, Oxford.

Ewald, François 1983, Old age as a risk: The establishment of retirement pension systems in France. In Anne-Marie Guillemard (ed.) *Old age and the welfare state*. Sage Publications, Beverly Hills, Calif., pp. 115–25.

Falk, Pasi 1994, *The consuming body*. Sage, Thousand Oaks, Calif.

Farb, Peter and Armelagos, George 1980, *Consuming passions*. Houghton Mifflin, Boston.

Finkler, Kaja 1980, Agrarian reform and economic development: When is a landlord a client and a sharecropper his patron? In P. F. Barlett (ed.) *Agricultural decision making: Anthropological contributions to rural development*. Academic Press, New York, pp. 265–88.

Flinn, Juliana 1985, Kinship, gender, and aging on Pulap, Caroline Islands. In D. A. Counts and D. R. Counts (eds) *Aging and its transformations*. University Press of America, Lanham, Md., pp. 65–82.

Foner, Nancy 1984, The old person as witch. In Nancy Foner *Ages in conflict*. Columbia University Press, New York, pp. 157–91.

Foster, George M. 1965, Peasant society and the image of limited good, *American Anthropologist*, 67 (2), 293–315.

Foster, John 1991, *The immaterial self*. Routledge, London.

Foucault, Michel 1970, *The order of things*. Random House, New York.

——— 1979, *Discipline and punish*. Vintage Books, New York.

Frank, Robert H. 1988, *Passions with reason*. Norton, New York.

Frankfurt, H. 1984, Necessity and desire, *Philosophy and Phenomenological Research*, 45 (1), 1–13.

Freud, Sigmund 1962 [1930], *Civilization and its discontents*, tr. and ed. James Strachey, 1st American edn. W. W. Norton, New York.

Friedman, Jonathan 1994, The emergence of the culture concept in anthropology. In Jonathan Friedman *Cultural identity and global process*. Sage, Thousand Oaks Calif., pp. 67–77.

Fujimoto, Akimi 1983, *Income sharing among Malay peasants*. Singapore University Press, Singapore.

Furstenberg, Frank F. 1966, Industrialization and the American family: A look backward, *American Sociological Review*, 31 (3), 326–37.

Garbarino, Joseph W. 1962, *Wage policy and long-term contracts*. Brookings Institution, Washington, DC.

Garrett, C. 1977, Women and witches: Patterns of analysis, *Signs*, 3 (2), 461–70.

Gaskin, J. C. A. 1994, Introduction. In Thomas Hobbes *The elements of law natural and politic*, ed. J. C. A. Gaskin. Oxford University Press, Oxford, pp. xi–xlii.

Gaunt, David 1983, The property and kin relationships of retired farmers in northern and central Europe. In R. Wall, J. Robin, and P. Laslett (eds) *Family forms in historic Europe*. Cambridge University Press, Cambridge, pp. 249–79.

Geertz, Clifford 1973, *The interpretation of cultures*. Basic Books, New York.

Gell, Alfred 1992, *The anthropology of time*. Berg, Oxford.

Gellner, Ernest 1964, *Thought and change*. Weidenfeld & Nicolson, London.

Genders, J. E. and Urwin, N. J. 1962, *Wages and salaries*. Institute of Personnel Management, London.

Gert, Bernard 1996, Hobbes's psychology. In Tom Sorell (ed.) *The Cambridge companion to Hobbes*. Cambridge University Press, Cambridge, pp. 157–74.

Giddens, Anthony 1984, *The constitution of society*. University of California Press, Berkeley & Los Angeles.

Ginzberg, Raphael 1952, The negative attitude toward the elderly, *Geriatrics*, 7 (5), 297–302.

Goodwin, Brian C. 1985, Constructional biology. In George Butterworth, Julie Rutkowska, and Michael Scaife (eds) *Evolution and developmental psychology*. Harvester Press, Brighton, pp. 45–66.

Goody, Jack 1986, *The logic of writing and the organization of society*. Cambridge University Press, Cambridge.

Gould, Stephen Jay 1990, *The individual in Darwin's world*. Edinburgh University Press, Edinburgh.

Gove, Walter R., Grimm, James W., Motz, Susan C., and Thompson, James D. 1973, The family life cycle: Internal dynamics and social consequences, *Sociology and Social Research*, 57 (2), 182–95.

Gow, Peter 1989, The perverse child: desire in a native Amazonian subsistence economy, *Man*, NS 24 (4), 567–82.

Graham, Thomas Francis 1968, *Anatomy of avarice*. Beacon-Bell, Canton, Ohio.

Gratton, Brian 1986, The new history of the aged: A critique. In David Van Tassel and Peter N. Stearns (eds) *Old age in a bureaucratic society*. Greenwood Press, New York, pp. 3–29.

Gray, John 1987, The economic approach to human behavior: Its prospects and limitations. In G. Radnitzky and P. Bernholz (eds) *Economic imperialism*. Paragon, New York, pp. 33–49.

Green, Maia 1994, Shaving witchcraft in Ulanga: Kunyolewa and the Catholic church. In Ray Abrahams (ed.) *Witchcraft in contemporary Tanzania*. African Studies Centre, Cambridge, pp. 23–45.

——1996, Medicines and the embodiment of substances among Pogoro

Catholics, Southern Tanzania, *Journal of the Royal Anthropological Institute*, 2 (3), 485–98.

Hacker, Andrew 1994, Unjust desserts? *New York Review of Books*, 3 March, 20–4.

Haddon, A. C. 1890. The ethnography of the western tribe of Torres Straits. *Journal of the Royal Anthropological Institute*, 19, 297–440.

Hagestad, Gunhild O. 1987, Parent–child relations in later life: Trends and gaps in past research. In J. B. Lancaster, J. Altmann, A. S. Rossi, and L. R. Sherrod (eds) *Parenting across the life span*. Aldine de Gruyter, New York, pp. 405–33.

Haines, Michael R. 1979, Industrial work and the family life cycle, 1889–1890. In Paul Uselding (ed.) *Research in Economic History*, vol. 4. JAI Press, Greenwich, Conn., pp. 289–356.

Hallowell, A. I. 1955, The self and its behavioral environment. In A. Irving Hallowell *Culture and experience*. University of Pennsylvania Press, Philadephia, pp. 75–110.

Hallpike, C. R. 1976, Is there a primitive mentality?, *Man*, NS 11 (2), 253–70.

Hammel, Eugene A. 1972, *The myth of structural analysis: Lévi-Strauss and the three bears*. Addison-Wesley, Reading, Mass.

Hammond, John and Marshall, F. H. A. 1952, The life cycle. In A. S. Parkes (ed.) *Marshall's physiology of reproduction*, 3rd edn. Longmans, Green and Co., London, vol. 2, pp. 793–848.

Hampshire, Stuart 1989, *Innocence and experience*. Harvard University Press, Cambridge, Mass.

Hannaford, Robert V. 1983, The theoretical twist to irresponsibility in business. In Wade L. Robison, Michael S. Pritchard, and Joseph Ellin (eds) *Profits and professions*. Humana Press, Clifton, NJ, pp. 101–12.

Hareven, Tamara K. 1982, *Family time and industrial time*. Cambridge University Press, Cambridge.

Harré, Rom (ed.) 1986, *The social construction of emotions*. Basil Blackwell, Oxford.

——1991, *Physical being*. Basil Blackwell, Oxford.

Harris, C. C. 1983, *The family in industrial society*. George Allen & Unwin, London.

Harris, William 1971, On war and greed in the second century B.C., *American Historical Review*, 76 (5), 1371–85.

Harrison, Bennett and Bluestone, Barry 1988, *The great U-turn*. Basic Books, New York.

Hart, Keith 2000, *The memory bank*. Profile Books, London.

Hartmann, Heidi 1981, The family as the locus of gender, class, and political struggle: The example of housework, *Signs*, 366–94.

Harwood, Alan 1970, *Witchcraft, sorcery and social categories among the Safwa*. Oxford University Press, London.

Head, Simon 1996, The new, ruthless economy, *New York Review of Books*, 43 (4), 47–52.

Heald, Suzette 1982, The making of men: The relevance of vernacular psychology to the interpretation of a Gisu ritual, *Africa*, 52 (1), 15–36.

Heckman, James J. 1976a, Estimates of a human capital production function embedded in a life-cycle model of labor supply. In Nestor E. Terleckyj (ed.) *Household production and consumption*. National Bureau of Economic Research, New York, pp. 227–64.

——1976b, A life-cycle model of earnings, learning, and consumption, *Journal of Political Economy*, 84 (4/II), S11–S44.

Heelas, Paul 1986, Emotion talk across cultures. In Rom Harré (ed.) *The social construction of emotions*. Basil Blackwell, Oxford, pp. 234–66.

Heller, Agnes 1976, *The theory of need in Marx*. St Martin's Press, New York.

Hendra, Tony 1994, *The book of bad virtues*. Pocket Books, New York.

Herlihy, David 1985, *Medieval households*. Harvard University Press, Cambridge, Mass.

Herrmann-Pillath, Carsten 1991, A Darwinian framework for the economic analysis of institutional change in history, *Journal of Social and Biological Structures*, 14 (2), 127–48.

Hess, Beth B. 1985, Aging policies and old women: The hidden agenda. In Alice S. Rossi (ed.) *Gender and the life course*. Aldine, New York, pp. 319–31.

Hirschman, A. O. 1977, *The passions and the interests*. Princeton University Press, Princeton.

Hobbes, Thomas 1914 [1651], *Leviathan*. Everyman edition, J. M. Dent, London.

——1994 [1640], *The elements of law natural and politic*, Part I: Human nature; Part II *De corpore politico*; Three lives, ed. with introduction by J. C. A. Gaskin. Oxford University Press, Oxford.

Hoffman, Martin L. 1984, Interaction of affect and cognition in empathy. In Carroll E. Izard, Jerome Kagan, and Robert B. Zajonc (eds) *Emotions, cognition, and behavior*. Cambridge University Press, Cambridge, pp. 103–31.

Holy, Ladislav 1990, Strategies for old age among the Berti of the Sudan. In Paul Spencer (ed.) *Anthropology and the riddle of the Sphinx*. Routledge, London, pp. 167–82.

Horii, Kenzo 1972, The land tenure system of Malay padi farmers, *Developing Economies*, 10 (1), 45–73.

Hsiao, J. C. 1975, The theory of share tenancy revisited, *Journal of Political Economy*, 83 (5), 1023–32.

Hume, David 1972, *A treatise of human nature: Being an attempt to introduce the experimental method of reasoning into moral subjects*. Book II [1739] Of the passions; Book III [1740] Of morals. Fontana Collins, London.

——1975 [1777], *Enquiries concerning human understanding and concerning the principles of morals.* Oxford University Press, Oxford.
Husserl, E. 1960, *Cartesian meditations: An introduction to phenomenology,* tr. Dorion Cairns. Martinus Nijhof, The Hague.
Huxley, Thomas Henry 1881, On the method of Zadig. In T. H. Huxley (ed.) *Science and culture, and other essays.* Macmillan, London, pp. 128–48.
Ingold, Tim 1990, An anthropologist looks at biology, *Man,* NS 25 (2), 208–29.
——1991, Becoming persons: Consciousness and sociality in human evolution, *Cultural Dynamics,* 4 (3), 355–78.
——1998, From complementarity to obviation: On dissolving the boundaries between social and biological anthropology, archaeology and psychology, *Zeitschrift für Ethnologie,* 123, 21–52.
Izard, Carroll E. 1984, Emotion–cognition relationships and human development. In Carroll E. Izard, Jerome Kagan, and Robert B. Zajonc (eds) *Emotions, cognition, and behavior.* Cambridge University Press, Cambridge, pp. 17–37.
Jackson, Michael 1983, Knowledge of the body, *Man,* NS 18 (2), 327–45.
Jacobs, Bruce 1990, Aging and politics. In Robert H. Binstock and Linda K. George (eds) *Handbook of aging and the social sciences,* 3rd edn. Academic Press, New York, pp. 349–61.
Johnson, Mark 1987, *The body in the mind.* Chicago University Press, Chicago.
Johnson, Paul, Conrad, Christoph, and Thomson, David (eds) 1989, *Workers versus pensioners.* Manchester University Press, Manchester.
Jorgenson, Dan 1985, Femsep's last garden: a Telefol response to mortality. In D. A. Counts and D. R. Counts (eds) *Aging and its transformations.* University Press of America, Lanham, Md., pp. 203–21.
Kagan, Jerome 1984, The idea of emotion in human development. In Carroll E. Izard, Jerome Kagan, and Robert B. Zajonc (eds) *Emotions, cognition, and behavior.* Cambridge University Press, Cambridge, pp. 38–72.
Kahn, Miriam 1986, *Always hungry never greedy.* Cambridge University Press, Cambridge.
Kant, Immanuel 1978 [1796], *Anthropology from a pragmatic point of view.* Southern Illinois University Press, Carbondale.
Kaplan, Robert D. 1994, The coming anarchy: How scarcity, crime, overpopulation, and disease are rapidly destroying the social fabric of our planet, *Atlantic Monthly,* February, 44–76.
Kelly, Michael J. 1994, *Lives of lawyers.* University of Michigan Press, Ann Arbor.
Kenny, Michael G. 1981, Mirror in the forest: The Dorobo hunter-gatherers as an image of the other, *Africa,* 51 (1), 477–95.
Kessler, Denis 1989, But why is there social security? In P. Johnson, C.

Conrad, and D. Thomson (eds) *Workers versus pensioners*. Manchester University Press, Manchester, pp. 80–90.

Kiefer, Christie W. 1990, The elderly in modern Japan: Elite, victims, or plural players? In Jay Sokolovsky (ed.) *The cultural context of aging*. Bergin & Garvey, New York, pp. 181–95.

Kingson, Eric R., Hirshorn, Barbara A., and Cornman, John M. 1986, *Ties that bind*. Seven Locks Press, Washington, DC.

Kinoshita, Yasuhito and Kiefer, Christie W. 1992, *Refuge of the honored*. University of California Press, Berkeley & Los Angeles.

Klein, Melanie 1975, *Envy and gratitude & other works 1946–1963*. Delacorte Press, New York, pp. 176–235.

Kotlikoff, Laurence J. 1989, *What determines savings?* MIT Press, Cambridge, Mass.

Kriegel, Annie 1978, Generational difference: The history of an idea, *Daedalus*, 107 (1), 23–38.

Krige, E. Jensen and Krige, J. D. 1943, *The realm of a rain-queen*. International African Institute/Oxford University Press, London.

Kroeber, Alfred 1948 [1923], *Anthropology*. Harcourt Brace, New York.

Kruse, Andreas 1984, The five-generation family: A pilot study. In V. Garms-Homolova, E. M. Hoerning, and D. Schaeffer (eds) *Intergenerational relationships*. C. J. Hogrefe, Lewiston, NY, pp. 115–24.

Kuper, Adam 1994, *The chosen primate*. Harvard University Press, Cambridge Mass.

Labouvie-Vief, Gisela 1984, Culture, language, and mature rationality. In Kathleen A. McCluskey and Hayne W. Reese (eds) *Life-span developmental psychology*. Academic Press, New York, pp. 109–28.

Lafleur, William R. 1992, *Liquid life*. Princeton University Press, Princeton.

Lakoff, George and Johnson, Mark 1980, *Metaphors we live by*. University of Chicago Press, Chicago.

Lambek, Michael 1998, Body and mind in mind, body and mind in body. In Michael Lambek and Andrew Strathern (eds) *Bodies and persons*. Cambridge University Press, Cambridge, pp. 103–23.

Laslett, Peter 1969, Size and structure of the household in England over three centuries, *Population Studies*, 23 (2), 199–223.

Leach, Edmund 1991, The social anthropology of marriage and mating. In Vernon Reynolds and John Kellett (eds) *Mating and marriage*. Oxford University Press, Oxford, pp. 91–110.

Le Play, Frédéric 1895, *L'organisation de la famille selon le vrai modèle signalé par l'histoire de toutes les races et de tous les temps*, 4th edn. Alfred Mame et Fils, Paris 1895.

Leavitt, John 1996, Meaning and feeling in the anthropology of emotions, *American Ethnologist*, 23 (3), 514–39.

Leder, Drew 1990, *The absent body*. University of Chicago Press, Chicago.

Lenin, V. I. 1964 [1899], *The development of capitalism in Russia*, 2nd rev. edn. Progress Publishers, Moscow.

Lerner, Richard M. and Hultsch, David F. 1983, *Human development*. McGraw Hill, New York.

Lévi-Strauss, Claude 1964 [1957], The principle of reciprocity. In Rose L. Coser (ed.) *The family*. St Martin's Press, New York, pp. 36–48.

Levine, David 1977, *Family formation in an age of nascent capitalism*. Academic Press, New York.

Lewis, Gilbert 1980, *Day of shining red*. Cambridge University Press, Cambridge.

——1986, The look of magic, *Man*, NS 21 (3), 414–35.

Lewis, Oscar 1964, *The children of Sánchez*. Penguin Books, Harmondsworth.

——1965, *La vida*. Random House, New York.

Lewontin, Richard 2000, *The triple helix: Gene, organism, and environment*. Harvard University Press, Cambridge, Mass.

Lewontin, R. C., Rose, S., and Kamin, L. J. 1984, *Not in our genes*. Penguin Books, Harmondsworth.

Lienhardt, Godfrey 1961, *Divinity and experience*. Clarendon Press, Oxford.

Lockwood, Michael 1989, *Mind, brain, and the quantum*. Basil Blackwell, Oxford.

Lopreato, Joseph 1984, *Human nature and biocultural evolution*. Allen & Unwin, London.

Lotka, Alfred J. 1956 [1924], *Elements of mathematical biology*. Dover, New York.

Loudon, J. B. 1977, On body products. In John Blacking (ed.) *The anthropology of the body*. Academic Press, London, pp. 161–78.

Lovejoy, Arthur O. 1996 [1930], *The revolt against dualism*. Transaction Publishers, New Brunswick.

Lubbock, Sir John 1875, *The origin of civilisation and the primitive condition of man*. Longmans, Green, London.

Lumsden, Charles J. and Gushurst, Ann C. 1991, Gene–culture coevolution: Humankind in the making. In James H. Fetzer (ed.) *Sociobiology and epistemology*. D. Reidel, Dordrecht, pp. 3–28.

Lupton, Tom and Bowey, Angela 1983, Salary systems and structures. In T. Lupton and A. Bowie *Wages and salaries*, 2nd edn. Gower Press, Aldershot, England, pp. 96–108.

Luttwak, Edward 1995, Turbo-charged capitalism and its consequences, *London Review of Books*, 2 November, 6–7.

Lutz, Catherine 1986, The domain of emotion words on Ifaluk. In Rom Harré (ed.) *The social construction of emotions*. Basil Blackwell, Oxford, pp. 267–88.

Lydall, Harold F. 1955, The life cycle in income, saving, and asset ownership, *Econometrica*, 23 (2), 133–50.

MacCormack, Carol 1980, Proto-social to adult: A Sherbro transformation. In Carol MacCormack and Marilyn Strathern (eds) *Nature, culture and gender*. Cambridge University Press, Cambridge, pp. 95–118.

MacCormack, Carol and Strathern, Marilyn (eds) 1980, *Nature, culture and gender.* Cambridge University Press, Cambridge.

Malinowski, Bronislaw 1960 [1941], *A scientific theory of culture.* Oxford University Press, London.

Malthus, Thomas 1970 [1798], *An essay on the principle of population.* Penguin Books, Harmondsworth.

Mannheim, Karl 1952, The problem of generations. In D. Kecskemeti (ed.) *Essays on the sociology of knowledge.* Routledge & Kegan Paul, London, pp. 276–322.

——1956, *From generation to generation: Age groups and social structure.* Free Press, Glencoe, Ill.

Marshall, Victor W., Cook, Fay Lomax, and Marshall, Joanne Gard 1993, Conflict over intergenerational equity: Rhetoric and reality in a comparative perspective. In Vern L. Bengtson and W. Andrew Achenbaum (eds) *The changing contract across generations.* Aldine de Gruyter, New York pp. 119–40.

Martin, Emily 1987, *The woman in the body.* Beacon Press, Boston.

——1992, The end of the body? *American Ethnologist,* 19 (1), 121–40.

Martinez-Alier, Juan 1971, *Labourers and landowners in southern Spain.* George Allen & Unwin, London.

Marwick, Max (ed.) 1970, *Witchcraft and sorcery.* Penguin Books, Harmondsworth.

Marx Karl 1973a [1939], *Grundrisse: Foundations of the critique of political economy (rough draft).* Penguin Books, Harmondsworth.

——1973b [1869], The Eighteenth Brumaire of Louis Bonaparte. In Karl Marx, *Surveys from exile.* Penguin Books, Harmondsworth, pp. 143–249.

Masters, John C. and Carlson, Charles R. 1984, Children's and adults' understanding of the causes and consequences of emotional states. In Carroll E. Izard, Jerome Kagan, and Robert B. Zajonc (eds) *Emotions, cognition, and behavior.* Cambridge University Press, Cambridge, pp. 438–63.

Matson, Wallace I. 1966, Why isn't the mind–body problem ancient? In Paul Feyerabend and Grover Maxwell (eds) *Mind, matter and method.* University of Minnesota Press, Minneapolis, pp. 92–102.

Matthews, Gareth B. 1994, *The philosophy of childhood.* Harvard University Press, Cambridge, Mass.

Mayer, Philip 1970, Witches. In Max Marwick (ed.) *Witchcraft and sorcery.* Penguin Books, Harmondsworth, pp. 45–64.

Mead, G. 1934, *Mind, self and society.* Chicago University Press, Chicago.

Mead, Margaret 1967 [1937], An investigation of the thought of primitive children, with special reference to animism. In Robert Hunt (ed.) *Personalities and cultures.* Natural History Press, New York, pp. 213–37.

Meade, J. E. 1966, Life-cycle savings, inheritance and economic growth, *Review of Economic Studies,* 33 (1), 61–78.

Medick, Hans 1976, The proto-industrial family economy: The structural function of household and family during the transition from peasant society to industrial capitalism, *Social History*, 3, 291–315.

Meillassoux, Claude 1972, From reproduction to production: A Marxist approach to economic anthropology, *Economy and Society*, 1 (1), 93–104.

——1981, *Maidens, meal and money*, Cambridge University Press, Cambridge.

——1983, The economic bases of demographic reproduction: From the domestic mode of production to wage-earning, *Journal of Peasant Studies*, 11 (1), 50–61.

Mendels, Franklin F. 1972, Proto-industrialization: The first phase of the industrialization process, *Journal of Economic History*, 32 (1), 241–61.

Mennell, Stephen 1997, On the civilizing of appetite. In Carole Counihan and Penny Van Esterik (eds) *Food and culture*. Routledge, London, pp. 315–37.

Merleau-Ponty, Maurice 1962 [1946], *Phenomenology of perception*, tr. Colin Smith. Routledge, London.

——1964, *The primacy of perception*. Northwestern University Press, Chicago.

Middleton, John 1960, *Lugbara religion*. Oxford University Press, London.

——(ed.) 1967, *Magic, witchcraft and curing*. Natural History Press, New York.

Middleton, J. and Winter, E. H. (eds) 1963, *Witchcraft and sorcery in East Africa*. Routledge & Kegan Paul, London.

Midgley, Mary 1995, *Beast and man*, rev. edn. Routledge, London.

Miller, Daniel 1997, *Capitalism: An ethnographic approach*. Berg, Oxford.

Miller, R. A. 1974, Are familists amoral? A test of Banfield's amoral familism hypothesis in a south Italian village. *American Ethnologist*, 1(4), 515–35.

Mines, Mattison 1981, Indian transitions: A comparative analysis of adult stages of development, *Ethos*, 9 (2), 95–121.

——1994, *Public faces, private voices*. University of California Press, Berkeley & Los Angeles.

Mintz, Sidney W. 1996, *Tasting food, tasting freedom*. Beacon Press, Boston.

Mitterauer, Michael and Sieder, Reinhard 1982, *The European family*. Basil Blackwell, Oxford.

Modigliani, Franco 1986, Life cycle, individual thrift, and the wealth of nations, *The American Economic Review*, 76 (3), 297–313.

Montgomery, Mark and Trussell, James 1986, Models of marital status and childbearing. In O. Ashenfelter and R. Layard (eds) *Handbook of labor economics*, vol. 1. Elsevier, New York, pp. 205–71.

Moore, Barrington 1967, *Social origins of dictatorship and democracy*. Penguin Books, Harmondsworth.

Moore, George Edward 1959 [1925], A defence of common sense. In G. E. Moore *Philosophical papers*. George Allen & Unwin, London, pp. 32–59.

Morgan, Elaine 1995, *The descent of the child*. Oxford University Press, Oxford.

Mueller, Dennis 1984, Further reflections on the invisible-hand theorem. In P. Wiles and G. Routh (eds) *Economics in disarray*. Basil Blackwell, Oxford, pp. 159–89.

Myles, John 1989, *Old age and the welfare state*, rev. edn. University of Kansas Press, Lawrence, Kansas.

Neu, Jerome 1980, Jealous thoughts. In Amelie O. Rorty (ed.) *Explaining emotions*. University of California Press, Berkeley & Los Angeles, pp. 425–63.

Newbery, D. M. G. 1975, Tenurial obstacles to innovation, *Journal of Development Studies*, 11 (4), 263–77.

Newman, Katherine S. 1988, *Falling from grace*. Free Press, New York.

Newton, Lisa H. 1983, The intractable plurality of values. In Wade L. Robison, Michael S. Pritchard, and Joseph Ellin (eds) *Profits and professions*. Humana Press, Clifton, NJ, pp. 23–36.

Noble, David 1979, The PMC: A critique. In Pat Walker (ed.) *Between labor and capital*. South End Press, Boston, pp. 121–42.

Noddings, Nel 1989, *Women and evil*. University of California Press, Berkeley & Los Angeles.

Nutton, Vivian 1993, Humoralism. In W. F. Bynum and Roy Porter (eds) *Companion encyclopedia of the history of medicine*, vol. 1. Routledge, London, pp. 281–91.

Onians, Richard Broxton 1951, *The origins of European thought about the body, the mind, the soul, the world, time and fate*. Cambridge University Press, Cambridge.

Oppenheimer, Valerie K. 1974, The life cycle squeeze: The interaction of men's occupational and family life cycles, *Demography*, 11 (2), May, 227–45.

Orloff, Ann Shola 1993, *The politics of pensions*. University of Wisconsin Press, Madison.

Ortner, Sherry B. 1974, Is female to male as nature is to culture? In Michelle Zimbalist Rosaldo and Louise Lamphere (eds) *Woman, culture, and society*. Stanford University Press, Stanford, Calif., pp. 67–87.

Oyama, Susan 1985, *The ontogeny of information*. Cambridge University Press, Cambridge.

Phillipson, Chris 1982, *Capitalism and the construction of old age*. Macmillan, London.

Polanyi, Michael 1969, *Knowing and being*, ed. Marjorie Grene. University of Chicago Press, Chicago.

Pratt, Henry J. 1976, *The gray lobby*. University of Chicago Press, Chicago.

Prichard, Harold A. 1968, *Moral obligation*. Oxford University Press, Oxford.

Prigogine, Ilya 1994, *Les lois du chaos*. Flammarion, Paris.

Quadagno, Jill S. 1986, The transformation of old age security. In David Van Tassel and Peter N. Stearns (eds) *Old age in a bureaucratic society*. Greenwood Press, New York, pp. 129–55.

Quadagno, Jill, Achenbaum, W. Andrew, and Bengtson, Vern L. 1993, Setting the agenda for research on cohorts and generations: Theoretical, political, and policy implications. In Vern L. Bengtson and W. Andrew Achenbaum (eds) *The changing contract across generations*. Aldine de Gruyter, New York, pp. 259–72.

Rabain, Jacqueline 1979, *L'enfant du lignage*. Payot, Paris.

Rex, John 1961, *Key problems of sociological theory*. Routledge & Kegan Paul, London.

Rhoads, Steven E. 1985, *The economist's view of the world: Government, markets, and public policy*. Cambridge University Press, Cambridge.

Ricardo, David 1971 [1821], *Principles of Political Economy*. Penguin Books, Harmondsworth.

Riesman, Paul 1986, The person and the life cycle in African social life and thought, *African Studies Review*, 29 (2), 71–138.

Riley, Matilda White 1978, Aging, social change, and the power of ideas, *Daedalus*, 107 (1), 39–52.

Riley, Matilda White, and Riley, John W. 1993, Connections: Kin and cohort. In Vern L. Bengtson and W. Andrew Achenbaum (eds) *The changing contract across generations*. Aldine de Gruyter, New York, pp. 169–89.

Robertson, A. F. 1978, *Community of strangers*. Scolar Press, London.

——1987, *The dynamics of productive relationships*. Cambridge University Press, Cambridge.

——1991, *Beyond the family*. Polity Press, Cambridge, and University of California Press, Berkeley & Los Angeles.

——1996, The development of meaning: Ontogeny and culture, *Journal of the Royal Anthropological Institute*, NS, 2 (4), 591–610.

Robertson, A. F. and Bray, F. A. 1980, Sharecropping in Kelantan, Malaysia. In G. Dalton (ed.) *Research in economic anthropology*, vol. 3. JAI Press, Greenwich, Conn., pp. 209–44.

Robertson, A. F. and Hughes, G. A. 1978, The family farm in Buganda, *Development and Change*, 9 (3), 415–38.

Rodeheaver, Dean and Datan, Nancy 1981, Making it: The dialectics of middle age. In Richard M. Lerner (ed.) *Individuals as producers of their own development*. Academic Press, New York, pp. 183–96.

Rose, Steven 1998, *Lifelines*. Oxford University Press, Oxford.

Rosen, Sherwin 1976, A theory of life earnings, *Journal of Political Economy*, 84 (4/II), S45–S67.

Rosenbaum, Jonathan 1993, *Greed*. British Film Institute, London.

Rosenberg, Harriet G. 1990, Complaint discourse, aging, and caregiving among the !Kung San of Botswana. In Jay Sokolovsky (ed.) *The cultural context of aging*. Bergin & Garvey, New York, pp. 19–41.

Rossi, Alice S. 1987, Parenthood in transition: From lineage to child to self-orientation. In J. B. Lancaster, J. Altmann, A. S. Rossi, and L. R. Sherrod (eds) *Parenting across the life span*. Aldine de Gruyter, New York, pp. 31–81.

—— 1993, Intergenerational relations: Gender, norms and behavior. In Vern L. Bengtson and W. Andrew Achenbaum (eds) *The changing contract across generations*. Aldine de Gruyter, New York, pp. 191–211.

Rothman, David J. 1998, The international organ traffic, *New York Review of Books*, 45 (5), 14–17.

Rousseau, Jean-Jacques 1911 [1762], *Emile, or Education*. Everyman edn, J. M. Dent, London.

Rowntree, B. Seebohm 1922 [1901], *Poverty: A study of town life*. 1922 edn reprinted by Howard Fertig, New York, 1971.

Russell, Bertrand 1961 [1946], *History of western philosophy*. George Allen & Unwin, London.

Ryan, Alan 1973, The nature of human nature in Hobbes and Rousseau. In Jonathan Benthall (ed.) *The limits of human nature*. Allen Lane, London, pp. 3–19.

Sahlins, Marshall 1972, *Stone age economics*. Aldine Atherton, Chicago.

—— 1976, *The use and abuse of biology*. University of Michigan Press, Ann Arbor.

—— 1999, Two or three things I know about culture, *Journal of the Royal Anthropological Institute*, 5 (3), 399–421.

Sarbin, Theodore R. 1986, Emotion and act: Roles and rhetoric. In Rom Harré (ed.) *The social construction of emotions*. Basil Blackwell, Oxford, pp. 83–97.

Schaeffer, Robert and Weinstein, James 1979, Between the lines. In Pat Walker (ed.) *Between labor and capital*. South End Press, Boston, pp. 143–72.

Schultz, T. Paul 1976, Comments on "Estimates of a human capital production function embedded in a life-cycle model of labor supply [by James J. Heckman]. In Nestor E. Terleckyj (ed.) *Household production and consumption*. National Bureau of Economic Research, New York, pp. 259–64.

Schultz, Theodore W. 1973, The value of children: An economic perspective, *Journal of Political Economy*, 81 (2/II), S2–S13.

—— (ed.) 1974, *Economics of the family*. National Bureau of Economic Research, University of Chicago Press, Chicago.

Schulz, James H. 1992, *The economics of aging*. Auburn House, New York.

Schumpeter, Joseph A. 1961 [1934], *The theory of economic development*. Oxford University Press, London.

Scott, James C. 1976, *The moral economy of the peasant*. Yale University Press, New Haven.

—— 1998, *Seeing like a state*. Yale University Press, New Haven.

Searle, John 1994, What's wrong with the philosophy of mind? In Richard Warner and Tadeusz Szubka (eds) *The mind–body problem*. Blackwell Publishers, Oxford, pp. 277–98.

—— 1997, *The mystery of consciousness*. New York Review of Books, New York.

Sekora, John 1977, *Luxury.* Johns Hopkins University Press, Baltimore.

Sen, Amartya 1977, Rational fools: A critique of the behavioral foundations of economic theory, *Philosophy and public affairs*, 6 (4), 317–44.

——1981, *Poverty and famines.* Clarendon Press, Oxford.

——1994, Freedoms and needs: An argument for the primacy of political rights, *New Republic*, Jan 10 & 17, pp. 31–8.

Shapiro, Susan P. 1987, The social control of impersonal trust, *American Journal of Sociology*, 93 (3), 623–58.

Shilling, Chris 1993, *The body and social theory.* Sage, London.

Silver, Alan 1985, "Trust" in social and political theory. In G. Suttles and M. Zald (eds) *The challenge of social control.* Ablex, Norwood, NJ, pp. 52–67.

Silverman, Sydel 1975, *The three bells of civilization.* Columbia University Press, New York.

Simmons, Leo W. 1945, *The role of the aged primitive society.* Yale University Press, New Haven.

Sinha, Chris 1985, A socio-naturalistic approach to human development. In George Butterworth, Julie Rutkowska, and Michael Scaife (eds) *Evolution and developmental psychology.* Harvester Press, Brighton, pp. 159–81.

Skinner, Quentin 1978, *The foundations of modern political thought.* Cambridge University Press, Cambridge.

Skultans, Vieda 1977, Bodily madness and the spread of the blush. In John Blacking (ed.) *The anthropology of the body.* Academic Press, London, pp. 145–60.

Smith, Adam 1970 [1776], *An enquiry into the nature and causes of the wealth of nations.* Penguin Books, Harmondsworth.

——1976 [1759], *The theory of moral sentiments.* Oxford University Press, Oxford.

Smith, James P. 1977, Family labor supply over the life cycle, *Explorations in economic research*, 4 (2), 205–76.

Smith, Richard M. 1981, Fertility, economy, and household formation in England over three centuries, *Population and Development Review*, 7 (4), 595–622.

Sobo, Elisa J. 1997, The sweetness of fat: Health, procreation, and sociability in rural Jamaica. In Carole Counihan and Penny Van Esterik (eds) *Food and culture.* Routledge, London, pp. 256–71.

Soper, Kate 1981, *On human needs.* Harvester Press, Brighton.

Spear, Norman E., and Campbell, Byron A. (eds) 1979, *Ontogeny of learning and memory.* Lawrence Erlbaum Associates, Hillsdale NJ.

Spicker, Stuart F. 1970, Introduction. In Stuart F. Spicker (ed.) *The philosophy of the body.* Quadrangle Books, Chicago, pp. 3–23.

Stewart, Frances 1985, *Planning to meet basic needs.* Macmillan, London.

Stich, Stephen 1983, *From folk psychology to cognitive science.* MIT Press, Cambridge, Mass.

Stini, William A. 1991, The biology of human aging. In C. G. N. Mascie-Taylor and G. W. Lasker (eds) *Applications of biological anthropology to human affairs*. Cambridge University Press, Cambridge, pp. 207–36.

Stocking, George W. Jnr. 1982, Franz Boas and the culture concept in historical perspective. In George W. Stocking Jnr. *Race, culture, and evolution*. University of Chicago Press, Chicago, pp. 195–233.

Stoller, Paul 1997, *Sensuous scholarship*. University of Pennsylvania Press, Philadelphia.

Strathern, Andrew 1982, Witchcraft, greed, cannibalism and death: Some related themes from the New Guinea Highlands. In M. Bloch and J. Parry (eds) *Death and the regeneration of life*. Cambridge University Press, Cambridge, pp. 111–33.

—— 1996, *Body thoughts*. University of Michigan Press, Ann Arbor.

Strathern, Marilyn 1988, *The gender of the gift*. University of California Press, Berkeley & Los Angeles.

Streeten, Paul 1981, *First things first*. IBRD/Oxford University Press, New York.

Symons, Donald 1989, A critique of Darwinian anthropology, *Ethnology and Sociobiology*, 10, 131–44.

—— 1992, On the use and misuse of Darwinism in the study of human behavior. In J. H. Barkow, L. Cosmides, and J. Tooby (eds) *The adapted mind*. Oxford University Press, New York, pp. 137–59.

Tansey, Geoff and Worsley, Tony 1995, *The food system*. Earthscan Publications, London.

Taussig, Michael T. 1980, *The devil and commodity fetishism in South America*. University of North Carolina Press, Chapel Hill.

Thomson, Andrew 1975, The structure of collective bargaining in Britain. In Angela M. Bowey (ed.) *Handbook of salary and wage systems*, 2nd edn. Gower Publishing, Aldershot, pp. 37–53.

Thomson, David 1986, Welfare and the historians. In Lloyd Bonfield, Richard M. Smith, and Keith Wrightson (eds) *The world we have gained*. Basil Blackwell, Oxford, pp. 355–78.

—— 1993, A lifetime of privilege? Aging and generations at century's end. In Vern L. Bengtson and W. Andrew Achenbaum (eds) *The changing contract across generations*. Aldine de Gruyter, New York, pp. 215–37.

Tooby, John and Cosmides, Leda 1992, The psychological foundations of culture. In J. H. Barkow, L. Cosmides, and J. Tooby (eds) *The adapted mind*. Oxford University Press, New York, pp. 19–136.

Toren, Christina 1993, Making history: The significance of childhood cognition for a comparative anthropology of mind, *Man*, NS 28 (3), 461–78.

Treas, Judith 1987, The effect of women's labor force participation on the distribution of income in the United States, *Annual Review of Sociology*, 13, 259–88.

Trempe, Rolande 1983, The struggles of French miners for the creation of retirement funds in the 19th century. In Anne-Marie Guillemard (ed.) *Old age and the welfare state*. Sage Publications, Beverly Hills, Calif., pp. 101–13.

Tuck, Richard 1996, Hobbes's moral philosophy. In Tom Sorell (ed.) *The Cambridge companion to Hobbes*. Cambridge University Press, Cambridge, pp. 174–207.

Tuleja, Tad 1985, *Beyond the bottom line*. Facts on File, New York.

Turnbull, Colin M. 1961, *The forest people*. Simon & Schuster, New York.

——1972, *The mountain people*. Simon & Schuster, New York.

Turner, Terence 1994, Bodies and anti-bodies: Flesh and fetish in contemporary social theory. In Thomas J. Csordas (ed.) *Embodiment and experience*. Cambridge University Press, Cambridge, pp. 27–47.

Veblen, Thorstein 1934 [1899], *The theory of the leisure class*. Random House, New York.

Venti, Steven F. and Wise, David A. 1990, But they don't want to reduce housing equity. In David A. Wise (ed.) *Issues in the economics of aging*. University of Chicago Press, Chicago, pp. 13–32.

Verbon, Harrie 1988, *The evolution of public pension schemes*. Springer Verlag, New York.

von Balluseck, Hilde 1983, Origins and trends of social policy for the aged in the Federal Republic of Germany and West Berlin. In Anne-Marie Guillemard (ed.) *Old age and the welfare state*. Sage Publications, Beverly Hills, Calif., pp. 213–49.

von Kondratowitz, Hans-Joachim 1984, Long-term changes in attitudes toward "old age." In V. Garms-Homolova, E. M. Hoerning, and D. Schaeffer (eds) *Intergenerational relationships*, C. J. Hogrefe, Lewiston, NY, pp. 27–40.

Wagner, Steven J. 1984, Descartes on the parts of the soul, *Philosophy and Phenomenological Research*, 45 (1), 51–70.

Wakoski, Diane 1969, *Greed*, parts 3 and 4. Black Sparrow Press, Los Angeles.

Walker, Alan 1990, The economic "burden" of ageing and the prospect of intergenerational conflict, *Ageing and Society*, 10 (4), 377–96.

——1993, Intergenerational relations and welfare restructuring: The social construction of an intergenerational problem. In Vern L. Bengtson and W. Andrew Achenbaum (eds) *The changing contract across generations*. Aldine de Gruyter, New York, pp. 141–65.

Wall, Richard 1983, The household: Demographic and economic change in England, 1650–1970. In R. Wall, J. Robin, and P. Laslett (eds) *Family forms in historic Europe*, Cambridge University Press, Cambridge, pp. 493–512.

Walser, Ferdinand 1982, *Luganda proverbs*. Dietrich Rimmer Verlag, Berlin.

Warner, Richard 1994, Introduction: The mind–body debate. In Richard Warner and Tadeusz Szubka (eds) *The mind–body problem*, Blackwell Publishers, Oxford, pp. 1–16.

Weinberg, Herman G. 1972, *The complete Greed of Erich von Stroheim*. E. P. Dutton & Co., New York.

White, Leslie A. 1949, *The science of culture*. Farrar, Straus, New York.

Willard, L. Duane 1983, Is action within the law morally sufficient in business? In Wade L. Robison, Michael S. Pritchard, and Joseph Ellin (eds) *Profits and professions*. Humana Press, Clifton, NJ, pp. 89–99.

Williams, Bernard 1973, A critique of utilitarianism. In J. J. C. Smart and B. Williams *Utilitarianism: For and against*. Cambridge University Press, Cambridge, pp. 77–150.

——1993, *Shame and necessity*. University of California Press, Berkeley & Los Angeles.

——1995, *Making sense of humanity and other philosophical papers 1982–1993*. Cambridge University Press, Cambridge.

Williams, George C. 1957, Pleiotropy, natural selection, and the evolution of senescence, *Evolution*, 11 (4), 398–411.

——1966, *Adaptation and natural selection*. Princeton University Press, Princeton N.J.

Wilson, Edward O. 1978, *On human nature*. Harvard University Press, Cambridge, Mass.

——1998, *Consilience: The unity of knowledge*. Vintage Books, New York.

Wilson, Edward O. and Lumsden, Charles J. 1991, Holism and reduction in sociobiology: Lessons from the ants and human culture, *Biology and Philosophy*, 4 (3), 401–12.

Wilson, Monica 1951, *Good company*. Oxford University Press, London.

Winter, Edward H. 1956, *Bwamba*. Heffer, Cambridge.

Winters, D. L. 1978, *Farmers without farms*. Greenwood Press, Westport, Conn.

Wise, David A. (ed.) 1990, *Issues in the economics of aging*. University of Chicago Press, Chicago.

Wolf, Eric 1969, *Peasant wars of the twentieth century*. Harper & Row, New York.

——1982, *Europe and the people without history*. University of California Press, Berkeley & Los Angeles.

Wolpe, Harold (ed.) 1980, *The articulation of modes of production*. Routledge & Kegan Paul, London.

Woodward, Kathleen 1995, Tribute to the older woman: Psychoanalysis, feminism, and ageism. In Mike Featherstone & Andrew Wernick (eds) *Images of aging*. Routledge, London, pp. 79–96.

World Bank 1994, *Averting the old age crisis*. Oxford University Press for World Bank, New York.

Worsley, Peter 1968, *The trumpet shall sound*. Schocken Books, New York.

Worthman, C. M. 1993, Bio-cultural interactions in human development. In M. E. Pereira and L. A. Fairbanks (eds) *Juvenile primates*. Oxford University Press, Oxford, pp. 339–58.

Wright, Erik Olin 1979, Intellectuals and the class structure of capitalist society. In Pat Walker (ed.) *Between labor and capital*. South End Press, Boston, pp. 191–212.

Wynn, Margaret 1970, *Family policy*. Michael Joseph, London.

Zelizer, Viviana A. 1985, *Pricing the priceless child*. Basic Books, New York.

Index

Tailpiece